Karl Barth, Catholic Renewal and Vatican II

T&T Clark Studies in Systematic Theology

Edited by

John Webster
Ian A. McFarland
Ivor Davidson

Volume 16

KARL BARTH, CATHOLIC RENEWAL AND VATICAN II

by
Benjamin Dahlke

BLOOMSBURY
LONDON · NEW DELHI · NEW YORK · SYDNEY

Bloomsbury T&T Clark
An imprint of Bloomsbury Publishing Plc

50 Bedford Square	1385 Broadway
London	New York
WC1B 3DP	NY 10018
UK	USA

www.bloomsbury.com

Bloomsbury is a registered trade mark of Bloomsbury Publishing Plc

First published 2012
Reprinted 2013
Paperback edition first published 2013

© Benjamin Dahlke, 2012

All rights reserved. No part of this publication may be reproduced or transmitted in any form or by any means, electronic or mechanical, including photocopying, recording, or any information storage or retrieval system, without prior permission in writing from the publishers.

Benjamin Dahlke has asserted his right under the Copyright, Designs and Patents Act, 1988, to be identified as Author of this work.

No responsibility for loss caused to any individual or organization acting on or refraining from action as a result of the material in this publication can be accepted by Bloomsbury or the author.

British Library Cataloguing-in-Publication Data
A catalogue record for this book is available from the British Library.

ISBN: HB: 978-0-567-60593-1
PB: 978-0-567-61686-9

Library of Congress Cataloging-in-Publication Data
A catalog record for this book is available from the Library of Congress.

Typeset by Deanta Global Publishing Services, Chennai, India

CONTENTS

Foreword by Bruce Lindley McCormack — vii
Preface by Benjamin Dahlke — x

Introduction — 1

1. *The Epistle to the Romans*: First Reactions to Karl Barth — 8
   1.1 Introduction — 8
   1.2 New Ways of Preaching: Joseph Wittig — 9
   1.3 The Anti-historical Revolution in Theology: Joseph Engert — 11
   1.4 Immanence, Transcendence and the *analogia entis*: Erich Przywara — 15
   1.5 God against Humanity: Karl Adam — 18
   1.6 Results — 22

2. Anti-Modern Modern: The Philosophical Presuppositions of Dialectical Theology — 25
   2.1 Introduction — 25
   2.2 The Tortuous Paths of Modern Theology: Michael Gierens — 27
   2.3 The Speechlessness of Dialectical Theology: Friedrich Maria Rintelen — 29
   2.4 The Christ of Faith: Karl Rahner — 31
   2.5 Barth's Conception of the Creature: Hermann Volk — 35
   2.6 Results — 38

3. Unity in Faith: The Münster Circle, Robert Grosche and the Periodical *Catholica* — 41
   3.1 Introduction — 41
   3.2 The Münster Circle — 42
   3.3 The Usefulness of Dialectical Theology: Robert Grosche — 44
   3.4 The Periodical *Catholica* — 47
   3.5 Results — 50

4. *Fides quaerens intellectum*: Barth's Essay on Anselm of Canterbury — 53
   4.1 Introduction — 53
   4.2 Anselm from a Neo-Scholastic Viewpoint: Franciscus Salesius Schmitt and Rudolf Allers — 54
   4.3 Worship in the Field of Thought: Anselm Stolz — 56
   4.4 Results — 59

CONTENTS

5. The Invention of the Antichrist? Catholic Reactions to Barth's Condemnation of the *analogia entis*   61
   - 5.1 Introduction   61
   - 5.2 The *Church Dogmatics* as a Curiosity: Bernhard Bartmann   66
   - 5.3 God and Being: Daniel Feuling   68
   - 5.4 A Thomistic Critique: Jakob Fehr   71
     - 5.4.1 Barth and Thomism   74
     - 5.4.2 God's Word in the Human Word   76
   - 5.5 Towards Salvation History: Gottlieb Söhngen   79
   - 5.6 *Analogia Entis* is not *analogia entis*: Erich Przywara   83
   - 5.7 The Rescue Attempt: Robert Grosche   88
   - 5.8 Results   90

6. Hans Urs von Balthasar's Contribution to the Renewal of Catholic Theology   95
   - 6.1 The Problem of Neo-Scholasticism   95
   - 6.2 Balthasar's Attempt to find a Solution   98

7. Balthasar's Perception of Barth's Line of Thought   103
   - 7.1 Balthasar's Dissatisfaction with the School Theology   103
   - 7.2 'Analogie und Dialektik' (1944)   108
   - 7.3 'Analogie und Natur' (1945)   113

8. Balthasar's Appropriation of Barth's Line of Thought (1948–1951)   121
   - 8.1 A Dialogue on a Circuitous Route: Barth and the *Nouvelle Théologie*   121
   - 8.2 *Karl Barth* (1951)   128
     - 8.2.1 A Contribution on Theological Methodology   128
     - 8.2.2 Barth's Theological Development   137
     - 8.2.3 On Bruce McCormack's Criticism of Balthasar   141
     - 8.2.4 On the Immediate History of its Effect and Reception   145

9. Balthasar's Later Writings on Barth's Thought (after 1951)   149
   - 9.1 The Relationship between Christology and Pneumatology   149
   - 9.2 God in His Revelation   150

Summary   156

Bibliography   161
Author Index   181
Subject Index   183

FOREWORD

While much has been written on Karl Barth's life-long engagement with Roman Catholic theology and the impact it had upon his own thinking, comparatively little has been written on the often tumultuous but eventually quite fruitful relationship between Barth and Catholicism starting from the other side. No full-length monograph on the history of German Catholic engagement with Barth's theology has existed – until now. But Benjamin Dahlke's fine study does much more than fill this lacuna. The story he tells – at least in outline form – is that of the evolution of German Catholic theology in the twentieth century in the run-up to the Vatican II. This is an important story to tell for many reasons – not least of which is that it helps to explain why, to this day, Thomism does not have the dominating influence among German Catholics which it enjoys elsewhere.

The story begins with so-called "Neo-scholasticism" – that version of Thomism which was dominant not just in Germany but in all Catholic theology from the end of the nineteenth century on through the end of the fourth decade of the twentieth. Neo-scholastic readers of Barth had eyes for one thing only – his talk (in the preface to the second edition of his *Romans*) of an infinite qualitative distinction between time and eternity. And on the basis of alleged entailments in this allegedly basic commitment, Neo-scholastics were able to find in Barth only a contradiction between the being of God and the being of the human. What they missed was the irony with which Barth's statement drips "... *if* I have a system, it is limited to a recognition of what Kierkegaard called the 'infinite qualitative distinction' between time and eternity' ... "[1] In truth, Barth had no "system" – *Romans* was an anti-metaphysical manifesto, not the elaboration of a purely negative metaphysical system. But, then, the Neo-scholastics also paid little or no attention to the clause which completes the just-cited sentence. "... and to my regarding this as possessing negative as well as positive significance."[2] The dialectic referred to in this statement was understood by Barth to be a witness to the God-world relation, not the thing itself. It did not rise to the level of a truly basic commitment. And its positive significance ought not to have been overlooked. If the dialectic of time and eternity prevented an identification of God's Self-revelation with any creaturely medium of it, it

---

[1] Karl Barth, *The Epistle to the Romans* (Oxford and New York: OUP, 1933), p.10.
[2] Ibid.

FOREWORD

did not eliminate the possibility that a positive relation between revelation and a historical event might nevertheless be established from God's side. And it is precisely at this point that the most basic shortcoming of Neo-scholastic readings emerges, viz. their failure to see that the dialectic of veiling and unveiling in revelation is far more basic to Barth's theology – already at this stage of his development – than is the dialectic of time and eternity.

And yet, Dahlke shows quite clearly that Neo-scholastic criticism of Barth was never an end in itself. Barth served as a useful foil in the battle against all forms of Catholic accommodation to modernity – and in that way, as a brake on all Catholic reform movements on into the 1940s. That Barth contributed to this state-of-affairs with his ill-advised description of the *analogia entis* as the invention of the Antichrist is clear. But power dynamics within the Catholic communion were even more significant. The struggle against modernity was, at the same time, a struggle for the supremacy of a particular school of theology.

A more positive, fruitful phase of engagement was made possible in large measure by Hans Urs von Balthasar. Dahlke traces Balthasar's discovery in Barth of a theologian who could provide resources for the creation of a new Catholic theology capable of supplanting Neo-scholasticism (which he regarded as much too closely allied with Enlightenment values like that of a disembodied universal reason to offer effective resistance to it). Dahlke's greatest contribution, in my view, lies just here. Armed with a close knowledge of neglected texts and unpublished letters, he is able to show (for example) that Balthasar's regard for *Church Dogmatics* II/1 was so high that he informed Barth (in a letter written in May 1940) that he regarded the Catholic dogmatics he had planned to write as having been rendered superfluous by it.

What Balthasar valued most in Barth was the latter's christological starting-point. The greatest need of Catholic theology as he saw it was a revised understanding of the relation of nature and grace found in the Neo-scholastics and he saw Christology as the proper arena for working out this revision. And yet, there were limits to how far he wished to keep company with Barth. Dahlke suggests that Balthasar only finally became acquainted with Barth's doctrine of election (which unleashed Barth's christocentrism in its mature form) in the late 40s. And when he did, he found that he had serious reservations – most especially in relation to Barth's claim that what is accomplished in the life, death and resurrection of Jesus is the *reality* of reconciliation and redemption and not merely their *possibility* (a possibility to be realized through the work of the Holy Spirit in and through the church). To be sure, Balthasar continued to prize a christological starting-point for the sake of constructing a new Catholic theology but Barth's doctrine of election and the soteriology it entailed were alien to his Catholic faith.

All of this provides important background knowledge for understanding the deepest-lying intentions which informed Balthasar's 1951 book,

FOREWORD

Karl Barth. This was a deeply Catholic book, written by a Catholic theologian for other Catholic theologians. Talk of a turn from "dialectics" to analogy, for example, was a way of granting to Barth's Neo-scholastic critics the validity of their criticism of Barth's *Romans* while insisting that Barth had left such "dialectics" behind. Catholics could and should take the mature Barth of analogical thinking with great seriousness.

Not surprisingly, Dahlke is less interested in questions surrounding the accuracy of Balthasar's historical reconstruction of Barth's development than he is in its sheer usefulness of that reconstruction in relation to a set of problems internal to the Roman communion. Balthasar was a significant figure in preparing the ground for Vatican II. By making Barth accessible to Catholics, he guaranteed that Barth too would play a role in that process, however indirect it might have been. The ecumenical significance of Bathasar's Barth book was immense – and that is the point its young Roman Catholic interpreter would like us to remember.

Dahlke has written a truly seminal work. He has succeeded in opening new avenues of inquiry while shedding light on a number of long standing questions. Doubtless, other works on Barth and Balthasar will be written; the relation of two great Swiss theologians is a topic of current interest in the English-speaking world especially. But all who follow will owe Dahlke a great debt. Certainly, the comprehensiveness of the research underlying his project sets an admirable standard which, it can only be hoped, others will seek to emulate.

Bruce Lindley McCormack

PREFACE

This work is based on a dissertation supervised by Prof. Leonhard Hell (Mainz) and Prof. Jörg Ernesti (Brixen) and accepted by the University of Mainz in the summer of 2009. Originally published in German[1], it has now been made available for an English-speaking public in a shortened and revised version, altered in some parts. I must thank the publishers for accepting it for inclusion in the T & T Clark series, "Studies in Systematic Theology". Likewise, I wish to thank Helen Heron, Prof. Alasdair Heron (Erlangen) and Dr. Kenneth R. Oakes (Tübingen) for the translation. Translations into English and newly-published literature were taken into consideration where possible. The faults, of course, remain my own.

I am grateful to Dr. Hans-Anton Drewes of the Karl Barth-Archive in Basel, Dr. Johannes Wischmeyer of the Institute for European History in Mainz, Princeton Theological Seminary – namely Prof. Bruce McCormack, Dr. Clifford Anderson and Kenneth Henke – and the parish of St. Paul's in Princeton, particularly its former curate Father Walter Nolan. Thanks are due also to the Academy of Sciences at Göttingen for granting the "Hanns-Lilje-Preis" in 2010. This book could hardly have been written without their manifold support and encouragement.

Bad Driburg (Westphalia),
October 2011
Benjamin Dahlke

---

[1] *Die katholische Rezeption Karl Barths. Theologische Erneuerung im Vorfeld des Zweiten Vatikanischen Konzils* (Tübingen: Mohr Siebeck, 2010). The reviews are listed on www.mohr.de.

INTRODUCTION

1 The Subject Matter and the State of Research

The distinguishing feature of a 'classic' is that it is resistant to interpretation; in other words, a 'classic' is so complex and rich in perspectives that it continually inspires new interpretations while simultaneously outlasting them.[1] By these criteria, the works of Karl Barth (1886–1968) already have a good chance of counting as 'classics' within theology. The *Epistle to the Romans* (1922) and the *Church Dogmatics* (1932–1967) in particular have generated and enjoyed diverse interpretations from their very publication, and the immense secondary literature surrounding them can no longer be surveyed at a single glance. Likewise, opinions regarding how Barth's works should be assessed hardly diverge to a lesser degree, for it is still debatable as to whether Barth's works constitute a forward-looking presentation of the Christian faith or a complete anachronism as regards the challenges modernity poses to Christianity.

It is by no means surprising that the answers to these questions remain controversial within Protestant theology even up until the present. Barth's way of thinking seems to contrast rather drastically with the main tendencies of recent Protestantism, particularly with those which can be traced back to Friedrich Schleiermacher (1768–1834). Striking comparisons such as these characterize research at least up to the immediate present.[2] There is, to put the matter simply, a dispute as to how Protestant theology should position

---

[1] Cf. George Steiner, *Errata. An examined life* (London: Phoenix, 1998), p. 22: 'It is as if the poem, the painting, the sonata drew around itself a last circle, a space for inviolate autonomy. I define the classic as that around which this space is perennially fruitful. It questions us. It demands that we try again. It makes of our misprisions, of our partialities and disagreements not a relativistic chaos, an "anything goes", but a deepening. Worthwhile interpretations, criticism to be taken seriously, are those which make their limitations, their defeats visible. In turn, this visibility helps make manifest the inexhaustibility of the object.'

[2] On this see Dietrich Korsch, 'Wort Gottes oder Frömmigkeit? Über den Sinn einer theologischen Alternative zwischen Karl Barth und Friedrich Schleiermacher', *ZDT* 5 (1989), pp. 195–216; Bruce McCormack, 'What Has Basel to Do with Berlin? Continuities in the Theologies of Barth and Schleiermacher', *Princeton Seminary Bulletin* 23 (2002), pp. 146–73; Jörg Dierken, 'Karl Barth (1886–1968)', in *Klassiker der Theologie*, ed. Friedrich Wilhelm Graf, vol. 2 (Munich: Beck, 2005), pp. 223–57; Christine Axt-Piscalar, 'Kontinuität oder Abbruch? Karl Barths Prolegomena zur Dogmatik im Lichte der Theologie des 19. Jahrhunderts – eine Skizze', *TZ* 62 (2006), pp. 433–51.

itself in modernity: should Protestant theology positively affirm the modern legacy, or should it critically distance itself from it?[3]

It should be noted, however, that Roman Catholics have also paid serious attention to Barth's work, and often to a remarkable extent. In what follows, I will examine both the *how* of this reception (i.e. the perception and appropriation of Barth's work, in Catholic German-speaking theology prior to Vatican II) and the *why* of this reception (i.e. why Barth's work was taken up and dealt with at all). This reception history is worth pursuing as, apart from a few brief surveys which are either far too broad[4] or far too narrow[5] in their focus, the topic has, up until now, not been worked on to any significant degree. Defining the scope of this undertaking is important, as the history of Barth's reception elsewhere and at different times would require another monograph.

Consideration of the Roman Catholic reception of Barth is worthwhile not only because it sheds light on the course of Barth's impact, but also because of the significant insight it offers regarding the current state of Catholic theology. A better understanding of Vatican II would require

---

[3] A critical evaluation of recent scholarship has been provided by Eberhard Busch, 'Weg und Werk Karl Barths in der neueren Forschung', *TRu* 60 (1995), pp. 273–99, 430–70; Bruce McCormack, 'Beyond Nonfoundational and Postmodern Readings of Barth's Critically Realistic Dialectical Theology', *ZDT* 12 (1997), pp. 67–95, 170–94; Arne Rasmusson, 'Historiography and Theology. Theology in the Weimar Republic and the Beginning of the Third Reich', *Kirchliche Zeitgeschichte* 20 (2007), pp. 155–80; Stefan Holtmann, *Karl Barth als Theologe der Neuzeit. Studien zur kritischen Deutung seiner Theologie* (Göttingen: Vandenhoeck und Ruprecht, 2007); ibid, 'Karl Barth als Theologe der Neuzeit. Die Deutungen Trutz Rendtorffs, Falk Wagners und Friedrich Wilhelm Grafs', in *Karl Barths Theologie als europäisches Ereignis*, ed. Martin Leiner and Michael Trowitzsch (Göttingen: Vandenhoeck und Ruprecht, 2008), pp. 331–47; Georg Pfleiderer, 'Karl Barths Dialektische Theologie als Paradigma des 20. Jahrhunderts. Versuch einer Selbstrezension eines Rezeptionsweges', *ZDT* 24 (2008), pp. 31–47.

[4] Cf. Grover Foley, 'The Catholic Critics of Karl Barth in Outline and Analysis', *SJT* 14 (1961), pp. 136–55; Emilien Lamirande, 'The Impact of Karl Barth on the Catholic Church in the Last Half Century', in *Footnotes to a Theology. The Karl Barth Colloquium of 1972*, ed. Martin Rumscheidt (Waterloo, Ontario: The Corporation for the Publication of Academic Studies in Religion in Canada, 1974), pp. 112–48; Philip J. Rosato, 'The Influence of Karl Barth on Catholic Theology', *Greg* 67 (1986), pp. 659–78; Geoffrey Bromiley, 'The Influence of Barth after World War II', in *Reckoning with Barth* [. . .], ed. Nigel Biggar (Oxford: Mowbray, 1988), pp. 9–23; Paolo Ricca, 'Barth di fronte al cattolicesimo e all'ecumenismo', in *Barth contemporaneo*, ed. Sergio Rostagno (Turin: Claudiana, 1990), pp. 197–211; Paul Brazier, 'Barth and Rome. A Critical engagement with Catholic thinkers', *Downside Review* 123 (2005), pp. 137–52; Denis Müller, *Karl Barth* (Paris: Cerf, 2005), pp. 207–16.

[5] Cf. Emilien Lamirande, 'Roman Catholic Reactions to Karl Barth's Ecclesiology', in *CJT* 14 (1968), pp. 28–42; and Alfons Nossol, 'Die Rezeption der Barthschen Christologie in der katholischen Theologie der Gegenwart', *EvT* 46 (1986), pp. 351–69.

INTRODUCTION

nothing less than in-depth research into the history of theology since the end of World War I. In fact, the interpretation and significance of this Council are still under debate, particularly as regards the validity and appropriateness of a 'hermeneutics of discontinuity' versus a 'hermeneutics of continuity'.[6] Discussions and debates surrounding the Council and its legacy all too often neglect its historical context. A closer investigation into this context could give mired debates new insights and avenues to explore.

2 The Historical Background

The history of the Roman Catholic Church from the middle of the nineteenth century to the middle of the twentieth is sometimes described as the '*Pianic age*'. The pontificates of Pius IX (1846–1858) to Pius XII (1939–1958) are connected by the same programme: outward expansion and inward consolidation, especially through the establishment of a self-contained Neo-Scholastic system which embraced both philosophy and theology.[7] In a world which was continually becoming more complex this programme became increasingly difficult to carry out. Thus the reorientation which Pope John XXIII (1958–1962) eventually introduced was simply inevitable. Shortly after his election he declared his intentions to convene a Council, the prime concern of which would be the '*aggiornamento*' of the Church. While this surprised many of the faithful, theology had long seen itself confronted with a complexity and plurality that the rigid Neo-Scholastic system could only incorporate with substantial difficulties. The outlines of this situation first became clear in Germany and then later in France.[8] It is thus hardly remarkable that bishops and theologians from these countries played a prominent part in the Council.[9]

---

[6] Cf. Nicholas Lash, 'What Happened at Vatican II?', in *Theology for Pilgrims* (Notre Dame, IN: University of Notre Dame Press, 2008), pp. 240–8; *Vatican II. Did Anything Happen?*, ed. David G. Schultenover (New York and London: Continuum, 2008); *L'Autorité et les autorités. L'herméneutique théologique de Vatican II*, ed. Gilles Routhier and Guy Jobin (Paris: Cerf, 2010).

[7] Cf. Gerald McCool, *The Neo-Thomists* (Milwaukee, WI: Marquette University Press, 1994); Christoph Theobald, 'De Vatican I aux années 1950: Révélation, foi et raison, inspiration, dogme et magistère infaillible', in *Histoire des dogmes*, vol. 4, ed. ibid and Bernard Sesboüé (Paris: Desclée, 1996), pp. 227–470; Giacomo Martina, *Storia della Chiesa. Da Lutero ai nostri giorni*, vol. 4 (Brescia: Morcelliana, ³2001).

[8] Cf. Étienne Fouilloux, 'I movimenti di riforma nel pensiero cattolico dal XIX al XX secolo', *Cristianesimo nella Storia* 24 (2003), pp. 659–76, 670–1.

[9] Cf. Melissa J. Wilde. *Vatican II. A Sociological Analysis of Religious Change* (Princeton, NJ and Oxford: Princeton University Press, 2007), pp. 33–5.

2.1 Between the Times: The Opening of German Catholicism, Karl Barth and Neo-Scholasticism (Chapters 1–5)

If, at the beginning of the 'Kaiserreich', Catholics were a marginalized and intellectually isolated minority, they soon started to enter the highest echelons of society, a process which reached its peak during World War I when the all-embracing mobilization of society broke down all earlier barriers.[10] Roman Catholics subsequently played a decisive role in the Weimar Republic.[11] Along with this new position came the necessity of adopting positions and judgements regarding other cultural forces, histories and trajectories. This necessity led to a lively study of not only contemporary literature and philosophy, but also of Protestant theology.

Previously there had been hardly any contact in this regard. Protestant theology was thought to have degenerated into a mere study of culture, for it seemed as if God and revelation no longer stood at the very centre of theology, but instead humanity's interpretation of itself and the world. In the eyes of Catholics at that time, Adolf von Harnack (1851–1930) and Ernst Troeltsch (1865–1923) were the personifications of this programme.[12] The advent of Dialectical Theology, however, signalled the arrival of a new situation, for now the difference between God and culture was emphasized.[13]

Dialectical Theology had its origins after World War I in a network of people who shared the same interests and formed a kind of study-group ('Arbeitsgemeinschaft').[14] Part of what connected them was the rejection of the

---

[10] Cf. Thomas F. O'Meara, *Church and Culture. German Catholic Theology, 1860–1914* (Notre Dame, IN and London: University of Notre Dame Press, 1992), pp. 195–6; Thomas Ruster, 'Theologische Wahrnehmung von Kultur im ausgehenden Kaiserreich', in *Antimodernismus und Modernismus in der katholischen Kirche. Beiträge zum theologiegeschichtlichen Vorfeld des II. Vatikanums*, ed. Hubert Wolf (Paderborn et al.: Schöningh, 1998), pp. 267–79; Anthony J. Steinhoff, 'Christianity and the creation of Germany', in *The Cambridge History of Christianity*, vol. 8, ed. Sheridan Gilley and Brian Stanley (Cambridge et al.: Cambridge University Press, 2006), pp. 282–300, 296–300; Claus Arnold, 'Internal Church Reform in Catholic Germany', in *The Churches*, ed. Joris van Eijnatten and Paula Yates (Leuven: Leuven University Press, 2010), pp. 159–84, 215–21.

[11] Cf. Thomas Ruster, *Die verlorene Nützlichkeit der Religion. Katholizismus und Moderne in der Weimarer Republik* (Paderborn et al.: Schöningh, 1994).

[12] See, for instance, Hermann Joseph Wurm, 'Protestantismus', in *Wetzer und Welte's Kirchenlexikon* 10 (1897), pp. 480–533, 506–16; and Hermann Lange, 'Protestantismus', in *Handlexikon der katholischen Dogmatik*, ed. Joseph Braun (Freiburg i.Br.: Herder, 1926), pp. 237–8.

[13] Cf. Heinrich Getzeny, 'Strömungen in der protestantischen Theologie der Gegenwart', *Der katholische Gedanke* 4 (1931), pp. 43–57, 43; Bernhard Bartmann, *Lehrbuch der Dogmatik*, vol. 2 (Freiburg i.Br.: Herder,[8] 1932), p. 525.

[14] For what follows see Dietrich Korsch, 'Dialektische Theologie', in *RGG*[4] 2 (1999), pp. 809–15.

INTRODUCTION

prevailing theology centred upon religious subjectivity, focused upon history and heavily psychologized. Even if in other matters Barth, Emil Brunner (1889–1966), Rudolf Bultmann (1884–1976), Friedrich Gogarten (1887–1967), Georg Merz (1892–1959) and Eduard Thurneysen (1888–1977) thought very differently, what united them and initially held them together was a severe and occasionally polemical antithesis and contradiction to what they identified as Liberal Theology or Neo-Protestantism.[15] Yet their gradual transition from the pastor's office to the professor's lecture hall, which already began at the start of the 1920s, marked the onset of a distinct change. At first its supporters found in this transition a corrective: Dialectical Theology was now forced to develop a well-rounded and pedagogically suitable programme. But internal differences only became all the more evident as the task moved further away from being critical of what had been inherited to offering a positive theological contribution. The fact that Dialectical Theology was less of a theological 'school' with a well-defined programme which joined them together but more of an extremely fragile union with a specific purpose accounts both for its initial success and for its disintegration at the beginning of the 1930s, which was primarily due to divergent opinions regarding natural theology. All of these events were, of course, attentively observed by Catholics.[16]

Catholics were already quite interested in Dialectical Theology when the movement first formed around Karl Barth after World War I. In contrast to Liberal Protestantism, Dialectical Theology gave theology once again the place of prominence now occupied by philosophy of religion; it explicitly concerned itself with dogmatics instead of with the mere history of dogmatic thinking; and it gave serious attention to and was determined by the Church. These factors help to explain why there was such a lively preoccupation with Barth. He gave off the impression that he was picking up where the Reformers had left off: with the question as to what the true faith is. It is remarkable in this regard that the model of a 'Protestant Catholicism' ('evangelische Katholizität') formulated at almost the same time by Friedrich Heiler (1892–1967) met with disapproval. Heiler taught religious studies in Marburg, was ordained a Bishop in order to stand within apostolic succession and offered a Protestantism oriented by the Lutheran Confession and liturgy for the sake of opposing liberal subjectivism and an individualistic Protestant culture. In this way he hoped to build a bridge to Catholicism.[17] His emphasis on external forms, however, only barely concealed his fundamentally liberal theological convictions, and for this reason his attempt was largely rejected

---

[15] On this term and its difficulties see Eilert Herms, 'Neuprotestantismus. Stärken, Unklarheiten und Schwächen einer Figur geschichtlicher Selbstorientierung des evangelischen Christentums im 20. Jahrhundert', *NZSTh* 51 (2009), pp. 309–39.
[16] Cf. Benjamin Dahlke, 'Das Zerbrechen der Dialektischen Theologie in katholischer Sicht', *Cath(M)* 64 (2010), pp. 67–78.
[17] Cf. Jörg Ernesti, *Ökumene im Dritten Reich* (Paderborn: Bonifatius, 2007).

on the Catholic side. Barth, by contrast, appeared to have far more dogmatic substance and to be closer to the Reformers.

There were, however, also critical voices which drew attention to the specifically modern elements in Barth's thinking that were difficult to bring in line with the Catholic theology of that time. One of these elements was, for example, the influence of Sören Kierkegaard (1813–1855). Yet what would prove more fatal for Barth's future impact upon Catholicism was the Preface to vol. I of the *Church Dogmatics*. Here Barth characterizes the *analogia entis* as the invention of the Antichrist and as the decisive reason why one could not become Roman Catholic.[18] This clearly thoughtless, casual aside led to Barth being regarded as the personification of Protestant intransigence. This impression determined and severely hampered the analysis of his thinking by German-speaking Catholic theologians.

Nevertheless, in spite of this flippant invective, the 1950s saw a renewed, intense consideration of Barth's thought which not only included a mere awareness of it, but a productive appropriation as well. This newfound attention to Barth within Catholicism can be essentially traced back to the work of Hans Urs von Balthasar (1905–1988). That Balthasar studied the *Church Dogmatics* while other Catholics saw no reason at all for so doing can be explained in part by his studies in France, where theology was particularly innovative at the time.

2.2 The Theological Change in Theology: Hans Urs von Balthasar, Karl Barth and the End of Neo-Scholasticism (Chapters 6–9)

The kind of readiness for change which French theology possessed can be seen in a brief article written by the Jesuit Jean Daniélou (1905–1974), published shortly after the end of World War II. In this article we can detect a return to the sources – meaning Scripture, the Church Fathers and the Liturgy – a great interest in modern philosophy, and the desire to move theology and preaching closer to life.[19] Insofar as it was a matter of widening Thomism

---

[18] Cf. KD I/1 (1932), pp. VIII–IX [English translation: CD I/1, p. XIII: 'I can see no third alternative between that exploitation of the *analogia entis* which is legitimate only on the basis of Roman Catholicism, between the greatness and misery of a so-called natural knowledge of God in the sense of the *Vaticanum*, and a Protestant theology which draws from its own source, which stands on its own feet, and which is finally liberated from this secular misery. Hence I have had no option but to say No at this point. I regard the *analogia entis* as the invention of Antichrist, and I believe that because of it it is impossible ever to become a Roman Catholic, all other reasons for not doing so being to my mind short-sighted and trivial.']

[19] Cf. Jean Daniélou, 'Les orientations présentes de la pensée religieuse', *Études* vol. 249 (1946), pp. 5–21.

INTRODUCTION

rather than a complete theological revolution, describing the kind of theology sketched out by Daniélou as *Nouvelle Théologie* is actually misleading.[20] But the sheer fact that the opponents of this school of thought coined such a term is an indication of how deeply suspect a more historical way of thinking was to them. The followers of Neo-Scholasticism favoured a theology that was completely focused on metaphysics, on a *philosophia perennis* which supposedly went back to Thomas Aquinas himself. They wanted to establish on this basis a system which could be contained because it was not dependent on history and therefore threatened by historical relativity. This project was undermined by the historical research of French Dominicans and Jesuits who gave prominence to the difference between Thomas and his later interpreters. It was the discovery of this difference which would finally bring about the breakdown of the Neo-Scholastic system.[21]

Initially, however, it looked as if the opponents of the *Nouvelle Théologie* had triumphed. In this regard we should mention the 1950 encyclical *Humani Generis*, a result of which was the restraining and silencing of many theologians.[22] Among these was Henri de Lubac (1895–1991), then working in Lyons. In his research he had historicized (and thus exposed the limitations of) the strict differentiation between nature and grace – the latter being understood as a higher nature – that had so characterized modern Thomism.[23] Hans Urs von Balthasar, who as a Jesuit had studied in Lyons in the 1930s and at that time befriended Lubac, adopted many of his insights. The highly intellectual Swiss, however, went far beyond the *Nouvelle Théologie* and in principle broke with the Thomist tradition, attempting to formulate what was Roman Catholic in a different way. He clearly was pleading for a *theological change in theology* when he emphasized the fact that theology should start with God's revelation in Jesus Christ instead of with abstract concepts. His study of Karl Barth fits within this context. Balthasar drew on impulses from the '*Church Dogmatics*' for the changing of Catholic theology.

---

[20] For an overview see Jürgen Mettepenningen, *Nouvelle Théologie – New Theology. Inheritor of Modernism, Precursor of Vatican II* (London and New York: T & T Clark, 2010).
[21] Cf. Gerald McCool, *From Unity to Pluralism. The Internal Evolution of Thomism* (New York: Fordham University Press, 1989), pp. 1–3, 200–33.
[22] Cf. Agnès Desmazières, 'Le sens d'une soumission. La réception française de l'encyclique *Humani generis* (1950–1951)', *RevThom* 105 (2005), pp. 273–306.
[23] Cf. Jean-Pierre Wagner, *Henri de Lubac* (Paris: Cerf, 2001).

1

THE EPISTLE TO THE ROMANS: FIRST REACTIONS TO KARL BARTH

1.1 Introduction

Rarely has a theological book had such a wide and sustained impact as Karl Barth's *Epistle to the Romans*. Within a short time Barth went from being a relatively unknown Swiss pastor in a small village to being one of the most prominent theologians in the German-speaking area. The first edition, published in 1919, had already given rise to an animated echo and to a large extent contributed to the fact that Barth was offered a position as an Honorary Professor in Göttingen.[1] The second edition of the *Epistle to the Romans*, published at the beginning of 1922, looked like a veritable revolution.[2] Several further editions of the work appeared within a very short time. While the dominant Protestant theology up until then had taken the human subject as its starting point, Barth now insisted upon the 'infinite qualitative difference between time and eternity'.[3] In theology, as in preaching, what is at stake is not humanity's interpretation of itself and the

---

[1] Karl Barth, *Der Römerbrief* (Bern: Bäschlin, 1919).
[2] RB (1922). Recently a critical edition was released, containing the various prefaces as well: *Der Römerbrief*, ed. Cornelis van der Kooi, Gesamtausgabe II. Akademische Werke (Zürich: Theologischer Verlag Zürich, 2010).
[3] Cf. RB (1922), p. XIII: 'Wenn ich ein System habe, so besteht es darin, daß ich das, was Kierkegaard den unendlichen qualitativen Unterschied von Zeit und Ewigkeit genannt hat, in seiner negativen und positiven Bedeutung möglichst beharrlich im Auge behalte'. On the background to this cf. Peter S. Oh, 'Complementary Dialectics of Kierkegaard and Barth. Barth's Use of Kierkegaardian Diastasis Reassessed', *NZSTh* 49 (2006), pp. 497–512.

world, but the divinity of God. Such was the central conviction which Barth never wearied of repeating.[4]

No less than the formation of the Dialectical Theology movement centred upon Karl Barth, the effect of the *Epistle to the Romans* within Protestantism, particularly in the context of academic theology, has been a subject of considerable research.[5] Nevertheless, it has not yet been made clear how these two phenomena were perceived by Catholics. This question is interesting not only because the reception history of the *Epistle to the Romans* began just a few months after it appeared, but also because the book gained such a prominent position. Here we must mention two journals, *Hochland* and *Stimmen der Zeit*, which circulated among the clergy and theologically open-minded lay persons. The *Lexikon für Theologie und Kirche*, which appeared at that time in its first edition, was addressed to the same circles. In view of the reputation and circulation of this reference book, as well as that of the two journals, we can attach considerable importance to the picture of Dialectical Theology contained in them.

1.2 New Ways of Preaching: Joseph Wittig

In contrast to many other Catholic theologians of the twentieth century, Joseph Wittig (1879–1949) has not yet been completely forgotten. Admittedly, however, this is only partially due to his academic contributions. Far more decisive in this regard was his excommunication in 1926 and his being unexpectedly reconciled shortly before death. Even up to the present, he is named as an example of the intransigence of the Catholicism of his day.[6]

Professor of Church History at the University of Breslau, Wittig saw his task less in the production of historical studies than in the writing of religious books. Particularly in the period immediately after World War I, he published, in addition to numerous stories, many contributions which were aimed at a

---

[4] Cf. John Webster, 'Karl Barth', in *Reading Romans through the Centuries. From the Early Church to Karl Barth*, ed. Jeffrey P. Greenman and Timothy Larsen (Grand Rapids, MI: Brazos Press, 2005), pp. 205–23; Dirk-Martin Grube, 'God or the Subject? Karl Barth's Critique of the "Turn to the Subject"', *NZSTh* 50 (2007), pp. 308–24.

[5] Cf. Cornelis van der Kooi, 'Karl Barths zweiter Römerbrief und seine Wirkungen', in *Karl Barth in Deutschland (1921–1935). Aufbruch – Klärung – Widerstand [. . .]*, ed. Michael Beintker et al. (Zürich: Theologischer Verlag Zürich, 2005), pp. 57–75; or Eckhard Lessing, *Geschichte der deutschsprachigen evangelischen Theologie von Albrecht Ritschl bis zur Gegenwart*, vol. 2 (Göttingen: Vandenhoeck und Ruprecht, 2004), pp. 21–48.

[6] On this see Karl Hausberger, 'Der "Fall" Joseph Wittig (1879–1949)', in *Antimodernismus und Modernismus in der katholischen Kirche. Beiträge zum theologiegeschichtlichen Vorfeld des II. Vatikanums*, ed. Hubert Wolf (Paderborn et al.: Schöningh, 1998), pp. 299–322.

more popular audience (or at least were not strictly academic). One of these articles, published in 1922, was to become his undoing. Wittig, motivated in part by his own experiences in pastoral care, emphasized the deliverance of Christians by the Easter Event over and against an apprehensive fixation on one's own sins.[7] This could be interpreted as criticism of the normal practice of confession at that time, and thus the reactions were vehement. Even if the criticism aimed at him was occasionally excessive and may have failed to detect his actual concerns, Wittig, who was even accused of Modernism, acted in a way which was not especially propitious. Although he had been expressly reprimanded by the Holy See in October 1923, he shortly afterwards published, again in *Hochland*, an article in which he took a critical look at the state of preaching in the Catholic Church. In this connection he also spoke of Barth's *Epistle to the Romans*.

As far as the state of preaching is concerned, Wittig's findings are exceedingly sobering.[8] Both in sermons and in religious books the same things had been said in the same way for decades. The vocabulary and style employed remained the same. The hearers and readers endured this monotony with quite admirable patience, but it is obvious to what a high degree the Church's proclamation had become estranged from the language of their actual addressees. Since homiletics are still at the state they were in the eighteenth and nineteenth centuries, sermons are often not much more than collages of texts from the Church Fathers or, at best, from Scripture. For Wittig, it is positively comforting that the 'pastoral voice' cultivated in Protestantism is even more platitudinous than the Catholic 'pulpit voice'. At any rate, nobody would think of voluntarily reading through a collection of sermons. The refined language of the sermon has crept into religious books, and very much to their disadvantage. Wittig proposes an alternative: one should not talk about religion as if one were reporting on something long-known, but rather in such a way that the inconceivability of what has been experienced continues to be reinforced.[9] The deeper reason as to why proclamation has become so linguistically worn, unimaginative and unappealing lies in the very fact that God has become conceivable.[10]

Wittig wants his view of the new religious literature to be understood with this proposal in mind. For Wittig, the force of the language is an indication of the power of the author's religious experience. This is why he is full of praise not only for the theologians of Eastern Orthodoxy or the representatives of religious socialism, including Friedrich Gogarten, but especially for Karl Barth. Wittig refers to Barth's *Epistle to the Romans*, as well as to some of

---

[7] Cf. Joseph Wittig, 'Die Erlösten', *Hochland* 19,2 (1922), pp. 1–26.
[8] On what follows see Joseph Wittig, 'Neue religiöse Bücher', *Hochland* 21,1 (1923/1924), pp. 415–30, 415–7.
[9] Cf. Wittig (1923/1924), pp. 424–5.
[10] Cf. Wittig (1923/1924), p. 416.

his other publications. He treats in detail, for example, Barth's 1919 lecture in Tambach in Thüringen.[11] While this lecture has received a great deal of attention in recent research because the leitmotifs of Dialectical Theology are already discernible in it in a highly concentrated and rhetorically brilliant form, Wittig was interested neither in the lecture's historical context nor in the course of its argumentation.[12] Instead he devotes his attention to the flow of the language and so he tacks quotation upon quotation for almost one and a half pages. Even if only briefly, Wittig also refers to Barth's lecture on the 'Poverty and Promise of Christian Proclamation', which appeared in the newly-founded journal of Dialectical Theology, the periodical *Zwischen den Zeiten (Between the Times)*.[13]

Clearly, however, it was not only Barth who was so noteworthy in comparison to what Wittig had otherwise read or heard on the Catholic side. In the closing section of his article, he remarks that many of the books he has presented are permeated with serious heresies (which means nothing more than that their authors were not Roman Catholic), yet he immediately adds that what he found in them (i.e. in Orthodox and Protestant authors) witnessed to a truly deep religious experience.[14]

1.3 The Anti-historical Revolution in Theology: Joseph Engert

With the collapse of the rationalistic metaphysics favoured by the Enlightenment at the end of the eighteenth century, there came an initial 'turn to the subject'. The nineteenth century, however, saw the development of what could be called 'historical awareness'. If one can only make claims about reality through a many-sided, highly subjective perspective, then one must be highly sensitive towards the historical interconnections in which claims about reality have formed and developed.[15]

---

[11] Cf. Wittig (1923/1924), pp. 420–1 with reference to RB (1922), or pp. 421–3 with reference to Karl Barth, *Der Christ in der Gesellschaft. Eine Tambacher Rede* (Würzburg: Patmos, 1920).

[12] For the so-called 'Tambacher Vortrag' cf. Bruce McCormack, *Karl Barth's Critically Realistic Dialectical Theology. Its Genesis and Development 1909–1936* (Oxford: Clarendon Press, 1995), pp. 195–202; Christian Link, 'Bleibende Einsichten von Tambach', in Beintker et al. (2005), pp. 333–46.

[13] Cf. Wittig (1923/1924), p. 423 with reference to Karl Barth, 'Not und Verheißung der christlichen Verkündigung', *Zwischen den Zeiten* 1 (1923), pp. 3–25.

[14] Cf. Wittig (1923/1924), p. 430.

[15] Cf. Karl Ameriks, *Kant and the Historical Turn. Philosophy as Critical Interpretation* (Oxford: Clarendon Press, 2006), pp. 1–12.

This development by no means passed by theology without leaving a trace. In the German Protestant Faculties especially, research on the Bible and dogma on the basis of the historico-critical method was increasingly taken as par for the course, and so the oftentimes so-called Liberal Theology that appealed to such methods came to dominate the theological scene.[16] Naturally, considerable uncertainties soon set in as the historicization of knowledge and thought always also means relativization. Within the writing of the history of theology and dogma, *speaking about speaking about God* took the place of *speaking about God*.

What may have been progress from a theoretical or academic viewpoint, as the differences between the pulpit and the university lectern were more clearly visible than before, proved to be far more problematic in another respect. Even if theology is taken to be systematic reflection on the Christian life of faith, it cannot reduce itself to merely retracing the genesis of the truth claims which happen to have been raised at some time in the past. Furthering and nurturing the Christian life and its creative power entails that theology must substantiate its truth claims. Answering questions regarding how this task could be fulfilled under the conditions of 'historical awareness', which soon developed into full-blown historicism, became an important task. Indeed, this question was equally virulent on both the Catholic and Protestant sides. Joseph Engert (1882–1964), Professor of Philosophy in Regensburg, is a fine example of one such Catholic who took up the challenges of historicism.[17] According to his own admission, the question of how theology was at all possible under modern conditions had troubled him for years.[18] It is in this connection that we should understand an article published at the beginning of 1924 which is essentially an analysis of Barth's *Epistle to the Romans*.[19]

As well as being a teacher, Engert was also active in pastoral care, and here it could be readily seen how historicism was more than a purely abstract academic problem. If the biblical texts were to be completely wrapped up in the context of their genesis and understood to be completely bound to a particular time and committed to a particular perspective, they would no longer have no immediate relevance for the present. It was, in fact, the impoverishment of preaching due to 'historical awareness' that had induced

---

[16] Cf. Thomas Albert Howard, *Protestant Theology and the Making of the Modern German University* (Oxford et al.: Oxford University Press, 2006), pp. 273–303.

[17] For biographical information see Otto Weiß, *Der Modernismus in Deutschland. Ein Beitrag zur Theologiegeschichte* (Regensburg: Pustet, 1995), p. 299.

[18] Cf. Joseph Engert, *Studien zur theologischen Erkenntnislehre* (Regensburg: Manz, 1926), p. IX.

[19] Cf. Joseph Engert, 'Metaphysik und Historismus im Christentum', *Hochland* 21,1 (1923/1924), pp. 502–17, 638–51. On this article's intention see Engert (1926), p. VII.

Engert to read the *Epistle to the Romans*.[20] For Engert, proclamation is impossible under the premises of historicism, which also explains why he thought it important to identify an alternative position. According to Engert historicism is on the verge of exhausting itself, for along with metaphysics another way of thinking is taking hold: belief in a transcendent truth and reality which lies beyond all human perception and which thus possesses a regulative and normative function towards all human action.[21] For Engert, Barth's *Epistle to the Romans* is a proof of the turn from historicism. He contrasts Barth's work with Friedrich Heiler's 1923 monograph on Catholicism.[22] Both authors had passed through the historico-critical school, but they subsequently went on to pursue very different lines. While Barth leaves behind a merely historical orientation, Heiler remains trapped within the intellectual world of the nineteenth century.[23]

The reason Engert devotes himself to the publications of two Protestants is that he is seeking a way of thinking which is truly appropriate for theology and thereby also makes proclamation possible. As he holds 'history' and 'truth' to be finally incompatible quantities, he rejects, in principle, a historical orientation within theology and pleads for a metaphysical one. Heiler appears to him to be the spokesman of historicism, and consequently pulls him to pieces. In his book on Catholicism, Engert is not simply offering criticisms of individual points but of the anti-metaphysical way of thinking as a whole.[24] A detailed examination of Heiler would basically be pointless, for he adheres to a concept of historicism which has long been overtaken and has no knowledge whatsoever of something like absoluteness. Heiler simply collects a vast number of details which cannot be connected into any kind of unity and thus finally has nothing to say to the present. Engert's verdict on Barth, however, is far more positive. He considers Barth to be an exponent of a metaphysical orientation within theology – although here, too, his approval is not unreserved. For alongside his systematic concern to define a way of thinking appropriate for theology and the proclamation resulting from it, Engert is also undertaking some theological polemics. He wants to clearly demonstrate that Catholic theology is far more in accordance with Pauline thought than is Protestant thought, represented, in this case, by Barth. Catholicism recognizes not only the absoluteness of God, which serves as the basis for a theology oriented to metaphysics, but also the absoluteness of God in his relationship to humanity. The very structure of his article corresponds to this sentiment. If initially he expounds the

---

[20] Cf. Engert (1923/1924), p. 502.
[21] Cf. Engert (1923/1924), p. 502. Also pp. 503–4.
[22] Cf. Engert (1923/1924), p. 502 with reference to RB (1922/²1923) and Friedrich Heiler, *Der Katholizismus. Seine Idee und seine Erscheinung* (Munich: Reinhardt, 1923).
[23] Cf. Engert (1923/1924), p. 502.
[24] Cf. Engert (1923/1924), pp. 638–50.

hermeneutics which arise from the absoluteness of God in the *Epistle to the Romans*, he then tests to what extent the absoluteness of God is also taken seriously as regards God's relationship to humanity.[25] In this context Engert turns to a theology of grace and then individually treats its implications for sacramentology, ecclesiology and, finally, ethics.[26]

As far as the first point is concerned, Engert understands Barth and his *Epistle to the Romans* as not only offering historical research in order, for example, to gain information about the situation in the first century CE. No less than Paul, Barth's is a more practical concern: the reality of the God beyond time who appeared within time in Jesus Christ.[27] Even if this fact can only be recognized and reflected upon in various perspectives, it still does not disappear. The limitedness of knowledge is indeed something different from the absoluteness of the reality which lets itself to be known. It is absolute because it is the reality of the eternal God himself, which the temporality of its appearance in no way changes.

This leads to the second point in Engert's argument: theocentrism. As God in his absoluteness stands at the centre of the Pauline letters, so too does the absoluteness of the divine action of grace.[28] Engert represents the position of a theology of grace which still understands the Reformers' leading distinction between the acts of God (*opera Dei*) and human works (*opera hominis*) as a sub-definition of the divine action. For if salvation is only granted when God alone is active, then the problem of a competition between God and humanity no longer arises.

Against such a background, Engert refers to the unreasonableness of Protestant accusations against Catholicism. Since baptism, which opens the way to the resurrection effected by God, is in a strict sense a work of God, Catholic teaching on the sacraments cannot be regarded as magic or wizardry.[29] As God in his sovereignty has intervened in human history, the Church is neither a merely human institution, as assumed in Protestantism, nor the institutionalized human attempt to take control of revelation, as formulated more even more sharply by Barth. Instead, the Church is the presence of salvation in history. Thus it is an oversimplification when Barth, on the one hand, equates the visible Church with the Church of Esau and gives her a merely human foundation, and, on the other hand, when he takes only the invisible Church of the Elect, here connected with the name of Jacob, to be the Church of God. Following Paul, one must consider the Church as the custodian of the secrets of redemption, as God's advocate towards

---

[25] Cf. Engert (1923/1924), pp. 504–6 or pp. 506–16.
[26] Cf. Engert (1923/1924), pp. 506–9 (theology of grace), pp. 509–11 (sacramental theology), pp. 511–5 (ecclesiology), pp. 515–6 (ethics).
[27] Cf. Engert (1923/1924), pp. 504–6.
[28] Cf. Engert (1923/1924), pp. 507, 509.
[29] Cf. Engert (1923/1924), p. 511.

humanity, which the Catholic Church can rightly lay claim to for herself.[30] Equally, the Catholic position regarding theological ethics corresponds far better to Pauline thought than does that of Barth. According to the *Epistle to the Romans*, human action is simply human action, not action made possible by God. Such a position does not satisfy the demands of theocentrism.[31]

To summarize, Engert thinks he can establish that Paul's Christianity cannot be understood without metaphysics. In this respect Catholicism has always been the true advocate of Pauline Christianity because it has most strongly represented the absolutely metaphysical and theocentric character of Christianity.[32]

In this way Engert pleads for a kind of thinking in which the apparent disintegration of all values and ideas into mere conditionals, the result of a deliberate demolition of reflection, can be countered by steadfast, lasting certainties. Hence he puts forward an account of the permanence of truth which understands that truth can only be recognized and reflected in various perspectives but cannot be dissolved without remainder into these perspectives.[33] He does not, however, explain how the perspectivity, and thus the limitedness of knowledge of truth, are compatible with the claim to a universal validity of what is known. Since Engert does not put forward any deeper philosophical criticism of historicism, one should consider his article less as a solution to the problem than as an indication of it.

1.4 Immanence, Transcendence and the analogia entis: *Erich Przywara*

At the end of September 1923, Eduard Thurneysen informed his friend Karl Barth of a recent publication which seemed to him absolutely remarkable. In a letter he says:

> Get ahold of issue 11 of 'Stimmen der Zeit', August 1923, Herder, Freiburg i. Br. In it there is a remarkably astute and detailed article about us from the side of our Catholic partner. It is interesting because it makes the Catholic viewpoint very clear. In it there are significant and detailed remarks on Augustine. The writer clearly knows what he

---

[30] Cf. Engert (1923/1924), pp. 514–5.
[31] Cf. Engert (1923/1924), p. 516.
[32] Cf. Engert (1923/1924), pp. 516–7.
[33] Cf. Engert (1923/1924), p. 502.

is talking about. We come off well, even if our most essential concerns are not detected.[34]

The article which Thurneysen recommends his friend to read came from the pen of Erich Przywara (1889–1972). An editor of *Stimmen der Zeit* since 1922, the Jesuit wrote numerous reviews and articles in which he explored almost every intellectual trend of his time. Przywara's enormous production can only be explained by the fact that it was his intent desire to show that Catholicism was *the* answer to the questions of the present.[35] The method that he used essentially remained the same: he constructed two alternative poles which tended towards the extremes and which could find their centre only in Catholicism. Indeed, such a method is readily recognizable in the very article in which he handles Dialectical Theology.[36]

Przywara argues that the question about God in the philosophy of religion and theology at that time had become acute in a new way.[37] Instead of merely going over the consequences of the idea of God as it had previously, it now dealt with the question of the reality standing behind this idea. The era of an Adolf von Harnack and an Ernst Troeltsch is past; a new generation of theologians is appearing, and Karl Barth and Friedrich Gogarten are singled out as noteworthy. In this way he acknowledged, not without some satisfaction, the end of the historicizing and psychologizing of the question of God.[38]

But if the *question* of God was again the centre of attention, it was still unclear which God was being discussed, or how the *conception* of God could be grasped concretely. In this regard Przywara saw a new age of denominational conflict approaching. The question of God was inevitably bound up with the question of the relationship between freedom and grace, and this relationship was understood very differently by Catholics and

---

[34] Cf. *Karl Barth – Eduard Thurneysen. Briefwechsel*, vol. 2, ed. Eduard Thurneysen, Gesamtausgabe V. Briefe (Zürich: Theologischer Verlag Zürich, 1974), p. 190 (Eduard Thurneysen to Karl Barth, letter dated 30 September 1923): 'Verschaff dir doch Heft 11 der 'Stimmen der Zeit', August 1923, Herder Freiburg. Dort ist ein merkwürdig scharfsinniger und ausführlicher Aufsatz über uns von Seiten des katholischen Partners. Er ist interessant, weil er den katholischen Standpunkt sehr deutlich sichtbar macht. Es fallen dabei wesentliche und eingehende Bemerkungen zu Augustin. Es ist ein Kenner, der da redet. Wir kommen gut weg, wenn auch unser eigentlichstes Anliegen nicht gesehen wird.'

[35] Cf. Thomas F. O'Meara, *Erich Przywara, S.J. His Theology and His World* (Notre Dame, IN: University of Notre Dame Press, 2002), pp. 33–41.

[36] On what follows see Erich Przywara, 'Gott in uns oder Gott über uns? (Immanenz und Transzendenz im heutigen Geistesleben.)', *StZ* vol. 105 (1923), pp. 343–62.

[37] Cf. Przywara (1923), p. 343.

[38] Cf. Przywara (1923), p. 343.

Protestants. Hence, instead of looking precipitately for convergences, one should first take a look at their differing conceptions of God.[39]

According to Przywara the Catholic conception of God gains its contours through its understanding of the relationship of God to the world.[40] Referring to Augustine (*Deus interior et exterior*), he understands God as the one who is both *in* everything and *beyond* everything, who is immanent as well as transcendent. These intuitions require a corresponding way of thinking that refrains from polar extremes and instead occupies the Catholic 'centre'. Thus the concept of God has both an orientating as well as a normative function. The extent to which the integration of both aspects – transcendence and immanence – is achievable represents, for Przywara, the decisive criterion for assessing theological proposals. When he uses this criterion to gauge recent outlines by Catholic and Protestant authors he comes to the conclusion that typically either immanence or transcendence is lost. For this reason Dialectical Theology is also judged to be inadequate, no matter how right it is in attacking liberal Protestantism, for in liberal Protestantism, as in Friedrich Heiler (whose thinking appears to Przywara to be just as abstruse as it does to Joseph Engert), immanence is awarded far too much emphasis.

The inadequacy of Dialectical Theology is grounded in the Protestant conception of God, which can be traced back to Martin Luther.[41] Characteristic of the German Reformer is an excessive emphasis on the 'God beyond us' and thus God's transcendence excludes his immanence.[42] According to Luther, a person cannot by his- or herself do anything with regard to God; all human acts and efforts are in the end sinful and must perish. Room is created for faith when our own attempts at self-justification before God cease and are seen to be impossible. Faith is an event in which the person is deeply stirred by God's work in Christ.[43] Przywara desires to understand Dialectical Theology from this angle as well. Here he sees Luther returning powerfully and with him the emphasis on 'God beyond us'.[44] The

---

[39] Cf. Przywara (1923), pp. 343–4.

[40] On what follows see Przywara (1923), pp. 344–7. Cf. Christophe Chalamet, 'Est Deus in Nobis? Die frühen Jahre der Barth-Przywara-Debatte', in *Karl Barths Theologie als europäisches Ereignis*, ed. Martin Leiner and Michael Trowitzsch (Göttingen: Vandenhoeck und Ruprecht, 2008), pp. 271–90, 274–5.

[41] For what follows see Przywara (1923), pp. 347–55. Przywara can speak of a unified Protestant conception of God because for him Calvinism and Lutheranism are, in the end, indistinguishable.

[42] Cf. Przywara (1923), p. 348.

[43] Cf. Przywara (1923), p. 349.

[44] Cf. Przywara (1923), pp. 350, 355. In later years Przywara still maintained that Barth resuscitates Luther's way of thinking. See the monograph *Das Geheimnis Kierkegaards* (Munich and Berlin: Oldenbourg, 1929), pp. 60–70 and his article 'Luther konsequent', *Scholastik* 12 (1937), pp. 386–92, especially pp. 390–1.

central idea of this theological movement around Barth was that God and humanity do not simply stand facing each other neutrally, but are positioned over and against each other in a hostile relationship. While, according to the Catholic understanding, there exists an *analogy* between the two, God is understood here as the *pure negation* of humanity.[45] On this basis there could never be a true unity between God and humanity, a fact which has serious implications for Christology and ecclesiology, as well as for any idea of human co-operation with the work of God.[46]

Przywara is content with these brief observations. To him, Dialectical Theology appears to be a part of the basic problem of Protestantism and by no means its solution. If transcendence and immanence are not placed in a balanced relationship the pendulum will constantly swing from one extreme to the other. Thus Dialectical Theology is merely a temporary phenomenon which sooner or later will be followed by a swing in the opposite direction of immanence. Przywara thus gives much more attention to contemporary Catholic theology.[47] Incidentally, the thinking of Joseph Wittig appears to him to be particularly inadequate as Wittig places too much emphasis on immanence.[48] Przywara emphasizes that only the God who is *in* and simultaneously *beyond* all is able to embrace all that is truly human. Apart from this God there can only be subjectivisms rendered absolute, meaning either anthropomorphized gods or idolized humans.[49] Przywara thinks that he can avoid either extreme with his concept of the *analogia entis*, an idea which was to move more and more into the centre of his thinking in the following years. To Przywara, the *analogia entis* was *the* answer to the questions of the present.[50]

1.5 God against Humanity: Karl Adam

Barely four years after the publication of *Epistle to the Romans*, Karl Adam (1876–1966), one of the foremost dogmaticians of his day in the German-speaking area, already thought that he could diagnose the book in *Hochland*:

> There is no doubt that now in Protestant Theology, which a few years ago might have appeared to the outside observer like a barren desert

---

[45] Cf. Przywara (1923), p. 350.
[46] Cf. Przywara (1923), p. 355.
[47] Cf. Przywara (1923), pp. 356–62.
[48] Cf. Przywara (1923), pp. 359–62.
[49] Cf. Przywara (1923), p. 362.
[50] Cf. Erich Przywara, 'Die Reichweite der Analogie als katholischer Grundform', *Scholastik* 25 (1940), pp. 339–62, 508–32, 339.

for long stretches over which the hot wind of unrestrained criticism raced, streams are suddenly springing up in an area where one might have least suspected them. A new sense for supernatural realities, for God and his revelation, for what is miraculous and for faith, is striving upwards and is fighting with incredible power and concentrated defiance against the old gods of earth and human blood.[51]

For the Tübingen dogmatician it is clear what has triggered this far-reaching change: the 'Theology of Crisis' as Adam, using a customary term at that time, called Dialectical Theology. Protestant theology, instead of working almost exclusively on the historical level and basing itself on human subjectivity, was now theology proper, dealing with serious theological questions and realities. Whether this change was caused by the 'breakthrough of the object' (as a philosophical counter-reaction to the 'turn to the subject' at the end of the eighteenth century) or by the apocalyptic atmosphere in the post-war years due to political, cultural and economic collapse is, according to Adam, a futile question, because at most there could be contributing factors. The real cause of the dramatic change within theology was Protestantism's rediscovery of the inheritance of the Reformation.

Although it cannot be proved unequivocally, there is reason to believe that Adam adopts Erich Przywara's interpretation of Dialectical Theology.[52] There are, for example, highly conspicuous elements common to both. Adam also approaches the theological movement around Barth with the categories of immanence and transcendence in hand.[53] Moreover, he also places much emphasis on the concept of God as a decisive point of difference between Catholic and Protestant theologies.[54] What connects Adam most of all to Przywara, however, is the goal that he pursues in his article: giving a genuinely Catholic assessment and evaluation of Dialectical Theology. To

---

[51] Cf. Karl Adam, 'Die Theologie der Krisis', *Hochland* 23,2 (1926), pp. 271–86, 271: 'Es ist kein Zweifel, daß in der protestantischen Theologie, die noch vor wenigen Jahren dem fremden Beobachter auf weite Strecken hin wie eine dürre Sandwüste erscheinen mochte, über die der heiße Wind hemmungsloser Kritik dahinfegt, nun auf einmal Quellen aufbrechen, die man gerade in ihrem Bereich am wenigsten vermutet hätte. Ein neuer Sinn für die übernatürlichen Wirklichkeiten, für Gott und seine Offenbarung, für das Wunder und für den Glauben strebt empor und kämpft mit unerhörter Gewalt und mit geballtem Trotz gegen die alten Götter aus Erde und Menschenblut.'

[52] An indication of this is not least Erich Przywara's assessment 'Neue Theologie? Das Problem protestantischer Theologie', *StZ* vol. 111 (1926), pp. 348–60, 356 fn 2 with reference to Adam (1926a). As far as what Adam has written about Dialectical Theology is concerned, he is completely in agreement with his interpretation.

[53] Cf. Adam (1926a), p. 272 and elsewhere. Also see p. 284: 'Der Gott über uns ist zugleich der Gott in uns.'

[54] Cf. Adam (1926a), p. 271 fn * with reference to RB (1922/³1924).

these ends, Adam first presents its basic ideas, beginning with the *Epistle to the Romans*.

In the end, Dialectical Theology is based on the 'infinite qualitative difference' between God and humanity.[55] Humanity, inevitably heading to death because of the Fall, stands in the greatest conceivable contrast to the God who is life. This has far-reaching consequences for theology, for neither the man Jesus, nor the Bible, nor creation, nor ethics, nor religion, nor even the Church itself, can lead to God, for all of them are subject to the questionability characteristic of everything worldly. If these realities are, nevertheless, by no means superfluous, it is only because they can still function, despite their dubious nature, as pointers to the God who is beyond the world. For Dialectical Theology, redemption is the fact that the person who has become aware of his own dubious nature, in extreme mortification and final brokenness, not only sees himself pulled to the edge of a precipice, but even dares to throw himself into the gaping void which opens up before him, and while in free fall he is caught up by the grace of God while remaining hovering over the abyss.

How is Dialectical Theology to be assessed from a Catholic point of view? According to Adam one must first stress that, in contrast to the Reformers, it does not primarily come out against Catholicism. Its real opponents are those currents in Protestantism which take up the ideas of Schleiermacher. These authors are concerned with humanity's interpretation of God and the world, instead of with God in his revelation, and in doing so they deprive theology of its true character. In this way there are even certain parallels between Dialectical Theology and Catholicism insofar as the latter is also concerned with combating the aberrations of modernity.[56] Moreover, there was a great deal of common ground in the doctrines of God and grace.[57] In spite of this common ground, however, in Adam's estimation there are serious differences. It is the acceptance of that 'infinite qualitative difference' which separates Catholic theology from Dialectical Theology.[58] Barth goes far beyond Luther and Calvin, who at least accepted a connection between God and humanity, no matter how tenuously, and regards God and humanity as completely disconnected from each other. In the process of disconnecting God and humanity, Barth has disconnected himself from the biblical basis of Christianity. What Barth thinks he can derive from the writings of Paul has, according to Adam, very little to do with what one actually finds in them. Paul does not portray the Christian as a person

---

[55] For what follows see Adam (1926a), pp. 271–5.
[56] Cf. Adam (1926a), pp. 276–7.
[57] Cf. Adam (1926a), pp. 277–8.
[58] Cf. Adam (1926a), pp. 278–82, especially p. 282 with reference to RB (1922/³1924), p. XIII.

who sinks into the deepest despair in the face of sin and only hears salvific words of forgiveness. For Paul, the Christian becomes in baptism a new creation who is no longer subjected to sin. Thus, while Barth thinks he must understand God as the complete and literal antithesis to the world, Catholic theology understands the relationship of both in the sense of similarity, and thus in the sense of the *analogia entis* which coordinates what is natural and what is supernatural. God and humanity are neither the same in essence nor irreconcilably opposed to each other. They are both differentiated from and, at the same time, related to each other inasmuch as their relationship is that of Creator and creation.[59] On the basis of the *analogia entis*, Catholicism can accept both the possibility of the natural recognition of God and the *potentia oboedientialis* understood as humanity's ever-present openness for the effects of grace. Thus the relationship of God and humanity need not be described, as in Barth, as a paradox or wonder, but can be seen as a relationship of a reciprocal kinship.[60]

Adam portrays the Catholic conception of God as straightforwardly rational and balanced. Dialectical Theology's highly Calvinistic conception of God, by contrast, seems to Adam to be entirely problematic, if not dangerous. Before a God who in his absolute superiority to the world and total freedom throws into question all that is earthly, one could have no confidence in oneself or in one's abilities. Such a person would then become either introverted and self-righteous, or worldly minded and addicted to earthly things.[61] The fresh streams which Adam initially had seen springing up in the barren, storm-tossed desert of Protestant theology have in the end proved to be a Fata Morgana. As Adam notes at the end of his article, Dialectical Theology is nothing less than hostile to life itself.[62]

For Adam, the topic of Barth was thereby dealt with in principle. Having finished off Barth, Adam's clash with the Lutheran Karl Heim (1874–1958) reads like a mere postscript. Like his Catholic colleague before him, the Tübingen systematician had published an essay on the nature of Christianity in 1925.[63] Adam commented on this piece in an extensive article which, just as the one on Dialectical Theology, also appeared in '*Hochland*' in 1926.[64]

---

[59] Cf. Adam (1926a), pp. 282–3.
[60] Cf. Adam (1926a), pp. 283–4.
[61] Cf. Adam (1926a), pp. 285–6.
[62] Cf. Adam (1926a), p. 286.
[63] Cf. Karl Heim, *Das Wesen des evangelischen Christentums* (Leipzig: Quelle und Meyer, 1925); or Karl Adam, *Das Wesen des Katholizismus* (Augsburg: Haas und Grabherr, 1924). For some helpful background see *Das Christentum der Theologen im 20. Jahrhundert. Vom 'Wesen des Christentums' zu den Kurzformeln des Glaubens*, ed. Mariano Delgado (Stuttgart: Kohlhammer, 2000).
[64] Cf. Karl Adam, 'Karl Heim und das Wesen des Katholizismus', *Hochland* 23, 2 (1926), pp. 447–69, 586–608.

German Protestant theology, Adam argues, is moving between two extremes. On the one hand, Barth in his extremely Calvinistic thinking is cutting any bond between God and the world.[65] On the other hand, Heim represents a spiritualist Lutheranism in which the distinction between God and the world finally becomes untenable.[66] The only appropriate conception of God is the one held by Catholicism, according to which God is both *beyond* and *in* creation.[67] Here, Adam simply adopts Przywara's formulation verbatim, revealing yet again how deeply he is indebted to the Jesuit for his interpretation of Barth. One can see how influential this interpretation was from the fact that already in 1928 a supporter of Dialectical Theology noted that for Catholics Barth was accused of looking exclusively to God and in the process forgetting humanity.[68] Only a short time later this interpretation was given a definitive air of authority by being included in the '*Lexikon für Theologie und Kirche*' by none other than Adam's assistant, Josef Rupert Geiselmann (1890–1970).[69]

1.6 Results

There are two likely reasons why Catholics were already giving attention to Dialectical Theology at the beginning of the 1920s. First, there was a clear awareness of the problematic areas within Catholicism, and it was hoped that Dialectical Theology might provide some insight into and way beyond these problems. In this connection we should specifically mention Joseph Wittig and Joseph Engert, both of whom were worried about the state of preaching at the time. Wittig recognized how pitiful preaching had become, for its sophisticated language had nothing in common with the typical speech of the average person in the pew. Similarly, Engert was haunted by the problem of how preaching could be carried out at all in the face of a relativistic historicism which reduced all truth and validity to a claim's historical origin and context. Thus what each valued in Barth's *Epistle to the Romans* was different. While Wittig was fascinated by Barth's prodigious linguistic power, Engert saw in him a turn away from historicism.

The second reason why Catholic theology took a critical look at dialectic theology at that time was incomparably more prosaic. The movement around

---

[65] According to Adam (1926b) Barth starts from a radically formulated principle of the *Deo soli Gloria* (p. 450) and aspires to restore a strict Calvinism (p. 469).
[66] Cf. Adam (1926b), pp. 453–4, 592–3.
[67] Cf. Adam (1926b), p. 608: '"über uns und in uns"'.
[68] Cf. Paul Schempp, 'Randglossen zum Barthianismus', *Zwischen den Zeiten* 6 (1928), pp. 529–39, 533–4 with reference to Przywara (1923) and Adam (1926a).
[69] Cf. Josef Rupert Geiselmann, 'Dialektische Theologie', in *LTK* 3 (1930), pp. 279–82.

Barth was unmistakably successful and thus constituted a theological-political factor which henceforth had to be taken into account. Erich Przywara and Karl Adam, unlike Wittig and Engert, did not aim at gaining insights from a systematic theological outline (appropriation), but rather at a critical estimation of a phenomenon within Protestantism (perception). An idealist Protestantism heavily indebted to historical criticism was quite clearly being beaten back, as Dialectical Theology seemed to be overwhelming the liberalism which until then had dominated the universities. If many Catholics had previously thought that it was no longer necessary to take a critical look at a Protestantism that was unconcerned with God in his revelation but merely satisfied itself with interpretations of the human subject, then Dialectical Theology marked the beginning of a completely new situation which demanded a response from its contemporaries. Even if Przywara, Adam and Geiselmann were keenly aware of how the theological movement around Barth was on the verge of ousting the hitherto dominant liberal line, they did not recognize within it anything relevant for Catholicism. This explains why, in the following period, they did not feel the need for sustained engagement with it. Certainly Przywara mentioned Dialectical Theology in many of his extensive analyses of the intellectual landscape of the Weimar Republic, but his perspective remained what it had been in his 1923 article, that of a critically dissociated observer.[70] Indeed, the fact that he met with Barth on several occasions was primarily due to Barth's initiative, not Przywara's, but we shall come back to this topic later.

If one looks at how Dialectic Theology was initially evaluated by Catholics one can see that there were two lines of interpretation which diverged to a rather large degree as regards their interest in its reception and their assessment of it. Barth himself was aware of this diversity of opinion, for in the Preface to the 1924 edition of the *Epistle to the Romans* he refers to the vastly diverging assessments of Przywara and Engert.[71]

---

[70] Cf. Erich Przywara, *Religionsbegründung. Max Scheler – J.H. Newman* (Freiburg i.Br.: Herder, 1923), p. 4 fn 1; ibid, 'Ringen um Gott', *StZ* vol. 107 (1924), pp. 347–52, 348–9; ibid, 'Neue Religiösität?', *StZ* vol. 109 (1925), pp. 18–35, 18–9; ibid, 'Neue Theologie? Das Problem protestantischer Theologie', *StZ* vol. 111 (1926), pp. 348–60, 356–7; ibid, 'Eschatologismus', *StZ* vol. 117 (1929), pp. 229–35.

[71] Cf. RB (1922/³1924), p. XXIV [English translation: *The Epistle to the Romans*, trans. Edwyn C. Hoskyns (London et al.: Oxford University Press, 1933), p. 21]: 'Catholic reviewers have, for the most part, displayed a genuine understanding of the point at issue. They have, moreover, conducted the discussion in a proper atmosphere of theological controversy – an atmosphere seemingly foreign to most of my reviewers on the other side of the great gulf. Now, what is the meaning of this fundamental, and to me quite unexpected, understanding? Erich Przywara, S.J., contrasts our "school"! with that of Otto and Heiler, judging it to be a "genuine rebirth of Protestantism", a reappearance of the "passionate fervor of the old Reformers". Joseph Engert, on the other hand, brings forward evidence to show that, apart from the doctrine of the

On the Catholic side, Przywara's interpretation of dialectic theology became the dominant one. Catholics, at least in the 1920s and 1930s, considered Przywara to be *the* interpreter of Protestantism, not only because of his obvious skill at trenchantly revealing lines of development and encapsulating them in useful phrases and formulae, but also because of his incessant literary production.[72] These two factors alone go some way towards explaining the ascendance of Przywara's interpretation of Dialectical Theology. In fact, it was not only taken over in a modified form by Adam and Geiselmann, but actually served as the basis for two dissertations on Dialectical Theology, one published at the beginning of the 1930s, the other at the end.[73]

At any rate, we must hold on to the fact that the *Epistle to the Romans* was read and received by Catholics in two fundamentally different ways. On the one hand we have the perception, analysis and evaluation of an interesting theological-political movement, and on the other we have the active adoption of a systematically relevant way of thinking. Catholic reception of Barth was to oscillate between these two perspectives in the following years.

Church elaborated in Chs. IX–XI, my commentary does not differ from the teaching of Thomas Aquinas, of the Council of Trent, and of the Roman Catechism; only my formulation of it is far more obscure and complicated. The two reviewers are clearly not saying quite the same thing.'

[72] For example, none other than Przywara wrote the article "Protestantismus II. Beurteilung vom Standpunkt des Katholizismus", in *RGG*² 3 (1930), pp. 1600–3, an assessment of Protestantism from the viewpoint of Catholicism.

[73] Cf. Georg Feuerer, *Der Kirchenbegriff der dialektischen Theologie* (Freiburg i.Br.: Herder, 1933) or Johannes Ries, *Die natürliche Gotteserkenntnis in der Theologie der Krisis im Zusammenhang mit dem Imagobegriff bei Calvin* (Bonn: Hanstein, 1939). Since the dissertation simply corroborated the arguments that Przywara had already put forth in the 1920s, the Jesuit could not find much fault with Ries's study. Unsurprisingly, then, his review in *StZ* vol. 137 (1940), p. 132 is rather positive. Hermann Volk, himself deeply indebted to Przywara, wrote another positive review in *TRev* 39 (1940), pp. 215–7.

2

ANTI-MODERN MODERN: THE PHILOSOPHICAL PRESUPPOSITIONS OF DIALECTICAL THEOLOGY

2.1 Introduction

Since the eighteenth century it has been clearly established that statements about *God* are *human* statements about God, meaning they are bound by the scope of reason and qualified by the historicity of understanding. Historical-critical exegesis exposed the multi-layeredness and plurality of biblical texts, the critique of knowledge seemed to spell the end of traditional metaphysics and a growing historical awareness gave all claims to a systematic validity a temporal context. Denominational theologies reacted to these developments in very different ways. Protestant theology attempted to talk about God under the assumptions of the Enlightenment and idealism. By contrast, Catholic theology, after similar attempts in the first half of the nineteenth century, witnessed the ascendance of medieval scholasticism (in the sense of the early modern schools) to the position of being the decisive authority.[1] Part of the growing influence of scholasticism was an implicit rejection of Kant's philosophy.[2]

---

[1] *The Blackwell Companion to Nineteenth-Century Theology*, ed. David Fergusson (Oxford et al.: Blackwell-Wiley, 2010) offers a survey of the various lines and currents on the Catholic as well as on the protestant side.

[2] Cf. *Kant und der Katholizismus. Stationen einer wechselhaften Geschichte*, ed. Norbert Fischer (Freiburg i.Br. et al.: Herder, 2005); Walter Schöpsdau, 'Philosoph des Protestantismus? Kant zwischen den Konfessionen', *Materialdienst des Konfessionskundlichen Instituts Bensheim* 62 (2011), pp. 10–3.

KARL BARTH, CATHOLIC RENEWAL AND VATICAN II

The clash between certain Catholics and Karl Barth should be understood against this backdrop. Themselves marked by Neo-Scholasticism, these Catholics not only recognized the completely different philosophical orientation of his thinking, but they also detected great problems in it. Their opinion is that while at its very best Dialectical Theology still maintains some of the central convictions of Christianity, it can no longer rationally penetrate and reveal them. Thus it is a question of the philosophical premises of theology: which philosophy is the appropriate one, and to what degree should it influence theology?

In 1930 the Jesuit Michael Gierens (1888–1937) published an article in which he classified Dialectical Theology historically within the context of recent Protestantism and subjected it to a systematic critique.[3] What moved the Professor of Dogmatics in Frankfurt (Sankt Georgen) to undertake such a task remains unknown. Almost as uncertain is the case of Friedrich Maria Rintelen (1899–1988), a priest in the archbishopric of Paderborn.[4] According to his own account, his doctoral studies qualified him for some of the leading tasks in the diocese.[5] The basic thesis of his 1934 dissertation was that the whole of modern Protestantism is decisively indebted to Kant.[6] The third theologian who will be discussed in what follows is Karl Rahner (1904–1984). In 1936, the now well-known Jesuit published an article on contemporary Protestant Christology, and it can be readily said that in doing so he desired to explore a topic which was, until then, unknown to him.[7] The fourth and final figure we should mention is Hermann Volk (1903–1988), later bishop of Mainz and indeed a cardinal. Volk maintains that even in

---

[3] Cf. Michael Gierens, 'Die ‚dialektische Theologie' in katholischer Sicht', *StZ* vol. 118 (1930), pp. 196–206. For biographical information see Dorothea Nebel, 'Die Lehrstuhlinhaber für Apologetik/Fundamentaltheologie und Dogmatik [...]', in *Die katholisch-theologischen Disziplinen in Deutschland 1870–1962. Ihre Geschichte, ihr Zeitbezug*, ed. Hubert Wolf (Paderborn et al.: Schöningh, 1999), pp. 164–230, 200.

[4] For biographical information see Clemens Brodkorb, 'Rintelen, Friedrich Maria', in *Die Bischöfe der deutschsprachigen Länder 1945–2001*, ed. Erwin Gatz (Berlin: Duncker und Humblot, 2002), pp. 347–9.

[5] Cf. Friedrich Maria Rintelen, *Erinnerungen ohne Tagebuch* (Paderborn: Bonifatius, ²1983), pp. 78–9.

[6] Cf. Friedrich Maria Rintelen, *Wege zu Gott. Eine kritische Abhandlung über das Problem des Gotterfassens in der deutschen protestantischen Theologie der Nachkriegszeit* (Würzburg: Becker, 1934).

[7] Cf. Karl Rahner, 'Die deutsche protestantische Christologie der Gegenwart', *Der Seelsorger* 1 (1936), pp. 189–202. Reprinted in his *Sämtliche Werke*, vol. 4 (Solothurn et al.: Benziger and Herder, 1997), pp. 299–312. On this article cf. Andreas R. Batlogg, 'Vom Mut, Jesus um den Hals zu fallen. Christologie', in ibid et al., *Der Denkweg Karl Rahners. Quellen – Entwicklungen – Perspektiven* (Mainz: Grünewald, 2003), pp. 277–99, 288; Michael Kappes, 'Die Bedeutung der Theologie Karl Rahners für die Ökumene. Ein vergessenes Thema?', *Cath(M)* 59 (2005), pp. 1–35, 3.

Barth's allegedly purely theological anthropology there are still philosophical elements (and certainly not scholastic ones) which play a decisive role.[8] Incidentally, at the end of 1936 Volk contacted Barth from Fribourg (where Volk had finished his doctorate in philosophy) and requested a meeting with the Swiss theologian. Their meeting took place shortly afterwards.[9]

2.2 The Tortuous Paths of Modern Theology: Michael Gierens

How Dialectical Theology should be judged from a Catholic point of view is the question Michael Gierens tries to answer. To this end he first places the movement around Karl Barth within the development of the history of Protestant theology and then subjects it to a systematic critique.[10]

In Gierens's estimation, Protestantism, marked by a rather free attitude towards dogmas and commandments, is made conspicuous by a continuous loss of what is specifically Christian.[11] At the beginning, its followers found themselves in a very comfortable situation: they could live off of the wealth of the traditions passed down to them from the medieval Church. The Reformers, however, already dealt with this inheritance quite liberally. While they held fast to some elements they regarded as essential, they discarded others as insignificant. More specifically, in the older Protestant orthodoxy doctrines such as the inspiration of Scripture, justification and predestination were given a significance which they had never had before, whereas other doctrines underwent massive modifications, including the idea of the priesthood, good works and, most importantly, the significance of ecclesiastical tradition and the Church's teaching office. The kind of consequences that such a selection principle would entail only came to light when Protestant theology was overtaken by the modern age. Historical-critical exegesis brought out the distance between today's believer and the biblical witness, rationalism eliminated the idea of the supernatural and critical epistemology banished the idea of independent objectivity.

As a result of the insight that statements about *God* are first and foremost statements by *humans* about God, there begins a process of transformation which, according to Gierens, constitutes the second phase of the history of Protestant theology and which is decisively connected with the name of

---

[8] Cf. Hermann Volk, *Die Kreaturauffassung bei Karl Barth. Eine philosophische Untersuchung* (Würzburg: Becker, 1938).
[9] Cf. KBA 9336.962 (Hermann Volk to Karl Barth, letter from 14 December 1936). As an entry in Barth's diary shows, a meeting took place in Basle on 6 January 1937. I would like to thank Hans-Anton Drewes (Basle) for this information.
[10] Cf. Gierens (1930), pp. 196–9 or pp. 199–206.
[11] For what follows see Gierens (1930), pp. 196–9.

Friedrich Schleiermacher. Since faith was no longer rational or justifiable through reference to objective data, Schleiermacher transferred its ground to emotion, to subjective moods. As a result, however, every material determination of the contents of the Christian faith through dogmatic propositions or ethical instructions does not obtain. It cannot be clearly determined what this Absolute now is, nor that it is identical with the Christian God; hence in Gierens's view, Schleiermacher was a pantheist. This is where Dialectical Theology comes into play. Its most conspicuous characteristic is the position it takes regarding Schleiermacher and the nineteenth-century theology which followed him. Alongside these historical judgements there is also Dialectical Theology's claim to be in agreement with the Bible and the Reformers; that is, to lend a voice to pre-modern Protestantism. The problematic position of modern Protestant theology is most clearly seen in preaching: only God's word *should* be preached, but only the human word *can* be preached; *something or other* is talked about, but *what is essential* is not given a voice. Dialectical Theology thinks it can solve this problem by emphasizing a subjective decision given its urgency by taking eschatology seriously.

Dialectical Theology therefore appears with the claim that, in contrast to the enervated Protestantism of modernity, it communicates the biblical Reformation message. Gierens objects that this only seems to be the case as Dialectical Theology is itself entangled in the modern premises.[12] He leaves his readers in no doubt that a truly Christian theology is impossible when modernity is accepted as its operative framework. To justify this argument he develops a systematic contrast between 'idealism' and 'realism'. If realism understands the discerning subject as *receptive*, and to this extent affected by the object, idealism views it as *productive*, for in a certain sense the subject produces its object (a thought which, incidentally, Gierens takes to be absurd). Whether theology takes realism or idealism as its epistemological presupposition is anything but insignificant.[13] These two options determine at the very outset how one will think of revelation – as a human construction or as a free gift from God to humanity. For Gierens there is no doubt that a coherent account of revelation as a revelation of *God* can only be maintained under the presupposition of realism. Thus he judges Dialectical Theology by the extent to which it has idealism or realism as its presupposition. By laying down this criterion Gierens arrives at an ambivalent result. Certainly, idealism would be overcome in principle by existential thinking, for the person who discovers that he or she is finite and sinful not only recognizes him- or herself as real, but also recognizes that God is neither finite nor sinful. In spite of this upshot, the representatives of

---

[12] On what follows see Gierens (1930), pp. 199–206.
[13] Cf. Gierens (1930), p. 200 with critical reference to CD (1927), p. 216.

Dialectical Theology leave idealism behind and do not accept realism as an epistemological presupposition. In order to defend itself against the monism which would inevitably arise if God were understood as a product of human cognition, a dualism was advanced, but it was a dualism which tacitly had monism as its presupposition. This dualism is expressed in the formula of the 'infinite qualitative difference' and spelt out in various ways, such as the difference between time and eternity.[14]

Gierens explores the cogency of these arguments through an engagement with the *Christian Dogmatics*. How is revelation to be understood?[15] On the one hand Barth assumes that God reveals himself, but on the other hand he denies that a person can achieve any knowledge of God, for God would then become a product of the human cognition. Barth thus slides into a problematic position, for if God is always beyond understanding then the concept of understanding also disappears and the logical consequence would then be agnosticism. If there is an insurmountable gulf between God and humanity then metaphysical certainties are impossible, which is the very definition of agnosticism. This conclusion can only be avoided if one chooses realism as one's epistemological presupposition. This presupposition can accept the difference between the infinite God and finite humanity without any difficulties and can render knowledge of God – understood here as the communicable knowledge of God, not the incommunicable – simultaneously incomplete and yet fundamentally true. Since Dialectical Theology is ensnared in idealism in spite of all claims to the contrary, it can only assert but not substantiate the contents of the Christian faith.

Four years later, Friedrich Maria Rintelen, in a similar manner to Gierens, would also cite the 'infinite qualitative difference' as his reason for rejecting Dialectical Theology.

2.3 The Speechlessness of Dialectical Theology: Friedrich Maria Rintelen

In his dissertation, Rintelen deals with philosophy of religion within the Protestant tradition since the end of World War I, paying close attention to the areas of knowledge of God and certainty of God in particular.[16] In so doing he also examines Dialectical Theology.[17]

---

[14] Cf. Gierens (1930), p. 206 with reference to RB (1922), p. XIII. Also pp. 201–4.
[15] On what follows see Gierens (1930), pp. 204–5 with reference to CD (1927).
[16] Cf. Rintelen (1934), p. V.
[17] Rintelen (1934), p. 132 does indeed speak of Barth as the real representative of the new movement within Protestant theology, so he talks of the 'Barthian line' (p. 138) rather than of Dialectical Theology. Even so, he devotes no more attention to Barth than he does to Brunner, Thurneysen and Gogarten – cf. also pp. X–XIV (Bibliography).

Rintelen structures his dissertation in the style of classical theological polemics ('Kontroverstheologie'). He first describes the positions of Protestant theologians so that he can then critically comment on them from a Catholic point of view. He sees the decisive difference between the two camps in that Catholic theology assumes that the human person entertains both a supernatural as well as a natural way to God; that is, faith and reason.[18] Recent Protestant theology, by contrast, is indebted to Luther for its religious outlook and to Kant for its philosophical presuppositions, and so denies that there is a natural way for human beings to reach God. Since the *ratio* is dethroned, the irrational prevails, at least in the way in which God is understood and frequently in the concept of God itself.[19] Behind this situation stands the figure of Kant, whose transcendental philosophy clearly has unlimited validity in Protestantism in spite of contrary and more recent developments in philosophy. Kant's authority is so strong that merely mentioning his name rules out any questions about the natural discernibility of God and that his objections to the proofs for God's existence can simply be parroted.[20] According to Rintelen, when deductive reasoning is eliminated as a way of knowing God, other spiritual aptitudes take the place of reason – for example, emotion, as in the case of those who follow Schleiermacher, or a kind of innate certainty of God as in Dialectical Theology.[21] On this point, however, its representatives are inconsistent. While on the one hand they accept a form of innate knowledge of God, on the other they make faith alone a way to God; the God of the philosophers has, in the end, nothing whatsoever to do with the God of Christianity.[22]

For Dialectical Theology, inferential reasoning offers no way to God; instead, God himself must reveal himself.[23] This idea was grounded on and likewise secured by the 'infinite qualitative difference', the central axiom of Dialectical Theology. Hopelessly subject to the temporal flux, the human person cannot find the eternal God by his or her own resources. Instead, he or she is permanently dependent on God, as one can never dispense with revelation.[24]

Yet Rintelen doubts whether this is really the case. The emotional way in which the representatives of Dialectical Theology express their convictions

---

[18] Cf. Rintelen (1934), p. 3.
[19] Cf. Rintelen (1934), p. 11. For Luther and Kant see pp. 9–11.
[20] Cf. Rintelen (1934), p. 12. According to Rintelen, Kant is *the* philosopher of Protestantism (p. 10).
[21] Cf. Rintelen (1934), pp. 35–6. For Dialectical Theology see pp. 39–41.
[22] Cf. Rintelen (1934), 39–40 fn 10 or p. 41 with fn 13. In this connection Rintelen also criticizes Barth's interpretation of Anselm (p. 48).
[23] For what follows see Rintelen (1934), pp. 130–46.
[24] Cf. Rintelen (1934), p. 132. Not here, but certainly elsewhere, there are references to the *Letter to the Romans*, namely, pp. 132–5 with reference to RB (1922/⁶1933), pp. 17, 73–4.

simply blurs the fact that their conception of God is more oriented by the Absolute of philosophy than by the God of revelation. The language they use is certainly religious, even prophetic, and yet the basic idea of their system is so far more indebted to German Idealism than to the Christian faith.[25] What presents itself as pure theology is, in fact, a theologically veiled philosophy. Revelation is thus not simply *explicated* by means of idealist conceptual tools, but it is already *conceived of* on idealist presuppositions. According to Rintelen, we should welcome the fact that the concept of revelation is, to all appearances, being taken seriously in Protestantism. Even so, there remain no points of contact between Dialectical Theology and Catholicism.[26] The acceptance of an 'infinite qualitative difference' between God and humanity prevents such a rapprochement.[27] In the end, Dialectical Theology leads to little more than speechlessness.[28]

2.4 The Christ of Faith: Karl Rahner

Like Michael Gierens and Friedrich Maria Rintelen, Karl Rahner also interprets Dialectical Theology on the basis of the *Epistle to the Romans*; in fact, not once does he refer to the *Church Dogmatics*. His primarily concern, however, is the systematic deciphering of the various Christological conceptions in German Protestant theology at the time, and not presenting the development or substance of Dialectical Theology.[29]

If Protestant theology has largely abandoned the search for a rational foundation of faith, this was primarily due to the fact that such a basis no longer seemed possible after the collapse of classical metaphysics in the eighteenth century and the development of historical awareness in the nineteenth. Christology in German Protestant theology therefore revolves around the catchphrase 'the Christ of faith'.[30] Accordingly, Rahner first depicts the understanding of faith which forms the basis of this Christological reflection and subsequently deals with the various conceptions of Christology.[31]

---

[25] Cf. Rintelen (1934), p. 141.
[26] Cf. Rintelen (1934), pp. 146, 158.
[27] Cf. Rintelen (1934), pp. 140–6. Rintelen writes (p. 146, translated): 'Dialectical Theology signifies a complete separation between God and humanity; Catholicism signifies the incarnation of God and the "deification of man": redemption, sanctification and deification of the whole comes through him who is the Head – Christ the Lord!' Erich Przywara also comes out in support of this in 'Religiöser und weltlicher Mensch', *StZ* vol. 129 (1935), pp. 200–2, 200.
[28] Cf. Rintelen (1934), p. 158.
[29] Cf. Rahner (1936), pp. 195–6. The various conceptions are presented on pp. 197–202.
[30] Cf. Rahner (1936), p. 189: 'Christus des Glaubens'.
[31] Cf. Rahner (1936), pp. 189–95 or pp. 195–202.

Two elements interlock in the Protestant understanding of faith: subjective experience and objective history.[32] It becomes clear, however, that the first element is dominant when one contrasts the Protestant understanding of faith with the Catholic. Here Rahner can fall back on the *analysis fidei*. In modern Catholic theology the problem of the foundation of faith has been discussed in detail under this catchphrase. In other words, Catholic theology deals with the question as to *what* the objective ground is for the believer's voluntary assent to the faith of the Church, and *how* this ground is recognized and affirmed in the act of faith. As far as this point is concerned, Rahner makes no differences between Catholic and Protestant theology, because it seems as if both affirm that the first and real cause of the acceptance of faith is nothing other than the God who reveals himself. The differences between the two appear quite clearly, however, with the question of relationship between the cause of the acceptance of faith and the ground of the credibility of faith. Protestant theology completely rejects a rational foundation for faith, for faith has no positive relationship to reason. By contrast, Catholic theology views the cognition of metaphysical and historical truths not as a sufficient condition for the act of faith, but certainly as a necessary one, for it considers the human person to be a rational being. To encapsulate the Catholic–Protestant antithesis under a formula, one could argue that if the credibility of faith is secured by *objective truths* for the former, then for the latter it is secured by *subjective certainties*.[33]

Thus, faith for Protestantism is simply an experience. But as experience can, in principle, only be subjective, the question arises as to how one can avoid the subjectivism of faith. Recent Protestant theology is not unaware of this problem, and in turn has seen in history an objective corrective. However, as Rahner immediately points out, this history can only be objective in a very limited sense, for it is necessary to reflect on events and to construct various connections between them. Subjectivism, then, is at best mitigated, but in no way is it entirely avoided. Rahner notes that it is possible to connect faith to history in two ways: one can either hold to a strict identity between revelation and history or identify a particular history as the history of God's saving grace. In the second case, one must not simply clarify *why* this particular history is revelation but, more importantly, *in what sense* God is part of the history. At this point there are three logical possibilities: history can be seen as revelation, as a veiling, or as both a revelation and a

---

[32] On what follows see Rahner (1936), pp. 189–95.

[33] There is a polemical undertone when Rahner (1936) speaks of the 'rational foundation of faith' (p. 192) in Catholic theology in contrast to the 'irrationality' (p. 190) of Protestant theology. On this see Karsten Kreutzer, 'Karl Rahners Kritik antiintellektualistischer Tendenzen in der deutschen Philosophie und Theologie während der nationalsozialistischen Ära', *TP* 76 (2001), pp. 410–20, especially p. 414.

veiling. Nevertheless, subjectivism still exists no matter how the relationship between subjective experience and apparently objective history is conceived of in the act of faith, for the concept of faith always determines what can be taken as a statement of faith.[34]

Rahner is well aware of the various problems that have confronted Protestant theology since the eighteenth century. The concrete solution to these, however, seems to him to be inadmissible, for if God is to be God then his freedom cannot find its limits in humanity's realm.[35] This theological axiom collides with the philosophical understanding of modernity, whereby the object remains a constitutive element of the subject.

Faith is emphasized in Protestant theology because it alone gives access to God's self-disclosure. Christ is the conclusive and decisive Word of God's Revelation; in Christ, God reveals himself to faith, in Christ faith has God himself. This is, for Rahner, the fundamental conviction of the whole of Protestant Christology and at the same time the fundamental impetus of its reflection. The question must be asked as to how faith should think of Christ so that faith actually has in Christ the God who reveals himself. At this point the concept of faith has a decisive significance for Christology, for every statement of faith is standardized by the concept of faith, and, furthermore, considering Christ as both a historical fact and yet as one who can only be grasped through faith entails defining the relationship between a *historical event* and an *experience of faith*.[36]

The varied conceptions of Christology, according to Rahner, arise from how one evaluates the aspects of the divine nature or transcendence ('above'), and the human nature or immanence ('below') in the person of the One who reveals himself. Five models can be identified in this regard: first, a *low Christology* in which Jesus is the revelation of the God who is immanent to the world in the immanence of the world; second, a *Christology from below*, which sees Jesus as a revelation of the transcendent from what is merely immanent; third, a *Christology from above*, where Christ is the entry of the transcendent into the immanent; fourth, a *Christology from below and from above*, in which Jesus is understood as a positive sign of the God who remains transcendent and thus also as an offence; and fifth, a *high Christology*, which regards Jesus simply as the judgement of the transcendent God over the world.[37]

In his article, Rahner pays only brief attention to Barth and Emil Brunner. Interestingly, he justifies this by saying that their way of thinking is already

---

[34] Cf. Rahner (1936), pp. 194–5.
[35] Cf. Rahner (1936), p. 195.
[36] Cf. Rahner (1936), p. 195.
[37] Cf. Rahner (1936), p. 196. This pattern consolidates one formulated earlier (pp. 195–6). Rahner then clarifies what this means in detail by giving examples (pp. 197–202).

known in Catholic circles. When Rahner also points out that Dialectical Theology is *not* identical with Protestant dogmatics, we can see the extent to which Dialectical Theology determined the perception of Protestantism in the mid-1930s.[38] For Rahner, however, it is simply a temporary phenomenon, as he sees a kind of Hegelian dialectic at work in the more recent history of Protestant theology. If liberal currents had dominated German Protestantism in the years before World War I, then Dialectical Theology represents its antithesis.[39] As the antithesis only reacts to a thesis, Rahner devotes particular attention to the approaches which attempt to mediate between the two and reach a synthesis. For this reason, he gives particular attention to Paul Althaus (1888–1966), who attempted to do something similar, although he reproaches Althaus with still being too closely attached to Barth.[40]

At any rate, we must note that Rahner thought of Dialectical Theology as a temporary extreme and a passing trend. He thus saw no need to pay much attention to it. He even gives a systematic reason for this judgement: Dialectical Theology differs from the other trends in Protestant theology in that it is anti-historical. History, which tends to be objective, is not seen as a corrective to what is in principle a subjective experience of faith, because indistinctness and inconsistency appear to be characteristic features of history.[41] Thus history, according to Dialectical Theology, cannot have a justifying function for faith because God reveals himself in a completely veiled way. This sentiment has, Rahner notes, considerable consequences for Christology. Since historical events in themselves are not unambiguous and therefore can be variously interpreted, human faith is not provoked into existence because of Jesus, but in spite of him.[42] Thus it cannot be shown *how* or even *that* God truly became man, for just as in the case of history and faith, the human and divine nature in Jesus Christ are not positively connected.[43] In him God still remains completely beyond and never really and truly becomes man.[44] The decisive systematic reservation which Rahner announces against Dialectical Theology is that at the most it can merely assert the doctrine of the incarnation, but cannot develop it more substantially.

---

[38] Cf. Rahner (1936), p. 189.

[39] Cf. Rahner (1936), p. 193: Rahner speaks here of the great line from Schleiermacher via Ritschl which had dominated humanitarian culturally optimistic Protestantism until the emergence of Dialectical Theology. Whether this 'great line' really existed should be discussed specifically. On this see Johannes Zachhuber, 'Friedrich Schleiermacher und Albrecht Ritschl. Kontinuitäten und Diskontinuitäten in der Theologie des 19. Jahrhunderts', *Zeitschrift für Neuere Theologiegeschichte* 12 (2005), pp. 16–46.

[40] Cf. Rahner (1936), p. 193. Rahner's critique of Althaus can be found on pp. 193–4, 196, 202.

[41] Cf. Rahner (1936), pp. 192–3.

[42] Cf. Rahner (1936), p. 201.

[43] Cf. Rahner (1936), p. 196.

[44] Cf. Rahner (1936), p. 202.

While Rahner criticized Dialectical Theology on theological grounds, Hermann Volk directly questioned its philosophical premises in his 1938 dissertation.

2.5 Barth's Conception of the Creature: Hermann Volk

Both philosophy and theology make claims about humanity. The question here is how to think of the relationship between these two forms of reflection. Hermann Volk develops this point in the preface to his study of Barth's conception of the creaturely (in fact, one can see in the preface the outlines of the rest of his analysis). In his view philosophy and theology stand in a close interrelation, where theology, in the end, has precedence over philosophy, ascribing, as it were, the role of *ancilla theologiae* to philosophy. He detects a very different conception of the relationship of theology and philosophy in Dialectical Theology, which maintains that the true situation of the human can only be deduced from revelation and thus to the exclusion of humanity's efforts to understand itself by its own powers.[45] Thus, when Volk allows philosophy a place *in* theology he is insinuating that the theological group around Barth wish to pursue theology *without* philosophy. That this is only supposedly the case is part of the central thesis Volk sets out to prove in his study, which argues that there are indeed philosophical elements (and decisive ones at that) in Barth's apparently purely theological anthropology.[46] To reveal these philosophical elements is Volk's declared aim, not to develop a standpoint opposed to Barth's.[47]

Barth's conception of the creature is understandable against the background of his central concern: giving prominence to God's otherness and divinity. Included in this concern is the desire to secure God's otherness and divinity in the face of the theology of the universities, which had essentially degenerated into a historically informed study of religion.[48] If God is always wholly other, then his revelation cannot be a supplement to human knowledge. Instead, revelation stands diametrically opposed to human knowledge; it is a complete paradox that enacts the abolition of all human knowing. As Barth understands it, the material content of revelation only remains secure if theology is completely separated from philosophy, and thus definitively removed from any harmful influence. Since one can only speak dialectically about a paradoxical revelation, this form of theologizing is rightly called 'Dialectical Theology'.[49] The programmatic statement of this

---

[45] Cf. Volk (1938), p. V.
[46] Cf. Volk (1938), pp. V, 20–1.
[47] Cf. Volk (1938), p. 23.
[48] Cf. Volk (1938), pp. 1–3.
[49] Cf. Volk (1938), pp. 3–4.

theological line is Barth's *Epistle to the Romans*, upon which Volk depends first and foremost for his reflections.[50]

Barth increasingly elaborates and expands upon his original intuition of keeping God and humanity strictly separate, and thus his theological development proceeds without any breaks.[51] He makes the recognition of God's otherness convincing by making a strict dualism between God and humanity the organizing principle of his theology. In the Preface to the *Epistle to the Romans* he describes this principle as the 'infinite qualitative difference'.[52] By this he means far more than that God and humanity are different; in his view they oppose each other like eternity and time, life and death, yes and no.[53] Understood in this way the expression has both a critical as well as a constructive function. It contains the criterion for examining the usefulness of theological tradition and represents the foundation upon which Barth intends to construct his own thoughts.[54]

As the supposed basic principle of Barth's theology, Volk thinks that the 'infinite qualitative difference' also stands behind Barth's anthropology.[55] This situation can be seen in Barth's conception of the creature, and its outlines become clearer when one asks how humanity can be described *in relation to God*, its *difference from God, in itself* and, finally, in its *situation before God*.[56] Volk expounds in several detailed studies how Barth answers these questions.[57] He comes to the conclusion that, as Barth understands it, the *duality* of God and humanity does not issue forth in a final *unity*. Neither is there any final dialectical unity, as Volk argues in a closing study which sums up the previous ones.[58]

Barth's central concern is to protect God from human interests, which should be achieved readily enough through the idea of the 'infinite qualitative difference'. But Barth did not come to the strict separation of God and humanity as expressed in this phrase through a purely theological reflection on revelation, but under the clear influence of particular philosophical traditions (Volk mentions, in particular, idealism, transcendentalism, scepticism and nominalism).[59]

---

[50] Volk (1938), pp. 10, 297 refers to the programmatic character of the *Epistle to the Romans*.
[51] Cf. Volk (1938), pp. 84–5, 101–2, 246.
[52] Cf. Volk (1938), pp. 3, 56.
[53] Cf. Volk (1938), pp. 56–72. Also p. 244.
[54] Cf. Volk (1938), pp. 4–6.
[55] Cf. Volk (1938), p. 7.
[56] Cf. Volk (1938), pp. 21–3.
[57] Cf. Volk (1938), pp. 24–54 (the creature in its coming from God), pp. 55–102 (the difference from God), pp. 103–46 (the material substance of the fallen creature), pp. 147–239 (the creature before God).
[58] Cf. Volk (1938), pp. 240–90, especially pp. 246–61.
[59] Cf. Volk (1938), pp. 294–305.

Of course Volk is concerned with more than just pointing out *that* there are indeed philosophical elements in Barth's allegedly purely theological thinking. What he finally wants to find out is *whether* the philosophy upon which Barth depends, or by which his thinking is at least stamped, is suitable as the basis of a theology desiring to be appropriate to revelation. What the answer will be is already made clear, according to Volk, by a look into history: theologies that maintained they could reason and do theology under the conditions of modernity had in the end disintegrated. In fact only medieval scholasticism was appropriate to revelation. Whether idealism, transcendentalism, scepticism and nominalism have really influenced Barth is thus not all that important. The concepts have a broader level of significance to the extent to which they describe historical-philosophical epochs. In the end Volk is concerned with the alternatives of a purely scholastic philosophy on the one hand, and with a later 'phenomena of decadence', together with modern philosophy, on the other. He hints that only the philosophy of scholasticism provides the philosophical prerequisite for a theology corresponding to revelation.[60] Barth, by contrast, opted for the *philosophy of modernity* and in particular for the philosophy of Kant.[61]

Volk asks us to consider the fact that Barth's close connection to idealism has serious consequences for his idea of the creature. This connection means that the difference between Creator and creature is interpreted as the difference between the idea and the reality.[62] Just as in the Marburg Neo-Kantianism which influenced Barth, the idea is put before the reality, causing a qualitative fall: Barth considers the condition of humanity as good before the Fall, and as evil after it.[63] In the process, the concept of creation, which otherwise ensures that even after the Fall humanity stands in a positive relationship to God, is levered out.[64] Volk's judgement is that Barth's apparently strictly theological anthropology is, in reality, a covert idealist philosophy.[65]

Volk merely hints in his conclusion at what an anthropology built on the tenets of scholasticism would be. Nevertheless, it appears that the concepts of transcendence, immanence and analogy would play a central part.[66] If the

---

[60] Cf. Volk (1938), pp. 305, 331–2.
[61] Cf. Volk (1938), pp. 294, 299, 303.
[62] Cf. Volk (1938), p. 296. In relation to the doctrine of creation, Volk (p. 295) argues that Barth was clearly influenced by the philosophy of origin put forth by the Marburg Neo-Kantian Hermann Cohen (1842–1918). On this see Johann Friedrich Lohmann, *Karl Barth und der Neukantianismus. Die Rezeption des Neukantianismus im ‚Römerbrief' und ihre Bedeutung für die weitere Ausarbeitung der Theologie Karl Barths* (Berlin and New York: Walter de Gruyter, 1995), pp. 280–306, 400–3.
[63] Cf. Volk (1938), p. 42.
[64] Cf. Volk (1938), p. 32.
[65] Cf. Volk (1938), p. 43.
[66] Cf. Volk (1938), pp. 305–32.

relationship between God and the human being is understood as a decidedly analogical relationship between Creator and creature, then a concept such as that of the 'infinite qualitative difference' is simply untenable. Barth, contrary to his own estimation and intention, is thus far too philosophical and too little theological, meaning that the philosophy he thinks can support his theology actually hinders his presentation of its theological content.

2.6 Results

Dialectical Theology attempts to talk about God under the conditions of modernity – such was the diagnosis of Michael Gierens, Friedrich Maria Rintelen, Karl Rahner and Hermann Volk. Its representatives deal with one of central problems of modernity when they maintain that one cannot say anything about God apart from revelation. Dialectical Theology, then, can be called *anti-modern modern*. Outwardly, it stylizes itself as the reviver of the genuine theology of Scripture and of the Reformers in complete contrast to decidedly modern lines of thinking, particularly in the tradition following Schleiermacher. It is, however, moving within a specifically modern framework, namely that of Kant.[67] Hence, Dialectical Theology, like all of the other trends in Protestantism, adopts the premises, and therefore also the problems of modernity, but is unwilling to accept their negative consequences. As a result, the function of the formula 'infinite qualitative difference' is to keep God and humanity apart in order to prevent God from being accessible to humanity.

Serious difficulties then follow. Gierens, Rintelen, Rahner and Volk all testify to the double speechlessness of dialectic theology: first of all, the strict separation of God and humanity prevents the human person from making true and not simply approximate dialectical statements about God; otherwise put, theology is impossible even *formally*. Accordingly, the epithets with which they label Dialectical Theology are 'agnosticism'[68], 'theologia negativa'[69] and 'subjectivism',[70] and the fundamental 'weakness' of its theological statements is also noted.[71] Second, the speechlessness can also be detected with regard to *content*. Central convictions of the Christian faith can no longer be articulated. The existence of revelation,[72] the personality

---

[67] An explicit reference to Kant can be found in Gierens (1930), 197; Rintelen (1934), pp. 12–20; Volk (1938), pp. 45–7, 284, 294, 299. Although his name is not mentioned, a material reference to Kant can also be found in Rahner (1936), pp. 191–2.
[68] Cf. Gierens (1930), p. 205.
[69] Cf. Rintelen (1934), p. 158.
[70] Cf. Rahner (1936), p. 194. Certainly the statement to the understanding of faith in more recent Protestant theologies is general, but Dialectical Theology is also meant.
[71] Cf. Volk (1938), p. 11.
[72] Cf. Gierens (1930), pp. 204–5.

ANTI-MODERN MODERN

of God and the reality of the Church,[73] the doctrine of the two natures, even of the incarnation at all,[74] and the creatureliness of humankind[75] cannot be conclusively explained. Dialectical Theology represents God as so overwhelming that in the end there is no room left for humanity. If this is perhaps understandable as a reaction against the problems with which theology sees itself confronted in modernity, then it nevertheless does not make for an acceptable and responsible form of Christian theology.[76]

In light of these assessments, it is unsurprising that none of the Catholic authors mentioned above gave further consideration to Barth. Gierens became the editor of two editions of a decidedly Neo-Scholastic dogmatic textbook in which Dialectical Theology was sharply criticized.[77] Rintelen first took over a position in the 'Bonifatiuswerk', a relief organization for Catholics in areas in which they live as a minority ('Diaspora'), shortly afterwards became vicar-general and, finally, auxiliary bishop of the archbishopric of Paderborn. (Incidentally, in October 1934 he gave a lecture in Magdeburg in which he supported the thesis that what was Christian in Protestantism was disintegrating as a result of false philosophical assumptions and thus the Catholic Church alone was the refuge of truth.[78]) Rahner devoted himself to questions in the realm of philosophy of religion and expressly dissociated himself from Protestant attempts in the field, not without mentioning Barth at least briefly.[79] Volk turned to Emil Brunner, a moderate representative of Dialectical Theology, in his subsequent writings for his academic qualifications.[80]

If Barth was met with rejection in Catholic theology, the main cause was the 'infinite qualitative difference' which he described in the *Epistle to the*

---

[73] Cf. Rintelen (1934), pp. 140–6.
[74] Cf. Rahner (1936), p. 202.
[75] Cf. Volk (1938), pp. 329–30.
[76] Cf. Gierens (1930), pp. 198, 206; Rintelen (1934), p. 146; Volk (1938), pp. 5, 7–8 or Gierens (1930), p. 206; Rintelen (1934), p. 158; Rahner (1936), p. 195; Volk (1938), p. 332.
[77] Cf. Joseph Pohle, *Lehrbuch der Dogmatik*, ed. Michael Gierens, 3 vols (Paderborn: Schöningh, [8]1931–1933). Here Gierens treats dialectic theology more closely at only one point in vol. 2 (1932), p. 509. He reproaches Barth for separating God and humanity too sharply. In the ninth edition of his textbook, which appeared only a few years later, Gierens explicitly criticized Barth's understanding of revelation; cf. vol. 1 (1934), p. 24 with reference to KD I/1 (1932), pp. 43ff. and *passim*.
[78] Cf. Friedrich Maria Rintelen, 'Das Verhängnis der protestantischen Theologie', *TGl* 27 (1935), pp. 453–65 with reference to RB (1922/[6]1933) and CD (1927).
[79] Cf. Karl Rahner, *Hörer des Wortes. Zur Grundlegung einer Religionsphilosophie* (Munich: Kösel-Pustet, 1941), pp. 37–8. How far Rahner later dealt with Barth still needs to be explored.
[80] Cf. Hermann Volk, *Emil Brunners Lehre von der ursprünglichen Gottebenbildlichkeit des Menschen* (Emsdetten: Lechte, 1939); ibid, *Emil Brunners Lehre von dem Sünder* [1943] (Münster: Regensberg, 1950).

Romans as the central idea of his thought. The strict separation of time and eternity, of God and humanity, gave the impression that this idea was taken more from philosophical reflection than revelation. Moreover, it had considerable consequences for theology, particularly for Christology, as the very reality of the incarnation appeared to be endangered. The fact that in the second half of the 1930s Barth began to reformulate his thinking in the light of the doctrine of election was not noted. Henceforward, Barth was considered a dialectical theologian even though he had actually adopted another course. At the very beginning of 1938's *Church Dogmatics* I/2 we find the following central statement:

> According to Holy Scripture God's revelation takes place in the fact that God's Word became a man and that this man has become God's Word. The incarnation of the eternal Word, Jesus Christ, is God's revelation. In the reality of this event God proves that He is free to be our God.[81]

---

[81] CD I/2, p. 1 (leading proposition to § 13. God's freedom for man), a translation of KD I/2 (1938), p. 1 (Leitsatz von § 13. Gottes Freiheit für den Menschen): 'Gottes Offenbarung ereignet sich nach der heiligen Schrift darin, daß Gottes Wort ein Mensch wurde, dieser Mensch also Gottes Wort gewesen ist. Die Fleischwerdung des ewigen Wortes, Jesus Christus, ist Gottes Offenbarung. In der Wirklichkeit dieses Ereignisses beweist Gott seine Freiheit, unser Gott zu sein.'

3

UNITY IN FAITH: THE MÜNSTER CIRCLE, ROBERT GROSCHE AND THE PERIODICAL *CATHOLICA*

3.1 Introduction

The thesis that the Catholic Church first turned to ecumenism with Vatican II has been increasingly questioned by recent studies.[1] How intense the struggle for unity already was before the Council can be seen in the animated exchange between Karl Barth and several intellectually alert and theologically open-minded Catholics. It appears that a debating circle completed with regular meetings was formed in 1927, a circle whose history has scarcely been explored.[2] Even Barth's call to the University of Bonn by no means spelt the end of the talks. The impetus for these meetings can be traced back to Robert Grosche (1888–1967), on whose initiative the polemical theological ('kontroverstheologisch') periodical *Catholica* was

---

[1] Cf. Tom Stransky, 'Roman Catholic Church and pre-Vatican II ecumenism', *Dictionary of the Ecumenical Movement*, ed. Nicholas Lossky (Genf: WCC Publishing,² 2002), pp. 996–8; Jörg Ernesti, *Ökumene im Dritten Reich* (Paderborn: Bonifatius, 2007); *Die Entdeckung der Ökumene. Zur Beteiligung der katholischen Kirche an der Ökumene*, ed. Jörg Ernesti and Wolfgang Thönissen (Paderborn: Bonifatius and Frankfurt a.M.: Lembeck, 2008).

[2] The only reconstruction comes from Wilhelm Neuser, *Karl Barth in Münster* (Zürich: Theologischer Verlag Zürich, 1985), pp. 37–40. Admittedly, at many points this work does not tally with the autobiographical sketch provided by Gottfried Hasenkamp, 'Erinnerungen an Robert Grosche. Wie es zur Gründung der CATHOLICA und zu deren Weiterführung nach dem Kriege kam', *Cath(M)* 37 (1983), pp. 163–71, 164–6. Bruce McCormack follows Neuser in his *Karl Barth's Critically Realistic Dialectical Theology. Its Genesis and Development 1909–1936* (Oxford: Clarendon Press, 1995), pp. 376–7, as does Lidija Matošević, *Lieber katholisch als neuprotestantisch. Karl Barths Rezeption der katholischen Theologie 1921–1930* (Neukirchen-Vluyn: Neukirchener, 2005), pp. 117–8.

published from 1932 onwards. From the very beginning, the main focus of this journal was debate with Dialectical Theology and so, naturally enough, its first articles dealt with its relationship to Catholicism.[3]

3.2 The Münster Circle

The origins of the Münster Circle go back to 1927, even if it is difficult to determine exactly when the meetings began.[4] Bernhard Rosenmöller (1883–1974), a well-known philosopher of religion, was a driving force behind them.[5] In the beginning, he and Gottfried Hasenkamp (1902–1990), together with their wives, met with Barth at one- to two-month intervals. Through Hasenkamp, then an editor at the Aschendorff publishing house, Robert Grosche gained entry to the Münster Circle (the two had actually been friends for years[6]). Grosche travelled specifically for the meetings from Cologne, where he was working as a university chaplain. His colleague in Münster, the Jesuit Ernst Böminghaus (1882–1942), also participated in the meetings occasionally. In the autumn of 1929, at the very latest, a young lady named Annemarie Nossen, who lived in Gladbeck and had converted to Catholicism, joined the group.[7] Like Barth, she had studied in Berlin under Adolf von Harnack and so they wrote to each other when their mutual teacher died in 1930.[8]

[3] Cf. Robert Grosche, 'Die dialektische Theologie und der Katholizismus', *Cath(M)* 1 (1932), pp. 1–18. Reprinted in his *Et intra et extra. Theologische Aufsätze* (Düsseldorf: Patmos, 1958), pp. 157–71.

[4] According to Hasenkamp (1983), p. 164, the discussions began before 1928 and went on until Barth's departure to Bonn. In fact, it can be proved that meetings already took place at the end of 1927, as seen from KBA 9327.630 (Gottfried Hasenkamp to Karl Barth, postcard dated 15 December 1927) and KBA 9327.451 (Bernhard Rosenmöller to Karl Barth, letter dated 9 October 1927).

[5] For biographical information see Emmanuel J. Bauer, 'Bernhard Rosenmoeller (1883–1974)', in *Christliche Philosophie im katholischen Denken des 19. und 20. Jahrhunderts*, ed. Emerich Coreth et al., vol. 3 (Graz et al.: Styria, 1990), pp. 159–71.

[6] Cf. Hasenkamp (1983), pp. 163–4. For Hasenkamp's biography see *Karl Barth – Charlotte von Kirschbaum. Briefwechsel*, vol. 1, ed. Rolf-Joachim Erler, Gesamtausgabe V. Briefe (Zürich: Theologischer Verlag Zürich, 2008), p. 91 fn 7.

[7] Cf. *Karl Barth – Eduard Thurneysen. Briefwechsel*, vol. 2, ed. Eduard Thurneysen, Gesamtausgabe V. Briefe (Zürich: Theologischer Verlag Zürich, 1974), pp. 677–80 (Karl Barth to Eduard Thurneysen, letter dated 6 October 1929), pp. 679–80; KBA 9329.488 (Annemarie Nossen to Karl Barth, letter dated 9 October 1929).

[8] Cf. KBA 9330.438 (Annemarie Nossen to Karl Barth, letter dated 24 July 1930); KBA 9230.190 (Karl Barth to Annemarie Nossen, letter dated 25 July 1930, copy); KBA 9330.454 (Annemarie Nossen to Karl Barth, letter dated 2 August 1930). Clearly, Nossen visited Barth even when he was already a professor in Bonn. On this cf. KBA 9330.595 (Annemarie Nossen to Karl Barth, letter dated 5 November 1930); KBA 9230.285 (Karl Barth to Annemarie Nossen, letter dated 24 November 1930, copy).

UNITY IN FAITH

Texts exchanged in advance formed the basis for the discussions.[9] The evening debates revolved around various theological problems, particularly the doctrine of grace. Barth repeatedly insisted upon the freedom of grace, which people may or may not grasp but which remains free even when they do. The Catholic participants were not prepared to accept this position.[10] In general, the discussions do not always seem to have proceeded harmoniously. After a meeting at the beginning of 1929, Rosenmöller assured Barth that no one had found him offensive.[11]

Barth must have welcomed the fact that the topics to be discussed were always explicitly dogmatic questions. When the discussion dealt with the reality of revelation, for example, the question was *how* one could speak about it theologically. It would have been difficult for Barth to have a similar debate with representatives of a Protestantism stamped by liberalism, historicism and philosophy of religion. Here the question would have been more a consideration of *whether* and *under which conditions* one could even think about something like revelation. It should be clear, then, that the Münster Circle was not a circle concerned with reform, liberally disposed or focused on modernity. It also did not desire to free the life of the Church or Catholic theology from possible encrustments by adopting more Protestant tendencies. Instead, the circle stood for an open-minded form of Catholicism. Its members were familiar with the theology of classical Thomism, and while they felt no kind of resentment against it they were also aware that they were bound to other thinkers such as Augustine, Johann Adam Möhler (1796–1838) and particularly Matthias Joseph Scheeben (1835–1888).[12] It is not at all surprising, then, that for Christmas 1928 Barth gave his friend Eduard Thurneysen a new edition of the four-volume dogmatics by the Neo-Scholastic Scheeben in Cologne.[13]

Barth's relationship to Bernhard Rosenmöller in particular was quite good. He appears to have found in the comprehensively learned and speculatively talented philosopher a congenial interlocutor. A letter from October 1929 allows us to see the warmth and closeness of this relationship.

---

[9] Cf. Hasenkamp (1983), pp. 165–6.
[10] Cf. Neuser (1985), p. 39.
[11] Cf. KBA 9329.14 (Bernhard Rosenmöller to Karl Barth, letter dated 6 January 1929).
[12] Cf. Hasenkamp (1983), p. 165 against Neuser (1985), p. 39. Grosche was in no way averse to Thomism. He sent Barth the book by Antonin Dalmace Sertillanges, *Der heilige Thomas von Aquin* (Hellerau: Hegner, 1928), which he himself had translated. In the accompanying letter we read: 'It appears to me unquestionable that a discussion between Catholic and Protestant theologians is possible on the basis of the *real* Thomas in a way quite different from what was previously possible.' Cf. KBA 9328.496 (Robert Grosche to Karl Barth, letter dated 16 November 1928): 'Daß von der Grundlage des *wirklichen* Thomas aus eine Diskussion zwischen katholischen und evangelischen Theologen in ganz anderer Weise als bisher möglich ist, erscheint mir als zweifellos.'
[13] Cf. Neuser (1985), p. 39.

At this point in time, Barth's move to the University of Bonn was certain and so it remarkable that Barth notes the Rosenmöllers are the only people in Münster whom he leaves with true reluctance.[14] Indeed, parting from the Catholic couple seems to have been harder for him than leaving his own colleagues in the Protestant faculty.

It was not to be Rosenmöller, however, who continued the discussion after Barth's departure from Münster. In 1937, he became Professor in East Prussian Braunsberg, and subsequently lost contact to an increasing degree.[15]

3.3 The Usefulness of Dialectical Theology: Robert Grosche

In the same year that Barth moved to the Rhineland, Grosche became parish priest in Brühl-Vochem, a small village only a few miles from Bonn. Almost immediately after he arrived he wrote to Barth and sought out contact with him.[16] There subsequently developed a pleasant exchange between the two, although Barth made no secret of the fact that he found Grosche's arguments only partially conclusive.[17] For instance, Barth was not at all convinced by what Grosche had presented in February 1932 in the course of Barth's seminar on Mariology.[18]

Before he became a parish priest, Grosche was a chaplain at the University of Cologne for almost ten years.[19] He thought that fulfilling this office provided him with a rather complex task. Many students had themselves experienced the horrors of World War I while, at the same time, the glitter of the *Golden Twenties* was being heralded. Grosche thus had to deal with both grave existential questions and fears and also with cultural

---

[14] Cf. Barth – Thurneysen (1974), pp. 677–80 (Karl Barth to Eduard Thurneysen, letter dated 6 October 1929), pp. 679–80.

[15] Cf. KBA 9353.161 (Bernhard Rosenmöller to Karl Barth, letter dated 2 April 1953). It is also the case that Barth and Rosenmöller corresponded near the end of 1935 about the awkward situation of the theologian Erik Peterson, who had converted to Catholicism several years earlier. The letters are accessible in Erik Peterson, *Ausgewählte Schriften*, vol. 9/2, ed. Barbara Nichtweiss (Würzburg: Echter, 2009), pp. 349–55. Whether they had further contact cannot be determined from the sources available.

[16] Cf. KBA 9330.439 (Robert Grosche to Karl Barth, letter dated 25 July 1930).

[17] Barth expressly related this ambivalence to Grosche; see KBA 9237.214 (Karl Barth to Robert Grosche, letter dated 29 December 1937, copy).

[18] Grosche published his seminar paper under the title 'Fünf Thesen zur Mariologie', *Cath(M)* 2 (1933), pp. 24–42. On this and Barth's reaction cf. Dahlke (2010), pp. 89–90.

[19] Cf. Richard Goritzka, *Der Seelsorger Robert Grosche (1888–1967). Dialogische Pastoral zwischen Erstem Weltkrieg und Zweitem Vatikanischen Konzil* (Würzburg: Echter, 1999), pp. 88–105.

developments coming thick and fast. In his sermons, then, he made use of modern literature in addition to philosophical and theological publications. His preoccupation with Karl Barth first becomes perceptible in a cycle of sermons given in the Winter Semester of 1924/1925. As Grosche candidly admits, he follows Barth closely, both in content and style.[20] He returned to Barth's publications again in other sermons he delivered in the second half of the 1920s.[21]

Even if sermon preparation made Grosche look more closely at Dialectical Theology, the initial reasons behind his engagement with the theological movement must be sought elsewhere. There are, in fact, three of them: (1) if the consideration of Dialectical Theology can be *useful for Catholicism*, then (2) it again enables the *possibility of a theological discussion between the denominations*, while (3) the polemics of Dialectical Theology against Catholicism raises the *necessity of Catholic apologetics*.

Dialectical Theology is *useful for Catholicism* inasmuch as it can reveal some of Catholicism's weak points.[22] Grosche's view of Church life, and particularly of the practice of faith, is sharpened by reading Barth, not so much because Grosche is an academic theologian, but more because he is a theologically interested pastor. Barth sensitized Grosche to the question of whether God was in truth always and everywhere given the honour due to him, or whether the human being does not simply please itself in the Church's display of splendour and its highly religious atmosphere.[23]

Yet Dialectical Theology does not simply challenge Catholicism to check its conscience, it also raises, once again, the *possibility of a theological discussion between the denominations*. Such a discussion is made possible because of the reversal of the disastrous development which Protestant theology underwent during and following the nineteenth century. Instead of 'God', Protestant theology took 'religion' for its principle concept and thus the human subject who delights in interpreting and objectifying its experiences.[24] Dialectical Theology turns its sights precisely against such a development. According to Grosche, Barth turns upside-down the theology of Schleiermacher, dominant

---

[20] Cf. Robert Grosche, *Der Kolosserbrief in Homilien erklärt* (Paderborn: Schöningh, 1926), p. 5. He frequently refers to Barth's writings: pp. 8–9, 21, 30, 33–7, 39, 43 fn 1, 56. Barth obviously read the sermons when they were later printed and wrote to Thurneysen that he should order them for himself as he thought them thought-provoking ('zu nachdenklicher Lektüre'); Barth – Thurneysen (1974), pp. 406–7 (Karl Barth to Eduard Thurneysen, letter dated 2.3.1926), p. 407.
[21] Cf. Robert Grosche, *Wenn du die Gabe Gottes kenntest* (Frankfurt a.M.: Verlag der Carolus-Druckerei, 1930), pp. 47 fn 1, 119, 127 with reference to Barth.
[22] Cf. Grosche (1926), p. 5; ibid (1932), p. 1.
[23] Cf. Grosche (1926), p. 56; ibid (1932), pp. 8, 16, 18.
[24] Cf. Grosche (1926), pp. 57–8; ibid, 'Augustin und die dialektische Theologie. Eine Auseinandersetzung mit Karl Barth', *Akademische Bonifatius-Korrespondenz* 45 (1930), pp. 86–98, 87–8; ibid (1932), pp. 3–14.

in Protestantism up to the present, and by doing so enacts a kind of return to the Reformation.[25] Scripture is no longer simply considered as some type of religious-historical document which must be researched historically and critically, but is now understood as the true Word of God; dogma and the confessions of the faith are again taken as binding authorities, and not as, at most, historically interesting documents of days long past.[26]

How Grosche can see in Dialectical Theology an opening for an ecumenical discussion can be explained against the background of the virtually diametrically opposite ways which the denominational theologies followed in the wake of the Enlightenment.[27] Catholic theology attempted to safeguard the Christian faith's claim to be true *formally*, meaning without any reference to its contents. It reacted to the intellectual loss of the Christian faith's plausibility by bestowing upon its contents authoritative guarantees such as the infallibility of its teaching and an inerrant, inspired Bible. Protestant theology, by contrast, began to understand the *content* of the Christian faith in a new way, based on the awareness of truth at that time. This is the great project of Protestant theology in the universities. As this particular brand of Protestant theology was highly reflexive, historically informed and philosophically committed to idealism, it was in a good position as regards the conflict of the faculties. If a discussion between the denominations could not be conducted in the light of such massive differences, this situation has, according to Grosche, fundamentally changed.[28]

For Grosche, however, Dialectical Theology does not simply open up the possibility of a discussion between the denominations: in turning away from the modern and to the Reformers, Dialectical Theology demands and elicits increased *apologetic efforts* from Catholics. There is, once again, an awareness that Protestantism is bound to Catholicism insofar as it came into being in protest against the traditional forms of Christianity. Grosche concludes that the time of denominational controversies and polemics has returned.[29] A lecture

---

[25] Cf. Grosche (1926), p. 58.

[26] Cf. Grosche (1932), pp. 5–7.

[27] On what follows see Wolfhart Pannenberg, *Problemgeschichte der neueren evangelischen Theologie in Deutschland. Von Schleiermacher bis zu Barth und Tillich* (Göttingen: Vandenhoeck und Ruprecht, 1997), pp. 32–5; Thomas Albert Howard, *Protestant Theology and the Making of the Modern German University* (Oxford et al.: Oxford University Press, 2006), or Aidan Nichols, *Catholic Thought Since The Enlightment. A Survey* (Pretoria: Unisa Press and Leominster, UK: Gracewing, 1998).

[28] Cf. Grosche (1930), p. 87.

[29] Cf. Grosche (1932), p. 14; ibid, 'Evangelisches Denken und Katholizismus', *Cath(M)* 1 (1932), pp. 191–3, 193; ibid, 'Katholizismus und Protestantismus', in *Pilgernde Kirche* (Freiburg i.Br.: Herder, 1938), pp. 109–16 (Radio lecture on the 'Deutsche Welle', 31 January 1933). What Grosche says here is later found in his editorial 'Zum Wiedererscheinen der "Catholica"', *Cath(M)* 9 (1952), pp. 1–3, 1. *Catholica* then appeared as an annual of polemical theology ('Kontroverstheologie') and not as a periodical.

which Barth had sent him in 1929 may have led him to this assessment. He was anything but pleased with it and consequently wrote:

> Dear professor, many thanks for your lecture on the Holy Spirit and the Christian life which, after your announcement (that it is probably the most un-Catholic piece which you have written), I immediately read with great excitement, as you can no doubt imagine. As I have merely skimmed it and not studied it thoroughly I can [...] not yet say very much about it. But in this case too I am experiencing my usual reactions: I entirely concur with half of what you say, i.e. with everything you have on your mind against the theology of immanence, to express it in an anti-modernistic way. Then, however, comes the other half, which I either do not understand – such as 'simul peccator et justus' – or cannot go along with. There is much which could be said. But I must have time.[30]

Indeed, it would take several months before Grosche got round to writing an answer. He sent it to Barth before it was published.[31]

His first move in the article is to reject as founded Barth's reproach against Catholic theology: that the difference between God and humanity is not taken into account, or only insufficiently so by means of a relationship which exhibits absolutely no dialectical tension. His second move is to turn the critical questions of Dialectical Theology back upon itself. He comes to the conclusion that Dialectical Theology actually does not speak dialectically about God and humanity, for it emphasizes the difference between the two so heavily that their relationship is no longer clear and so all dialectic tensions effectively disappear.[32]

3.4 *The Periodical* Catholica

While today there are an impressive number of ecumenical periodicals, the beginning of the century had few, if any. The High Church Ecumenical

---

[30] KBA 9329.662 (Robert Grosche to Karl Barth, letter dated 23 December 1929, translated).

[31] Cf. KBA 9330.439 (Robert Grosche to Karl Barth, letter dated 25 July 1930). Barth replied immediately and spoke of the correctness of his interpretation of Augustine in KBA 9230.198 (Karl Barth to Robert Grosche, letter dated 1 August 1930, copy). Grosche, however, stuck to his criticism; cf. KBA 9330.559 (Robert Grosche to Karl Barth, letter dated 21 October 1930).

[32] Cf. Grosche (1930), especially pp. 88–98 with reference to Karl Barth, 'Der heilige Geist und das christliche Leben'; ibid and Heinrich Barth, *Zur Lehre vom heiligen Geist* (Munich: Kaiser, 1930), pp. 39–105. Grosche's text is reprinted under the title 'Gott und die Welt. I. Zum Werk eines Theologen', ibid (1938), pp. 77–95.

Alliance (*Hochkirchlich-ökumenischer Bund*), a supradenominational organization, which arose in 1924, attempted to close the gap.[33] It was responsible for the periodical *Una Sancta*, and Catholics were among its editors and staff.[34] When the Catholics had to withdraw from participation in its production on instructions from the Holy Office (today the Vatican's Congregation for the Doctrine of Faith), the periodical was discontinued. *Religiöse Besinnung* cautiously attempted to carry on this tradition but in the end was unsuccessful.[35] To be able to conduct a dialogue with Barth, a new – but unsuspicious – forum had to be found.

The idea of founding their own periodical came from Gottfried Hasenkamp and Robert Grosche, two members of the Münster Circle.[36] To put this into effect, however, they first had to find a publisher. Hasenkamp approached the then director of the diocesan seminary in Paderborn, Max ten Hompel (1882–1960). At that time ten Hompel was the president of the Winfriedbund, an organization founded in 1920 which is still around today with headquarters in Paderborn. Its aim is reunification in faith. He willingly took up the suggestion of launching a periodical and also agreed to entrust editorship to Grosche. Thus, from 1932 onwards, *Catholica. Quarterly for Kontroverstheologie* appeared in the publishing house of the Winfriedbund.

The title of the periodical is highly revealing and, in fact, programmatic: a critical debate with Protestantism should be conducted from a determinedly Catholic viewpoint. *Catholica* has no desire to take the course of denominational confrontation or pacifying compromise, neither should it use an all too narrow understanding of what is Catholic or take up some kind of superdenominational metaperspective. Instead the teaching of the authentic Roman Catholic Church should be set forth in dialogue with Protestantism. In this way *Catholica* dissociated itself not only from periodicals such as *Una Sancta* or *Religiöse Besinnung*, but at the same time from the model of a 'Protestant Catholicity' ('evangelische Katholizität') associated with the name of Friedrich Heiler. Without formally converting, Heiler, who later became Professor of Religious Studies in Marburg, professed the Lutheran faith from 1919 onwards. He did not, however, consider this in any way to be a break with Catholicism, but an ecumenical gesture. The Church that he envisaged, and which he desired to make a reality, not least through his engagement in the initially extremely influential 'Hochkirchlichen Vereinigung', stood

---

[33] On what follows see Dominik Burkard, '... Unam Sanctam (Catholicam?). Zur theologiegeschichtlichen Verortung des Ökumenismusdekrets "Unitatis redintegratio" aus der Sicht des Kirchenhistorikers', in *Glaube in der Welt von heute. Theologie und Kirche nach dem Zweiten Vatikanischen Konzil*, Festschrift Elmar Klinger, ed. Thomas Franz and Hanjo Sauer, vol. 1 (Würzburg: Echter, 2006), pp. 57–109, 65–83.

[34] Una Sancta. Zeitschrift des Hochkirchlich-Oekumenischen Bundes 1 (1925) – 3 (1927).

[35] Religiöse Besinnung 1 (1928) – 5 (1933).

[36] Cf. Hasenkamp (1983), p. 166.

UNITY IN FAITH

above the existing denominations.[37] *Catholica* distanced itself very clearly from such a wishful ecclesiology.[38] Incidentally, Karl Barth also indicated his fundamental distance to Heiler at the same time.[39] If there is to be Church unity, it can only be reached on the basis of a dogmatically understood confession of faith. This was the conviction which connected them.

The aim of *Catholica* is not confrontation or compromise, but polemical theological dialogue ('Kontroverstheologie'). This dialogue was understood in the sense of Johann Adam Möhler's most famous work, the 1832 *Symbolik*, which at that time was being given considerable attention.[40] Since the theological treatment of Protestantism was by no means a self-evident or self-justifying pursuit, it was clearly necessary to connect this activity to historical precedents. Hence *Catholica*, by appealing to *Symbolik*, could insert itself into a larger context of theological history. At first glance, Möhler admittedly does not appear to play a significant part. Grosche, for example, the driving force behind the periodical, only occasionally quotes from his writings.[41] Moreover, it was only years after the founding of the periodical that there appeared an article in which the *Symbolik*, together with the controversy which had developed over it between Möhler and his Protestant colleague in Tübingen, Ferdinand Christian Baur (1792–1860), was opened up for inter-denominational dialogue.[42] Hence one could actually think that the connection of *Catholica* to Möhler was simply an historical-theological expedient. What prevents such an interpretation, however, is a programmatic article by Bernhard Rosenmöller in which he explains the understanding of polemical theology ('Kontroverstheologie') to which the periodical is committed.[43] For Rosenmöller, polemical theology in general

---

[37] Cf. Ernesti (2007), pp. 30–9, 44–6.

[38] Grosche (1932), p. 192 thus represents Heiler as the vanishing point of the long-since overtaken world of the nineteenth century. The dialogue between Catholicism and Protestantism cannot take place on the basis of some kind of diffuse *religious experience*, no matter how much it is trimmed to High Church standards, but on the solid basis of the *dogma of the Church*. Grosche stresses this in his article 'Die katholisch-protestantische Auseinandersetzung', *Cath(M)* 1 (1932), p. 96.

[39] Cf. KD I/1 (1932), p. 106 [English translation: CD I/1, p. 104].

[40] On this see Josef Rupert Geiselmann, *Johann Adam Möhler. Die Einheit der Kirche und die Wiedervereinigung der Konfessionen. Ein Beitrag zum Gespräch zwischen den Konfessionen* (Wien: Friedrich Beck, 1940), pp. 89–95.

[41] Cf. Grosche (1932), 191; ibid, 'Zum Gespräch zwischen den Konfessionen', *Cath(M)* 8 (1939), pp. 85–6.

[42] Cf. Ludwig Lambinet, 'Das Prinzip des Protestantismus nach J. A. Möhler', *Cath(M)* 7 (1938), pp. 37–53.

[43] Cf. Bernhard Rosenmöller, 'Katholische Kontroverstheologie', in *Cath(M)* 2 (1933), p. 48. In the estimation of Siegfried Wiedenhofer, 'Ökumenische Theologie (1930–1965). Versuch einer wissenschaftsgeschichtlichen Rekonstruktion', *Cath(M)* 34 (1980), pp. 219–48, 224 fn 15, this article is one of the earliest reflections on the method and aim of polemical theology.

is a *form of dialogue between the denominational theologies*.[44] Catholic polemical theology sees itself as simultaneously facing several tasks: first, it must bring out clearly and precisely what connects and what separates the partners in the dialogue in order to measure it against the question of truth; second, it must critically question its Protestant dialogue partner and in such a way that the partner is able to give an answer; third, it must listen to the questions which Protestantism directs against Catholicism so that it can answer them appropriately. This programme is precisely what Möhler attempted in his *Symbolik*: bringing out the fundamental differences in between the denominations starting from a phenomenological reflection.

Since they could not sufficiently prove their purely academic, apolitical character to the satisfaction of the National Socialist regime, *Catholica* was discontinued in September 1939.[45] There was thus no longer a Catholic forum for dialogue with Dialectical Theology. Certainly in 1943 Grosche was already giving thought as to which authors and questions would be possible for future issues, and shortly after the end of the war Hasenkamp made contact with him and ten Hompel in the hope that *Catholica* could reappear as soon as possible, but the periodical's full return still only took place in 1958.[46] The publisher was now the Johann Adam Möhler Institute, which had been established shortly before in Paderborn. Academic discussion of the ecumenical process remains until today one of its most important tasks.[47]

3.5 Results

Catholica was first founded as a periodical for polemical theology ('Kontroverstheologie') and re-established after World War II. Since its twenty-second anniversary in 1968, it has appeared as a *Journal for Polemical Theology and Ecumenics* ('Kontroverstheologie und Ökumenik'). The renewed ecclesiology of Vatican II made it appear that the periodical's previous programme needed to be supplemented: along with polemical theology, which worked on the differences between the denominations, there now appeared ecumenics, which stressed the elements that connected them and those they held in common.[48] It should be noted, however, that in the 1930s polemical theology was understood less as apologetics and more as a denominational 'science', or academic pursuit. It was, therefore, in no way opposed to the

---

[44] Where Rosenmöller (1933) talks of a 'discussion' ('Aussprache') between Catholic and Protestant Theology, Grosche (1939) calls it a 'conversation between the denominations' ('Gespräch zwischen den Konfessionen').
[45] Cf. Ernesti (2007), p. 177 with fn 524.
[46] Cf. Hasenkamp (1983), pp. 167–8; Ernesti (2007), p. 179.
[47] Cf. Aloys Klein, 'Möhler-Institut', in *LTK*³ 7 (1998), p. 375.
[48] On this see Wiedenhofer (1980), pp. 224–6 with fn 17.

ecumenical movement and in fact could be understood as making its own contributions to the unity of the Church. For Bernhard Rosenmöller and Robert Grosche, the confrontation with Dialectical Theology was actually a boon.[49] Behind this lies the act/potential distinction of scholastic philosophy, according to which the *actus* is the developed reality and the *potential* the real possibility or ability – even if itself undeveloped – to fulfil the *actus*. Applied to theology, this distinction entails that what the Catholic Church always already is *potentialiter* – namely, the true Church – she must become more clearly *actualiter*, in her own self-realization and perfection. To do so, dialogue with Protestantism could prove very useful. Interestingly, the act/potential pattern can also be found in other significant ecumenical publications of the 1930s.[50]

Barth himself had no problem with the 'dogmatic intolerance' (as he put it) of the circle around Rosenmöller and Grosche. In fact this 'intolerance' appeared to him to be the prerequisite for a productive inter-denominational dialogue:

> In a theological conflict, the opponents are still together in Christ and therefore still within the Church when it is clear that they are separated in Christ and that they contend, not about the respective rights of their Churches, or tendencies within their Churches, or only their own personal opinions, but about the right of the Church against heresy, which makes this dispute necessary. At this point we may refer expressly to the Roman Catholic *Vierteljahrsschrift für Kontroverstheologie*, published since 1932 by Robert Grosche under the title *Catholica*. For its contributors the presupposition of controversy is that Catholic theology is *the* theology of the Church, that the Evangelical opponent is therefore a heretic, and that as such he must be treated with real seriousness. Behind this presupposition of the Roman theologians who write in *Catholica* lies the further presupposition that they are dealing with an Evangelical theology which for its part is prepared to accept responsibility as the one theology of the one Church, and not merely to play the part of one theology of one Church. And from the contents of this very journal we can satisfy ourselves whether it is not the case that even on this very 'intolerant' presupposition, with an attitude which is actually and not merely verbally confessional, it is still possible to conduct the controversy between Roman Catholicism and Protestantism in a way which is not merely worthy of the participants but of the matter which both sides confess to be indisputably at stake,

---

[49] Cf. Rosenmöller (1933).
[50] Cf. Yves Congar, *Chrétiens désunis. Principes d'un'œcuménisme' catholique* (Paris: Cerf, 1937), pp. 277–308 and Arnold Rademacher, *Die Wiedervereinigung der christlichen Kirchen* (Bonn: Hanstein, 1937), pp. 37–8.

and therefore in a way which is Christian in a unity even in disunity. Conversely, there is no question that in the shadow of an ecumenicism whose basic principle is that no Church should take itself or other Churches with final seriousness, the different wild beasts of an all too human egoism will, as occasion offers, bare and use their claws with all the greater abandon. It is only where adversaries are opposed with genuine dogmatic intolerance that there is the possibility of genuine and profitable discussion. For it is only there that one confession has something to say to the other.[51]

Yet Barth was not to be caught up in this dialogue. This had less to do with the fact that from 1935 onwards he was living in Basle and no longer allowed to enter Germany, but that he, and the theologians allied with him, had already been deliberately kept out of the ecumenical movement. When Catholic-Protestant consultations took place in 1934 in Berlin-Hermsdorf, and subsequently in 1936 in Chichester (England), liturgically oriented and dogmatically conservative Lutherans represented Protestantism, among them Wilhelm Stählin (1883–1975), who was anything but well-disposed to Barth.[52] Representatives of other theological circles such as liberal and Dialectical Theology were initially not invited and included in the dialogue. This selective choice of the partner in ecumenical dialogue continued when Stählin, in the meantime regional bishop of Oldenburg, together with Lorenz Jaeger (1892–1975), archbishop of Paderborn, founded an association of Protestant and Catholic theologians after World War II.[53] Meanwhile, however, there emerged in the German and also in the English-speaking area a revival of liberal Protestantism. In this case ecclesial agreement, frequently reached only with great difficulty, seems to be irrelevant, because if dogma and confessions are not really normative, then doctrinal agreement is not of much help. The question should be raised, however, whether the very structure of the ecumenical process is not responsible for this situation.

---

[51] CD I/2, p. 826–7, a translation of KD I/2 (1938), p. 924.
[52] Cf. Ernesti (2007), pp. 42–134.
[53] Cf. Barbara Schwahn, *Der ökumenische Arbeitskreis evangelischer und katholischer Theologen 1946 bis 1975* (Göttingen: Vandenhoeck und Ruprecht, 1996).

4

FIDES QUAERENS INTELLECTUM: BARTH'S ESSAY ON ANSELM OF CANTERBURY

4.1 Introduction

The validity and conclusiveness of the ontological argument which Anselm of Canterbury (1033–1109) expounds in the *Proslogion* for the existence of God have been debated up to the present. Hence it seems reasonable to conclude that it is hardly possible to assess and interpret Anselm's thought definitively and exhaustively.[1] Relevant attempts to do so thus say at least as much about his interpreters as about the erudite monk and bishop himself; every *interpretation* of Anselm allows the systematic preliminary decisions of Anselm's *interpreter* to be revealed.

This is no less true of Barth's 1931 essay *Fides quaerens intellectum*.[2] It is still debatable whether this work is simply a theological-historical investigation or a programmatic description of his own theology.[3] Barth himself, at any rate, made no explicit statement in relation to this problem. While in the Preface to *Fides quaerens intellectum* he emphasized that he wanted simply to interpret Anselm and nothing else, many years later he conceded that his analysis of the *Proslogion* proved highly significant for his own intellectual formation, particularly as regards the *Church*

---

[1] Cf. Rolf Schönberger, *Anselm von Canterbury* (Munich: Beck, 2004), pp. 151–4.
[2] Karl Barth, *Fides quaerens intellectum. Anselms Beweis der Existenz Gottes im Zusammenhang seines theologischen Programms* (Munich: Kaiser, 1931).
[3] An example of the controversy is the critique by Bruce McCormack, *Karl Barth's Critically Realistic Dialectical Theology. Its Genesis and Development 1909–1936* (Oxford: Clarendon Press, 1995), pp. 421–48 of the interpretation which goes back to Hans Urs von Balthasar, *Karl Barth. Darstellung und Deutung seiner Theologie* (Cologne: Hegner, 1951). Balthasar's position has admittedly been reinforced recently by Timothy Stanley, 'Returning Barth to Anselm', *Modern Theology* 24 (2008), pp. 413–37. On the background to this debate cf. Chapter 8.2.3.

Dogmatics.⁴ Indeed, in both works he understands theology as a human re-consideration of divine revelation.⁵ Reason would disappear into a void without a previously *given* revelation by which it could orient itself. If cognition signifies first and foremost re-cognition, then any form of a natural cognition of God is impossible.

It was probably this rather unusual role given to philosophy within theology which made the Catholic readers of *Fides quaerens intellectum* sit up and take notice. Both determined supporters of Neo-Scholasticism, such as Franciscus Salesius Schmitt and Rudolf Allers, and others such as Anselm Stolz, whom it is much more difficult to categorize, looked critically at Barth's interpretation of Anselm in the 1930s.

4.2 Anselm from a Neo-Scholastic Viewpoint: Franciscus Salesius Schmitt and Rudolf Allers

If Neo-Scholasticism increasingly became the dominant line in Catholic theology in the course of the nineteenth century, it was not only due to ecclesial or political-theological intrigues. Rather, Neo-Scholasticism appeared to provide the answers to questions the Church saw itself facing at the time. Rationalism, which sceptically opposed or even rejected the idea of a historically contingent revelation, was found to be particularly worrying.⁶ To combat atheism and agnosticism, Neo-Scholasticism first attempted to safeguard rationally the thought of God, as such, so that it could then supplement this thought with the supernatural cognition of God on the basis of faith.⁷ This historical context helps to explain why readers stamped by a philosophically inclined Neo-Scholastic theology could make such little sense of Barth's Anselm essay.

At this point we must mention Franciscus Salesius Schmitt (1894–1972), a Benedictine monk in the Silesian Abbey in Grüssau. Schmitt worked on

---

⁴ Cf. Barth (1931), p. VIII or Karl Barth, *Fides quaerens intellectum. Anselms Beweis der Existenz Gottes im Zusammenhang seines theologischen Programms* (Zollikon: Evangelischer Verlag, ²1958), p. 10.

⁵ Cf. Barth (1931), pp. 37–60 or KD I/1 (1932), pp. 261–310 (§ 7. Das Wort Gottes, das Dogma und die Dogmatik). How little Barth adhered to fideism can already be seen in KD I/1 (1932), pp. 89–128 (§ 4. Das Wort Gottes in seiner dreifachen Gestalt); there is a dialectical relationship between the one Word of God and its different forms.

⁶ Cf. Gerald McCool, *Catholic Theology in the Nineteenth Century. The Quest for a Unitary Method* (New York: Seabury, 1977), pp. 32–5.

⁷ Examples of this are Bernhard Bartmann, *Lehrbuch der Dogmatik*, vol. 1 (Freiburg i.Br. et al.: Herder, ⁷1928), pp. 80–96 and Franz Diekamp, *Katholische Dogmatik nach den Grundsätzen des heiligen Thomas*, vol. 1 (Münster: Aschendorff, ⁶1930), pp. 95–118. Both Bartmann (pp. 85–7) and Diekamp (pp. 108–18) tackle in detail what they consider to be false approaches, first and foremost among these being modern Atheism.

the critical edition of Anselm's works, and when Barth's *Fides quaerens intellectum* appeared he was working on the *Proslogion* in particular, which may explain why he became aware of and then reviewed Barth's essay.[8] There can be no doubt as to what Schmitt actually thinks of *Fides quaerens intellectum*: he did not think highly of it. Although the essay offers a wealth of suggestions and prescient observations, the work as a whole, and its main conclusions, are hardly satisfactory. At the end of the day the piece simply is not an interpretation of the *Proslogion* but an explanation of Barth's own theological programme.[9]

The Benedictine expressly contradicts Barth's thesis that there is absolutely no ontological proof for God's existence in the *Proslogion*. As Schmitt argues, Anselm actually overestimates the powers of reason insofar as he does not limit the flow and scope of his argument before elements of the faith, such as the Trinity and the incarnation, which are only accessible through revelation. Anselm, then, actually has a rationalist tendency. At any rate the *Proslogion* allows of no other interpretation than the traditional one Barth attempts to discredit. Anselm developed a conclusive, rationally comprehensible proof which works just fine without adding any statements of faith, and thus Anselm's embedding of the argument within a prayer is merely a literary artifice.[10]

Schmitt was in no way alone in making such an evaluation. Rudolf Allers (1883–1963) also considered the *Proslogion* to be a purely philosophical document.[11] In 1936, the learned psychotherapist and writer produced an introduction to Anselm in which he also offered his own translations of Anselm's works.[12] While he discusses in detail the ontological proof for God's existence in Thomas Aquinas, Descartes and Kant, references to *Fides quaerens intellectum* are confined to footnotes. Allers turns decisively against the thesis that Anselm starts out from doctrines which he already assumes are true.[13] In fact, Allers represents the opposite position and argues that Anselm stands firmly on the ground of the Church's teaching (most recently affirmed at Vatican I) that the cognition of the existence of God is attainable

---

[8] Cf. the review article by Franciscus Salesius Schmitt, 'Der ontologische Gottesbeweis Anselms', *TRev* 32 (1933), pp. 217–23. Schmitt's critical edition of Anselm's *Liber Proslogion* [...] (Bonn: Hanstein, 1931) only appeared after *Fides quaerens intellectum*, for Barth (1931), pp. VIII–IX expressed his regret that he did not have the long-heralded edition before him.

[9] Cf. Schmitt (1933), p. 217.

[10] Cf. Schmitt (1933), p. 221.

[11] For biographical information see 'Allers, Rudolf', in *Deutsche Biographische Enzyklopädie* 1 (1995), p. 91.

[12] Cf. Rudolf Allers, *Anselm von Canterbury. Leben, Lehre, Werke* (Wien: Thomas-Verlag Jakob Hegner, 1936), pp. 11–250 (Introduction) with pp. 565–639 (notes).

[13] Cf. Allers (1936), pp. 593–4 related to fn 1, 594–5 related to fn 3, 598–9 related to fn 25.

by human reason.[14] At no point does Anselm assume faith; his arguments are solely philosophical.[15]

Hence, Allers desires to understand the *Proslogion* in the context of the Constitution on Revelation, *Dei Filius*, which was directed against atheism and agnosticism. According to this document, reason allows one to know with certainty God's existence from created things.[16] The Vatican Council admittedly acknowledged that God has revealed himself in a supernatural way, but this point was far less emphasized in its reaction to 'modernism', which appeared to be entering Catholic theology along with modern relativism.[17] But the more the rationality of faith was emphasized, the more its unavailability appeared to fade into the background. There were, of course, some who thought that this tactic was problematic,[18] and among them stood Anselm Stolz.

4.3 Worship in the Field of Thought: Anselm Stolz

Like Franciscus Salesius Schmitt and Rudolf Allers, Anselm Stolz (1900–1942), who taught in Rome for the greater part of his life, has been almost completely forgotten.[19] However, anyone who deals with the work of the Benedictine from the Abbey Gerleve close to Münster will encounter one of the most interesting and certainly one of the most unconventional Catholic dogmaticians of the twentieth century. His unfinished Latin Dogmatics is remarkable; its speculative power and breadth of thought clearly distinguishes it from comparable works at the time.[20] For all his tremendous erudition, Scholz did not think of theology as just an intellectually engaging hobby. As he concentrated on the monastic schools of the early Middle Ages, and not the epistemological ideals of the modern university, he considered prayer to be the beginning and end

---

[14] Cf. Allers (1936), p. 598 related to fn 25: 'Anselm steht durchaus auf dem Boden der von der Kirche stets, zuletzt im *Vaticanum* (Denz. 1806) vertretenen Lehre, daß der menschlichen Vernunft die Erkenntnis vom Dasein Gottes erreichbar sei.'

[15] Cf. Allers (1936), p. 599 related to fn 25.

[16] Cf. DH 3004. On the document's interpretation see Fergus Kerr, 'By reason alone: what Vatican I never said', *New Blackfriars* 91 (2010), pp. 215–28.

[17] According to the anti-modernist oath introduced in 1910 and obligatory until 1967, the natural cognition of God is *the* Catholic doctrine (DH 3537–8).

[18] Cf. Heinrich Weiswieler, 'Natur und Übernatur in Glaube und Theologie', *Scholastik* 14 (1939), pp. 346–72, 347. Weiswieler expressly refers to the newly awakened interest in Anselm of Canterbury.

[19] For biographical information see Pius Engelbert, *Geschichte des Benediktinerkollegs St. Anselm in Rom* [...] (Rom: Pontificio Ateneo S. Anselmo, 1988), pp. 140–2, 154–64.

[20] Cf. Anselm Stolz, *Manuale theologiae dogmaticae*, 6 vols (Freiburg i.Br.: Herder, 1939–1943).

of all theological reflection.[21] Such an intuition can also be seen in his interpretation of Anselm. The central thesis driving his interpretation is that Anselm's method in the *Proslogion* was neither that of thinking *towards* revelation (philosophy) nor thinking *about* it (theology), but approaching the living God on an intellectual level. Anselm's method is a matter of worship in the field of thought.

In a way, Barth actually anticipated Stolz, as the Benedictine was still dealing with the *Proslogion* at the time. In his review of Barth's book for the journal *Divus Thomas*, Stolz certainly reported and commented upon the train of thought in *Fides quaerens intellectum*, but it appears that he took the review more as an occasion for expounding his own view of things.[22] As far as Anselm's theological programme in general is concerned, Stolz was of the same opinion as Barth. He quite rightly diverges from Johannes Brinktrine (1889–1965), a strict Neo-Scholastic. Brinktrine's translation rests on the false assumption that the *Proslogion* is a purely philosophical document.[23] Barth, by contrast, brought out the consistently theological character of the argument, which presupposes the revelation of the name of God and does not simply reconstruct it rationally. Stolz agrees with his Reformed colleague's interpretation and regards the popular Catholic interpretation as incorrect. But Stolz differs from Barth in relation to the *special* methods which form the basis of the *Proslogion*. Stolz argues that Anselm develops neither a purely philosophical nor a simply theological proof for God's existence, but instead endeavours to gain an insight into the being of the God taught by faith.[24] He was, to be sure, highly aware that such a position needed to be justified in more detail, but we can already see taking shape in this review his idea that the *Proslogion* is not a *rational proof* but more a *mystical experience*. For Stolz it is not a question of whether Anselm has produced a philosophical or a theological proof for God's existence. The *Proslogion*

---

[21] Cf. Fabio Bressan, 'Alla ricerca della figura spirituale della teologia e del teologo: l'Introductio in *Sacram Theologiam* di Anselm Stolz o.s.b. (1900–1942)', *Benedictina* 48 (2001), pp. 61–96.

[22] Cf. the review by Anselm Stolz in *DT* 10 (1932), pp. 560–1. By his own admission the exegete and Church historian Erik Peterson, who in the interim had converted to Catholicism, had urged Stolz to work on *Fides quaerens intellectum*. Erik Peterson, *Ausgewählte Schriften*, vol. 9/2, ed. Barbara Nichtweiss (Würzburg: Echter, 2009), pp. 325–7 (Erik Peterson to Karl Barth, letter dated 15 October 1932), p. 326.

[23] Cf. Stolz (1932), p. 561 with reference to Anselm von Canterbury, *Proslogion. Zum erstenmal ins Deutsche übertragen und mit Einleitung und Anmerkungen versehen von Dr. J. Brinktrine* (Paderborn: Schöningh, 1925). As Barth (1931), p. X notes, this translation is in no respect a significant achievement.

[24] Cf. Stolz (1932), p. 561. The same reflections can be found in Hermann Keller's review for *Benediktinische Monatsschrift* 14 (1932), pp. 324–5. Keller (1905–1970), a monk in the archabbey in Beuron, was Stolz's favourite pupil. They had, presumably, exchanged views regarding how to interprete of the *Proslogion* previously. As far as we can tell, Keller published no further articles on Anselm.

aims for an 'insight' into the cognition of God that lies beyond knowledge, however won; such a recognition is nothing less than a *vision*.

In a longer article which appeared in *Catholica* in 1933, Stolz explained that the *Proslogion* should be interpreted as a kind of intellectual mysticism.[25] He agrees with Barth that the *Proslogion* is not a philosophical document in which something like an ontological argument for God's existence is developed;[26] but with that the common ground is exhausted. The disagreement can already be intimated when Stolz addresses the question of how Anselm actually does theology in the *Proslogion*, and answers that theology happens in prayer.[27] In this way the text differs in form from Anselm's other works and cannot, in Barth's opinion, be interpreted in the context of any general theological programme. According to Stolz, Anselm desires to attain a vision of God himself through reflection upon what he says about God. *Rational cognition* strives for *mystical experience*.[28] This is why Stolz, just like Barth, rejects the Neo-Scholastic interpretation of the *Proslogion*.[29] Anselm is not concerned with offering a proof for God's existence.[30]

With such an interpretation, Stolz takes up the position of a complete outsider.[31] Contradictions were promptly offered. One came from the brilliant medievalist Étienne Gilson (1884–1978), who pointed out that the *Proslogion* could not be definitely assigned either to philosophy, theology or even to mysticism.[32] Stolz insisted in his 1935 riposte that the whole text consisted of orations and meditations, but this position seems rather contrived and serves as a sign of how exiguous the basis of his argument was.[33]

---

[25] Cf. Anselm Stolz, 'Zur Theologie Anselms im Proslogion', *Cath(M)* 2 (1933), pp. 1–24.

[26] Cf. Stolz (1933), pp. 1–2.

[27] Cf. Stolz (1933), p. 2.

[28] Cf. Stolz (1933), pp. 3, 8. For Stolz, the *Proslogion* is an example of mystical theology. A few years later the Benedictine published his own *Theologie der Mystik* (Regensburg: Pustet, 1936).

[29] Cf. Stolz (1933), pp. 19–21.

[30] Cf. Stolz (1933), p. 24. Stolz also stresses this point in his article '"Vere esse' im Proslogion des hl. Anselm"', *Scholastik* 9 (1934), pp. 400–9, 408–9.

[31] Cf. Arthur C. McGill, 'Recent Discussions of Anselm's Argument', in *The Many-Faced Argument. Recent Studies on the Ontological Argument for the Existence of God*, ed. ibid and John Hick (New York: Macmillan, 1967), pp. 33–110; Elmar Salmann, 'Die Anselm-Interpretation bei A. Stolz', in *La Teologia mistico-sapienziale di Anselm Stolz*, ed. ibid (Rom: Pontificio Ateneo S. Anselmo, 1988), pp. 101–24.

[32] Cf. Étienne Gilson, 'Sens et nature de l'argument de saint Anselme', *Archives d'Histoire doctrinale et littéraire du Moyen Âge* 9 (1934), pp. 5–51. By his own admission (p. 5), the Frenchman had turned to Anselm after having been stimulated by the articles of Barth and Stolz.

[33] Cf. Anselm Stolz, 'Das Proslogion des hl. Anselm', *RBén* 47 (1935), pp. 331–47, 336, 346–7.

Thus, Stolz took *Fides quaerens intellectum* simply as a peg on which to hang his own interpretation; Barth was, for him, less a dialogue partner than a stimulus. This point is made completely clear in an introduction Stolz wrote in 1937 for a translation of selected writings by Anselm.[34] In one section he refers to the varying interpretations of the *Proslogion*. Stolz at least mentions Barth's purely theological exegesis, but does not consider it to be of any great relevance.[35]

4.4 Results

Barth wrote a new preface to *Fides quaerens intellectum* when the second edition appeared at the end of the 1950s. Reflecting on the history of the work, Barth admits, though without mentioning any names, that criticism from the Catholic side tended to be more objective, more sympathetic and more worthy of consideration than that from the Protestant side.[36] Such an assessment is somewhat surprising given that *Fides quaerens intellectum* certainly received attention from Catholic theologians rather quickly, but Barth's book was usually taken as an opportunity for more general reflection upon the congency and veracity of Anselm's thinking.[37] This helps to explain why interest in Barth's Anselm book faded just as quickly as it had kindled. In fact, a dissertation from 1939 already historicized the debate on how to properly interpret Anselm which had only begun a few years before. Adolf Kolping (1909–1997), later professor in Münster and Freiburg, developed his own interpretation alongside the previous attempts to read the *Proslogion* either as a philosophical or as a theological work.[38] He was particularly sceptical of the interpretations offered by Barth and Stolz as they appeared to him to come more from a negative attitude

---

[34] Cf. Anselm Stolz, 'Einleitung', in *Anselm von Canterbury* (Munich: Kösel-Pustet, 1937), pp. 7–43.
[35] Cf. Stolz (1937), p. 16.
[36] Cf. Barth (1958), p. 10.
[37] Representative examples included a review by August Deneffe in *Scholastik* 7 (1932), p. 608 and a contribution by Maieul Cappuyns, 'L'argument de saint Anselme', *Recherches de Théologie Ancienne et Médiévale* 6 (1934), pp. 313–30, 313–4, in which Barth (1931) is only briefly mentioned. Instead, the central question is to what extent the ontological argument obtains. For Franciscus Salesius Schmitt, in comparison, Anselm had a rationalist tendency. Having first formulated the thesis in 1933 – cf. Schmitt (1933), p. 221 – the Benedictine held to it fast as long as he lived; see the lexicon article 'Anselm v. Canterbury', in *LTK²* 1 (1957), pp. 592–4, 593 and his 'Der ontologische Gottesbeweis und Anselm', *Analecta Anselmiana* 3 (1972), pp. 81–94, 93–4.
[38] Cf. Adolf Kolping, *Anselms Proslogion-Beweis der Existenz Gottes. Im Zusammenhang seines spekulativen Programms* Fides quaerens intellectum (Bonn: Hanstein, 1939), pp. 1–9.

towards any philosophical proof of God than from a purely historical analysis of the sources.[39]

Fides quaerens intellectum was, at any rate, read as an essay about Anselm. What place it had in Barth's own theological development or whether it was a theological programme played no part at all in subsequent discussions.[40] One might conclude, then, that the discussion surrounding Barth's work primarily involved the historical veracity of his interpretation of Anselm.[41] In reality, however, this only constitutes the first aspect of the three dimensions of Catholic reception of *Fides quaerens intellectum*. Alongside the appropriateness of Barth's interpretation there was, second, the debate as to what kind of work the *Proslogion* actually was. While for Fransiscus Salesius Schmitt and Rudolf Allers it was a purely philosophical tract, Anselm Stolz saw in it an induction to intellectual mysticism. We can already sense, however, that discussions regarding historical and hermeneutical matters also had a third, much more fundamental dimension.

If Schmitt and Allers, following Neo-Scholasticism, emphasized the inner subordination of the *ordo naturalis* to the *ordo supernaturalis*, Stolz stressed that faith is more than a finely balanced system of true statements. Neither side, however, could make much sense of Barth's interpretation of Anselm. It was either too 'modern' insofar as it denied, in contrast to Neo-Scholastic theology, the possibilities of a *theologia naturalis* or *praeambula fidei*, or it was too 'conservative' insofar as it remained within the neat and tidy differentiation of philosophy and theology, and nature and grace, instead of finally leaving this framework of thought behind completely.

---

[39] Cf. Kolping (1939), p. VI.
[40] Only Erich Przywara touches upon it in his otherwise somewhat unwieldy article 'Sein im Scheitern – Sein im Aufgang', *StZ* vol. 123 (1932), pp. 152–61, 158–9 with reference to Barth (1931).
[41] Cf. Dietrich Korsch, 'Intellectus fidei. Ontologischer Gottesbeweis und theologische Methode in Karl Barths Anselmbuch' [1989], in *Dialektische Theologie nach Karl Barth* (Tübingen: Mohr, 1996), pp. 191–213, 191.

5

THE INVENTION OF THE ANTICHRIST? CATHOLIC REACTIONS TO BARTH'S CONDEMNATION OF THE *ANALOGIA ENTIS*

5.1 Introduction

At the beginning of July 1968, Barth was visited by a group of students from the Church College in Wuppertal. In response to a question about the preface to *Church Dogmatics* I/1, where he had unequivocally declared that he considered the *analogia entis* to be the invention of the Antichrist and the only legitimate reason for why one could not become Roman Catholic, he answered:

> It is true that that was such a punch-line. I wrote it on the Monte Pincio in Rome itself after seeing St. Peter's in the radiant dawn between 5 and 6 in the morning, and then it slipped from my pen: Aha! That is the *analogia entis* over there! And those in Germany should hear this. It was rather pedantic, the way I dashed it off. And when I heard how it had raised a thousand-fold echo in the theological world and that everyone was racking their brains; *analogia entis, analogia fidei*... etc., I said: 'Well, prattle on more about all this nonsense! I did not mean it in that sense! [...]'. Of course we had other quite different things to do than to fight against Catholicism.[1]

---

[1] Cf. *Karl Barth. Gespräche 1964–1968*, ed. Eberhard Busch, Gesamtausgabe IV. Gespräche (Zürich: Theologischer Verlag Zürich, 1997), pp. 472–521 (conversation with students from Wuppertal on 1 July 1968), pp. 484–5 in relation to KD I/1 (1932), p. VIII: 'Das war so eine Pointe, gelt. Ich habe das niedergeschrieben auf dem Monte

Unfortunately Barth's rather breathless account of the writing of his infamous invective is mistaken. He had actually written the preface in his native Switzerland, not in the glow of a Roman sunrise.[2] Barth can, nevertheless, be excused for his poor memory, for he actually had good reason to play down what he wrote in his preface. By that time there had already appeared numerous articles and monographs which took his condemnation of the *analogia entis* as their primary theme. The preface to *Church Dogmatics* I/1 itself became essential reading-matter and had such force that the rest of work was interpreted in its light.[3] Such a hermeneutic is, however, in no way necessary. If one reads both the preface and the main text on their own then a quite different perspective comes to light. It quickly becomes clear how different the polemics against the *analogia entis* in the preface are from the actual analysis of the concept in the main text. The discussion of the *analogia entis* in the main text revolves around a metaphysical concept, allegedly used in Catholic theology, which makes possible true statements about God in complete independence from revelation; in the preface, however, the concept simply serves as a convenient catchword Barth can use to dissociate himself and the work from Catholicism. This differentiation also explains Barth's later retraction that he did not mean his statement *in that way*. The *analogia entis* is not a doctrine that can divide denominations; it does not present a *punctum stantis et cadentis ecclesiae*.[4]

Pincio in Rom selber, habe da im Morgenglanz zwischen 5 und 6 Uhr am Morgen den Petersdom gesehen, und dann ist mir das so in die Feder gerutscht: aha! Das ist die analogia entis, da drüben!, und das sollen die in Deutschland nur hören! Es war mehr so ein bißchen literarhaft, wie ich das so hingeschrieben habe. Und als ich dann hörte, wie das ein tausendfältiges Echo erweckte in der theologischen Welt und alle sich nun den Kopf zerbrochen haben: analogia entis, analogia fidei . . . usf., habe ich gesagt: na ja, schwatzt ihr weiter über das Zeug! So habe ich's nicht gemeint! [. . .] Natürlich haben wir ganz anderes zu tun gehabt, als gegen den Katholizismus zu kämpfen.' Barth indicated something similar in another interview four years earlier. Cf. ibid, pp. 10–20 (Interview by Dietmar Schmidt on 18 February 1964), pp. 16–7.

[2] See Eberhard Busch's comments in Barth (1997), p. 484 fn 48. Parts of *Nein! Antwort an Emil Brunner* (Munich: Kaiser, 1934) were probably written in Rome: pp. 32–45. Ever since Martin Luther declared that the Adversary sits on the papal throne, the term 'Antichrist' was frequently used in Protestant polemics. On this cf. Gottfried Seebaß, 'Antichrist. IV. Reformations- und Neuzeit', in *TRE* 3 (1978), pp. 28–43.

[3] When we mention the *Church Dogmatics* in what follows in this chapter, KD I/1 (1932) is meant.

[4] In recent years, particularly in the English-speaking world, the problem of the *analogia entis* has attracted much attention. The more important contributions include John R. Betz, 'Beyond the Sublime: The Aesthetics of the analogia entis', *Modern Theology* 21 (2005), pp. 367–411 and 22 (2006), pp. 1–50; Kenneth R. Oakes, 'Three Themes in Przywara's Early Theology', *The Thomist* 74 (2010), pp. 283–310; Keith L. Johnson, *Karl Barth and the Analogia Entis* (London and New York: T & T Clark, 2010); ibid, 'Reconsidering Barth's Rejection of Przywara's *analogia entis*', *Modern Theology* 26

THE INVENTION OF THE ANTICHRIST?

Barth's judgement that the *analogia entis* represents the fundamental form of what is Roman Catholic can be definitively ascribed to his acquaintance with the Jesuit Erich Przywara, for the term in question does not appear in the textbooks which Barth otherwise used in the *Church Dogmatics* to understand and illustrate the positions of Catholic theology.[5] Furthermore, other publications at the time at most dealt briefly with an 'analogy of being' ('Seinsanalogie' or 'Analogie des Seins').[6] Przywara's entire system of thought, however, revolved around the *analogia entis*, or at least around what he understood by this term. Barth met with the Jesuit in 1929 and 1931 and so had the opportunity to learn at first how Przywara understood the *analogia entis*.[7] As their relationship was characterized by mutual respect, it is all the more necessary to explore what moved Barth to speak of the *analogia entis* as the invention of the Antichrist.

The exact background to Barth's infamous declaration has not yet been completely clarified, yet the clash with Georg Wobbermin (1869–1943) clearly played an important part.[8] Wobbermin, professor in Göttingen, considered himself committed to liberal Protestantism and to Schleiermacher in particular. At quite an early date he saw in Barth a vast collection of views diametrically opposed to his own. Initially, however, he had to swallow the

---

(2010), pp. 632–50; *The Analogy of Being. Invention of the Antichrist or the Wisdom of God?*, ed. Thomas Joseph White (Grand Rapids, MI and Cambridge: Eerdmans, 2011). As regards the several works listed, I soon hope to publish an article handling all of them in detail. In this study, however, I shall only be developing my own perspective.

[5] In the *Church Dogmatics* as a whole, not simply in the prolegomena, Barth relies on Bernhard Bartmann, *Lehrbuch der Dogmatik*, 2 vols (Freiburg i.Br. et al.: Herder, [7]1928) and Franz Diekamp, *Katholische Dogmatik nach den Grundsätzen des heiligen Thomas*, 3 vols (Münster: Aschendorff, [6]1930). He does not take into account the later, partly revised editions of the two textbooks.

[6] Cf. Christian Pesch, *Gott der Eine und Dreieine. Dogmatische Darlegungen* (Düsseldorf: Schwann, 1926), p. 48; Gallus Maria Manser, 'Das Wesen des Thomismus', *DT* 6 (1928), pp. 385–404 and *DT* 7 (1929), pp. 3–30, 322–47, 373–99; Josef Santeler, 'Die Lehre von der Analogie des Seins', *ZKT* 55 (1931), pp. 1–43. It is quite possible that it was through Barth's trenchant comparison of the *analogia entis* and the *analogia fidei* that the conceptual apparatus of Neo-Scholasticism was sharpened. On this see Dahlke (2010), p. 95 fn 7.

[7] Cf. Dahlke (2010), pp. 81–6; Amy Marga, *Karl Barth's Dialogue with Catholicism in Göttingen and Münster. Its Significance for His Doctrine of God* (Tübingen: Mohr Siebeck, 2010).

[8] Cf. Matthias Wolfes, *Protestantische Theologie und moderne Welt. Studien zur Geschichte der liberalen Theologie nach 1918* (Berlin and New York: Walter de Gruyter, 1999), pp. 322–7; Brent A. R. Hege, 'Liberal Theology in the Weimar Era. Schleiermacher and the Question of Religious Subjectivity in the *Methodenstreit* between Georg Wobbermin and Karl Barth', *TZ* 64 (2008), pp. 33–48. Also Marga (2010), p. 51: 'Surely the angry tone about Catholicism and the *analogia entis* in the preface to the *Church Dogmatics* I/1 received some of its energy from these kinds of attacks.'

steadily increasing influence of Dialectical Theology without being able to do anything against it. The opportunity to cross to the offensive came in 1932 when two well-known theologians converted to Catholicism. After Erik Peterson (1890–1960), a church historian in Bonn, had become Catholic, Oskar Bauhofer (1897–1976) decided to do the same. An ordained Reformed theologian, who worked for the European Headquarters for Church Relief Action in Geneva, Bauhofer had also taken an active part in the ecumenical movement. At Pentecost, 1932, he was accepted into the Catholic Church.[9] For Wobbermin this was a welcome opportunity to attack Dialectical Theology. In an open letter he maintained that there was a connection between Dialectical Theology and these conversions. Both Peterson and Bauhofer had earlier had suspicious ties to Dialectical Theology and before they formally converted already had an understanding of dogma which was completely un-Protestant and quite close to that of Catholic scholasticism.[10] Even the daily newspapers reported on the violent exchanges which developed between Wobbermin and Barth as a result.

Barth clearly wanted to make his distance from Catholicism unmistakeably clear once again when he wrote the preface to the *Church Dogmatics* in August 1932. Thus, immediately after his polemic against the *analogia entis*, he responds to a constant and longstanding accusation to which he had been subjected: that in the form and content of his thinking he was following the paths of scholasticism and thus was a crypto-Catholic.[11] Wobbermin might actually be the one Barth has in mind at this point, for he had already insinuated that Barth's theology caused Protestants to become Catholic. Thus the condemnation of the *analogia entis* as found in the preface has also the function of removing from the very outset any impression that the *Church Dogmatics* promotes Catholicism. After all, it was a work which appeared with the express claim that it was churchly and not liberal, dogmatics and not doctrine ('Glaubenslehre').

The identification of the *analogia entis* as a basic form of what is Roman Catholic in the main body of the *Church Dogmatics* has a quite different function from that in the preface. While Catholicism did not play a part in the 1927 *Christian Dogmatics*, in the work published five years later Barth develops the true Protestant faith by dissociating it from two 'heresies': Roman Catholicism and liberal Neo-Protestantism. A truly Protestant theology, one appropriate to the revelation attested to in Scripture, stands between these

---

[9] For biographical information see Roger Liggenstorfer, 'Bauhofer, Oskar', in *Historisches Lexikon der Schweiz* 2 (2003), p. 96.

[10] Cf. Georg Wobbermin, 'Ein neuer Fall "Peterson"', *Das Evangelische Deutschland* 9 (1932), p. 180. Incidentally, Bauhofer himself did not consider that he was particularly close to Dialectical Theology. He explains this in his article '"Katholische Tendenzen im Protestantismus?"', *Schweizerische Rundschau* 32 (1932/1933), pp. 562–4, 563.

[11] Cf. KD I/1 (1932), pp. IX–X [English translation: CD I/1, p. XIII–XIV].

two heresies.[12] Interestingly, Barth thought Catholicism to be the lesser evil when compared with Neo-Protestantism, for at least Catholicism did not consider the reality of the divine to be a human construct. Catholicism, then, presents the main problem that needs to be tackled. The strategy Barth adopts in engaging Catholicism could be called 'dialectic catholicity'.[13] When Barth contrasts the realism which, in his view, characterizes the Roman Church's understanding of the bible, grace and dogma with the sovereignty of God so emphasized by the Reformers, he wins an understanding of a critically broken orthodoxy which sees itself as determinedly Protestant. Barth is, of course, admittedly constructing his own adversary. The picture he paints of Catholicism is certainly not a caricature, but more like a woodcut, for it would simply not be expedient to develop his opponent's position in detail.

Furthermore, at this time Przywara was, for Barth, the very embodiment of everything Catholic. However, it is almost tragic that the Jesuit had in fact modified his position just before the *Church Dogmatics* appeared, and that he had done so because of his meetings with Barth. According to his own admission, Przywara was sufficiently stimulated by these encounters with Barth that he began to emphasize the theological aspects of the *analogia entis*.[14] In his 'magnum opus' published in the summer of 1932, the *Analogia entis*, Przywara altered his usual shorthand for the *analogia entis* in order to give a clearer prominence to the distance between God and humanity. Instead of speaking about 'God in-beyond the creature', Przywara now writes about 'God beyond-in the creature'.[15] Barth was most likely unaware of this very serious shift of emphasis. This is a point to which we shall return later.

As we have seen, Barth's rejection of natural theology and the *analogia entis* as the (alleged) quintessence of Catholicism formed part of his attempt to reach a genuinely Protestant way of thinking. Against liberal Protestantism, Barth insisted that God is not simply available to humanity; God is God and humanity is humanity. By contrast, what Catholic theology was emphatically stressing at the time was the human being's transcendence of its finite nature. This is partially due to the fact that the fears of Catholicism were quite different than that God would become merely available to humanity; instead they stemmed from the practical and theoretical atheism and the agnosticism which first became socially acceptable in the eighteenth century and then had met with approval in all classes of society in the nineteenth century. In the light of these developments, Catholic theology attempted to secure the very

---

[12] Cf., for instance, KD I/1 (1932), pp. 23–43 (§ 2 Die Aufgabe der Prolegomena zur Dogmatik), and Alexander Maßmann, 'Ein ambivalentes Erbe. Karl Barth zwischen Neuprotestantismus und Katholizismus', *EvT* 68 (2008), pp. 144–9.

[13] Cf. Hütter (2000), p. 142.

[14] Cf. Erich Przywara, *Analogia Entis. Metaphysik*, vol. 1 (Munich: Kösel and Pustet, 1932), p. VI.

[15] Cf. Przywara (1932), pp. 58–60, 153–4 or p. 42 with fn 2.

idea of God in the first place. Metaphysics was thought to be a particularly suitable helpmate in this endeavour, and thus Neo-Scholasticism favoured a concept of being which encompassed God and humanity alike.[16]

This historical background also explains why almost all the Catholic theologians who paid attention to the *Church Dogmatics* could do little with it. What Barth developed on hundreds upon hundreds of pages seemed stimulating and erudite, but in the end it merely floated in the air without any real connection to earth. If revelation means the unveiling of God for humanity, humanity must be able to recognize this and understand what it means. Without a previous rational presentation of the idea of God (*praeambula fidei*) revelation has absolutely no connection to humanity; it remains alien and unclear. At least such was the conviction of the vast majority of Catholic theologians who worked on the *Church Dogmatics* in the 1930s, particularly Bernhard Bartmann, Daniel Feuling and Jakob Fehr. In this respect, the one exception was Heinrich Weisweiler (1893–1964), a professor in the Jesuit seminary in Valkenburg. In his review of the *Church Dogmatics* he mentions neither the *analogia entis* nor the *analogia fidei*, although he certainly understands the work to be putting critical questions to Catholicism.[17]

5.2 The Church Dogmatics as a Curiosity: Bernhard Bartmann

When Bernhard Bartmann reviewed the *Church Dogmatics*, he could look back on a lengthy and successful career as an academic. He had been professor in the philosophical-theological academy in Paderborn since 1898, and had put his stamp on a whole generation of students. His *Lehrbuch der Dogmatik*, a kind of theological manual, was also very popular. Revised once again, it was available in several editions, and translations were soon to follow. But it was not only Catholic students of theology who fell back on the two-volume work in order to learn about the teaching of the Catholic Church. Barth likewise consulted the textbook in its seventh edition, which appeared at the end of the 1920s.[18]

As already noted, Barth developed his thought in *Church Dogmatics* I/1 through a critical distancing of his theology from the 'heresy' of Roman

---

[16] A good example of this tendency can be found in Bernard Kälin, *Lehrbuch der Philosophie*, vol. 1 (Sarnen: Benediktinerkolleg Sarnen, ⁵1957), pp. 68–9.

[17] Cf. Heinrich Weisweiler's review in *Scholastik* 8 (1933), pp. 599–601.

[18] Cf. the passages listed in KD I/1 (1932), p. 521 (index) each relating to Bernhard Bartmann, *Lehrbuch der Dogmatik*, 2 vols (Freiburg i.Br.: Herder, ⁷1928–1929). In CD (1927) Barth used the sixth edition of the textbook which appeared in 1923.

Catholicism. In the process, he elaborates a critically broken orthodoxy which sees itself as determinedly Protestant, and he does so by holding fast to the sovereignty of God, given such prominence by the Reformers, over and against the objectivism which characterizes the Catholic understanding of Scripture, grace and dogma. We can see this distancing tactic in the *Church Dogmatics* as Barth quotes extensively from dogmaticians who were popular in Catholic theology at that time and who were typically used in university teaching. In total he cites Bartmann's textbook seven times, and thus the most frequently. This textbook focused on biblical texts, Patristics and the history of dogma, and thus represents a 'positive' as opposed to a speculative methodology. Dogmatic tenets are provided with a great deal of biblical, patristic, scholastic and academic references. It thus fits very well into the picture Barth had of Catholicism.

In his review of the *Church Dogmatics*, which is on the whole rational, direct and informative, Bartmann makes no mention of the fact that his textbook was frequently quoted.[19] The reader is concisely and accurately informed about the author of the *Church Dogmatics*, his theological concerns and the content of the work.[20] As Bartmann frequently offers us quotations from quite different sections of the *Church Dogmatics*, he allows us to infer that he had read the work thoroughly.

Bartmann understands the central theme of Barth's theology to be the strict differentiation of God and humanity. Only if God actively reveals himself to humanity can humanity speak about God properly: humanity could never do this by itself. In this connexion we can also understand the harsh polemics against the *analogia entis*.[21] These polemics have their origin in external circumstances: Barth saw himself confronted with the accusation of 'crypto-Catholicism' and apparently felt he had to prove his solid allegiance to Protestantism. He was undoubtedly successful in proving this allegiance, Bartmann dryly comments. Of course, Barth's polemic was not only motivated by such a strategy: as Catholicism understands there to be an analogous transference of creaturely perfections to the divine being, it unacceptably levels out the difference between God and humanity.

In the end, then, Barth condemns the *analogia entis* on theological grounds. Bartmann's response is to quote authorities, in particular the Vatican Council, Augustine and Paul, which Barth clearly thinks he can ignore. Already at the time of Augustine, Catholic theology had talked of a *theologia naturalis*, and thus a natural way to God, which believers can

---

[19] Cf. Bernhard Bartmann, 'Die Dogmatik von Karl Barth', *TGl* 26 (1934), pp. 205–13.
[20] Cf. Bartmann (1934), pp. 205–6 containing a biographical sketch; pp. 207–10 with reference to KD I/1 (1932), pp. 47–310 (§§ 3–7) or pp. 210–2 with reference to KD I/1 (1932), pp. 311–514 (§§ 8–12).
[21] On what follows see Bartmann (1934), pp. 206–7 quoting KD I/1 (1932), p. VIII.

employ to Christianize already religious pagans. Even Barth's supporters advised him to develop a natural theology. If they did not succeed it was because Barth understood the human being to be incapable of entering into a relationship with God. Humanity is completely restricted and confined to itself and its world; a relationship to God beyond these realities is constantly denied.[22] The fact that Paul teaches something quite different in his letter to the Roman congregation clearly did not worry Barth. The two passages which Bartmann cites in this connexion – Rom 1.20 and 2.14f – are the traditional prooftexts for natural theology. The former verse was already interpreted in this way at the First Vatican Council.[23]

To be sure, Bartmann is quite satisfied with what he reads in Barth regarding individual dogmatic questions – for example, that the Trinity is recognized as dogma or that Thomas Aquinas is not only quoted thirty-five times but also, for the most part, approvingly. However, on the whole he considers the *Church Dogmatics* to be wordy, in some respects even challenging, but in the end inconsistent. He finds it inconsistent because revelation cannot actually reveal anything. If the difference between God and humanity is as severe as Barth makes it, then even faith itself does not provide any possibility of knowing God, for like revelation itself, faith must also be believed. Bartmann thus sees in Barth's theology an infinite regress or a logical circle, and nothing else Barth said could convince him otherwise.[24] In the end Bartmann finds the *Church Dogmatics* to be an exotic oddity.[25] Daniel Feuling, a monk in the Benedictine abbey at Beuron, was to come to virtually the same conclusion.

5.3 God and Being: Daniel Feuling

Daniel Feuling (1882–1947) first taught at the University of Salzburg and then at the College of the Order in Beuron.[26] In spite of all his open-mindedness and intellectual breadth, he was firmly committed to Neo-Scholasticism. For him it was an established fact that one could only speak meaningfully of revelation on the basis of natural theology. Thus his particular interest was in metaphysics, and he later produced an extensive monograph on the

---

[22] Cf. Bartmann (1934), p. 207 quoting KD I/1 (1932), p. 251.
[23] Cf. DH 3004 quoting Rom.1.20.
[24] Cf. Bartmann (1934), p. 213, with Bartmann alluding to KD I/1 (1932), p. 190 [English translation: CD I/1, p. 183].
[25] Cf. Bartmann (1934), p. 213 quoting Werner Petersmann, 'Die "Theologie der Krisis" in Japan', *Christliche Welt* 48 (1934), pp. 27–30, 27.
[26] For biographical information see Johannes Schaber, 'Der Beuroner Benediktiner Daniel Feuling (1882–1947)', *Freiburger Diözesan-Archiv* 124 (2004), pp. 73–84.

subject.[27] Metaphysics is also the perspective from which Feuling assesses the *Church Dogmatics*.

The learned monk actually sent his review of *Church Dogmatics* to Barth before it appeared in the *Benediktinische Monatsschrift* in 1934. The accompanying letter is warm and testifies to a great regard and respect.[28] The same can be said of the review, for Feuling considers Barth to be the pioneer of faithful Protestant dogmatics. He not only acknowledges the richness of Barth's thought, but also emphasizes his by no means inappreciable originality.[29] What makes him think particularly well of Barth's work, however, is his clear rejection of the modernist (i.e. Neo-Protestant) position. For Barth, revelation is not, as it is for the Neo-Protestants, a product of the humanity's experience of itself and the world, but rather a gift from God.[30] Feuling goes on to say, however, that there still lingers a central theological question: how can the finite human being in any way understand the message of the infinite God.[31] In Feuling's view, Barth continually struggles with the problem of the comprehensibility of revelation in the *Church Dogmatics*.[32]

As Feuling explains, Catholic theology solves this problem by starting from the metaphysics of cognition.[33] Accordingly, the understanding spirit refers to everything which *is*, or being. This being is simultaneously one and many in its becoming in different entities, which exist only because being is one. Being is a unified variety to the extent to which it is the relationship of several becomings to one another, and thus it is in itself analogous (*analogia entis*). It is a manifold unity insofar as it can be comprehended by means of what becomes on the basis of an idea of being, which is also analogous (*analogia cognitionis*). In Feuling's view, this metaphysical picture explains how the revelation of the infinite God becomes understandable for the finite human being. Insofar as God exists, he *is*, and his existence can be understood even by a human who shares, in a finite way, in the infinite being. Yet neither God's essence nor his actions lie within reach of human cognition: they are a part of revelation. The knowledge of God achieved through reason and the knowledge won through faith do not stand side by side, completely separated; rather, each one is inwardly connected to the other. As the one being is the basis of the various becomings, it becomes recognized in the cognition of the becoming. 'Recognized' has a double meaning here: if being

---

[27] Cf. Daniel Feuling, *Hauptfragen der Metaphysik. Einführung in das philosophische Leben* (Salzburg and Leipzig: Pustet, 1936).
[28] Cf. KBA 9334.343 (Daniel Feuling to Karl Barth, letter dated 12 March 1934).
[29] Cf. Daniel Feuling, 'Das Gotteswort der Offenbarung', *Benediktinische Monatsschrift* 16 (1934), pp. 123–30, 124.
[30] Cf. Feuling (1934), pp. 124–5, refering to KD I/1 (1932), p. 62.
[31] Cf. Feuling (1934), p. 125.
[32] Cf. Feuling (1934), pp. 125–6.
[33] On what follows see Feuling (1934), pp. 126–8.

is on the one hand *revealed* as the basis of becoming as the latter would not exist at all without the former, it is also simultaneously *concealed* as it is in itself not becoming. Concealing is inevitably connected to revealing. God is thus revealed to the world as the unfathomable basis of its very knowledge. God is *revealed* because all becomings have a cause, and thus there must be a Creator, and he is also *concealed* insofar as he is not becoming and thus his inner essence and action remain outside of this circle of knowing and being. Human beings may be able to recognize *that* a God exists, but not *how* he exists in himself. God is only truly known as he actively allows himself to be known, by making himself the object of human recognition and taking on the human understanding of being. There can only be knowledge of revelation when revelation is possible on the basis of (note: not because of) the knowledge of being. Only then, along with the *analogia entis* and the *analogia cognitionis*, does the *analogia fidei* come upon the scene and with it the analogy between the individual statements of faith. As the mere recognition of being hardly means revelation, the latter is still unthinkable without the former; otherwise revelation would merely be some human word with nothing to say about God, instead of the Word of God which concerns the human person. Feuling, then, simply cannot understand why Barth opposes the *analogia fidei* to the *analogia entis*. What Feuling read in the preface to the *Church Dogmatics* must have seemed to him particularly incomprehensible.[34] Clearly, Barth has completely misunderstood what is meant by the *analogia entis*, and is judging and condemning something he does not really understand. In fact, Barth's position is self-contradictory insofar as he assumes that God and humanity are in a real ontological community through faith and grace, but at the same time denies that there is any ontological connexion between God and humanity. As Feuling stresses, the *analogia entis* precisely guarantees the reality of the connexion between God and humanity in revelation, and that Barth cannot finally deny the ontological presuppositions of the analogy of recognition.[35] Admittedly, the Benedictine in no way desired that his criticism be understood as theological polemics, but rather as a friendly invitation to Barth to look more closely at the Catholic position.

Feuling's review of the *Church Dogmatics* allows us to see the fundamental contrast which exists between theology based on the concept of being and one founded upon on a non-metaphysical basis. Jakob Fehr, who, like Feuling, is a determined Thomist, also lays great stress on the incompatibility of the two perspectives. The separation of metaphysics and revelation, programmatically enforced in the *Church Dogmatics* with the rejection of all natural theology, was simply incomprehensible to him. For

---

[34] Cf. Feuling (1934), p. 129 with reference to KD I/1 (1932), p. VIII.
[35] Cf. Feuling (1934), pp. 129–30.

Barth, there could not be a *duplex ordo cognitionis* as decreed by Vatican I and taught by Neo-Scholasticism.[36]

5.4 A Thomistic Critique: Jakob Fehr

In 1939, Jakob Fehr (1907–1971) published a monograph[37] on Dialectical Theology which received considerable attention in the Swiss media.[38] The monograph was actually the end result of several years of reading and thinking about the upstart theological movement. Fehr himself sent the work to a variety of people including Oskar Bauhofer, whose conversion probably caused Barth to condemn the *analogia entis* in the preface of *Church Dogmatics* I/1. In the summer of 1939, Bauhofer wrote a letter to Barth in an obvious attempt to pacify him:

> I am somewhat surprised at the extent of Fehr's inability to 'win' anything from your theology. But it seems to me that it has become inevitable that he makes absolutely no attempt to relax the language of the Thomism into more unconventional, biblical words and in this way find a common basis, a common 'language' with you. Here one is punished if, as a Catholic theologian, one believes one may conduct a conversation ad extra on the basis of Thomism or any of the other ready-made systems. I don't doubt Thomism – but it is not the judgement seat before which one could bring Protestant theology just like that; one too easily forgets that a direct comparison or comparability is not possible between a highly-developed system with a 'ready-made' group of concepts and a theology which is supported directly by the actuality of Holy Scripture. (That Protestant theology visualizes its Catholic

---

[36] Cf. for instance, KD I/1 (1932), p. 194 (Leitsatz von § 6. Die Erkennbarkeit des Wortes Gottes) [English translation: CD I/1, p. 187 (leading thesis of § 6. The Knowability of the Word of God): 'The reality of the Word of God in all its three forms is grounded only in itself. So, too, the knowledge of it by men can consist only in its acknowledgment, and this acknowledgment can become real only through itself and can become intelligible only in terms of itself.'].

[37] Cf. Jakob Fehr, *Das Offenbarungsproblem in dialektischer und thomistischer Theologie* (Freiburg i.Ue. and Leipzig: Verlag der Universitätsbuchhandlung Freiburg, 1939). For biographical information see the note in *Karl Barth – Eduard Thurneysen. Briefwechsel*, vol. 3, ed. Caren Algner, Gesamtausgabe V. Briefe (Zürich: Theologischer Verlag Zürich, 2000), p. 144 fn 13.

[38] See the reviews of Walter Nigg in *Neue Zürcher Zeitung* (25 October 1939); Werner Tanner in *Kirchenblatt für die reformierte Schweiz* 96 (1940), pp. 26-9; and Paul Wyser, in *DT* 19 (1941), pp. 332-40.

opponent in Thomism for example is, on the contrary, quite in order – it must hold on to a particular concretion of what is Catholic.)[39]

In this missive, Bauhofer identified the fundamental problem fairly accurately: what is the relationship between metaphysics and revelation? While metaphysics relates to the general and necessary, revelation is concerned with historical particularity and freedom. There is no inevitable conflict between the two, but nor can they simply coincide. Fehr's own preferences and leanings, however, were pretty clear and well defined, not least because of his time of study in the theological faculty in Fribourg, which was led by Dominicans and counted as one of the most important centres of Neo-Thomism.[40]

After Fehr acquired his licentiate, he spent a further year of study in various German universities; the winter semester of 1930/31 found him in Tübingen, where as a matter of priority he attended Karl Adam's lectures. He spent the following summer semester in Bonn, where he participated in Barth's seminar and made a positive impression on the professor.[41] Fehr subsequently returned to Fribourg, and in 1932 received his doctorate on the basis of a thesis dealing with Dialectical Theology's doctrine of revelation. While he was curate in Basle-Riehen he participated in meetings of a discussion group which had formed around Eduard Thurneysen. The topic of the meetings was the 'essence' of Catholicism, with Karl Adam's 1924 book of the same name serving as the basis for discussion.[42] Fehr was, however, not invited back to the group after his first two evenings with them, as no constructive debate with Fehr had arisen.[43] Clearly the meetings did not proceed as harmoniously as Thurneysen had hoped. It is difficult

---

[39] KBA 9339.438 (Oskar Bauhofer to Karl Barth, letter dated 24 July 1939, translated).

[40] On the Thomism which the Dominicans in Fribourg, Toulouse and Rome supported, cf. Henry Donneaud, 'Une école thomiste en sa tradition contemporaine. XIXe–XXe siècles', in Serge-Thomas Bonino et al., *Thomistes ou de l'actualité de saint Thomas d'Aquin* (Paris: Parole et Silence, 2003), pp. 255–64.

[41] Cf. *Karl Barth – Eduard Thurneysen. Briefwechsel*, vol. 3, ed. Caren Algner, Gesamtausgabe V. Briefe (Zürich: Theologischer Verlag Zürich, 2000), pp. 140–6 (Karl Barth to Eduard Thurneysen, letter dated 29 May 1931), p. 144. Barth is full of praise in the report which he wrote for Fehr after his semester in Bonn. A copy of this report can be found in KBA 9231.201 (report by Karl Barth for Jakob Fehr on 15 July 1931, copy).

[42] Thurneysen informed Barth about the meetings in several letters, viz. *Karl Barth – Eduard Thurneysen. Briefwechsel*, vol. 3, ed. Caren Algner, Gesamtausgabe V. Briefe (Zürich: Theologischer Verlag Zürich, 2000), pp. 629–38 (Eduard Thurneysen to Karl Barth, letter dated 18 May 1934), 636; ibid, pp. 652–4 (Eduard Thurneysen to Karl Barth, letter dated 23 May 1934), p. 654.

[43] Cf. *Karl Barth – Eduard Thurneysen. Briefwechsel*, vol. 3, ed. Caren Algner, Gesamtausgabe V. Briefe (Zürich: Theologischer Verlag Zürich, 2000), pp. 660–6 (Eduard Thurneysen to Karl Barth, letter dated 20 June 1934), pp. 664–5.

to determine for certain whether these events induced Fehr to take up a certain position towards Dialectical Theology. At any rate, from 1936 to 1939, alongside his pastoral work, he published six articles in which he brought Dialectical Theology's understanding of revelation face to face with that of Thomism.[44] Having also written a review of the Prolegomena to the *Church Dogmatics* in the meantime, he finally compiled all the articles in the monograph mentioned earlier.[45]

Taken as a whole, Fehr's analysis of dialectic theology is rigidly systematic. He discusses whether its spokesperson's understanding of revelation is really consistent. He uses Thomism as both a contrasting system and as a criterion for his assessment.[46] As Fehr explores the particular historical context of the ideas he covers, he initially places Dialectical Theology within the context of the more recent history of theology. In his view, there was a dramatic change in Protestantism during the nineteenth century which has had serious subsequent consequences for it. No longer was *God* in his revelation seen as the object of theological reflection, but the *human being* as deeply and religiously stirred. The theological movement around Barth in the twentieth century is the antithesis to this development: it is attempting to retrieve revelation as the true subject of theology.[47] For Fehr, however, the question is: is it actually succeeding in doing so?

---

[44] Cf. Jakob Fehr, 'Der Weg zur dialektischen Theologie', *DT* 14 (1936), pp. 163–80; ibid, 'Zweierlei Offenbarung? Gedanken zu einer protestantischen Kontroverse', *DT* 14 (1936), pp. 399–420; ibid, 'Die Offenbarung als "Wort Gottes" bei Karl Barth und Thomas von Aquin', *DT* 15 (1937), pp. 55–64; ibid, 'Offenbarung und Analogie. Ihr Verhältnis in dialektischer und thomistischer Theologie', *DT* 15 (1937), pp. 291–307; ibid, 'Offenbarung und Glaube. Ihr Verhältnis in dialektischer und thomistischer Theologie', *DT* 16 (1938), pp. 15–32; ibid, 'Offenbarung, Heilige Schrift und Kirche. Ihr Verhältnis in dialektischer und thomistischer Theologie', *DT* 16 (1938), pp. 309–30. Fehr also published a review-article in which he treated KD I/1 (1932) and KD I/2 (1938): '"Offenbarungstheologie". Eine Buchbesprechung', *DT* 17 (1939), pp. 99–107.

[45] Cf. Fehr (1939a). In detail: ibid (1936a) = ibid (1939a), pp. 1–18; ibid (1936b) = ibid (1939a), pp. 19–40; ibid (1937a) = ibid (1939a), pp. 41–50; ibid (1937b) = ibid (1939a), pp. 51–68; ibid (1938a) = ibid (1939a), pp. 69–86; ibid (1938b) = ibid (1939a), pp. 87–108; ibid (1939b) = ibid (1939a), pp. 109–22. The articles were reprinted essentially unchanged and unrevised apart from two small additions to the text which did not change the content significantly; cf. for the one ibid (1937b), p. 307 with ibid (1939a), pp. 67–8, for the other ibid (1939b), 107 with ibid (1939a), pp. 117–22. The monograph was not, as is frequently assumed, Fehr's doctoral dissertation; on this cf. Dahlke (2010), p. 109 fn 68.

[46] Cf. Fehr (1936a), p. 163 fn 1; ibid (1939a), pp. V–VI.

[47] Cf. Fehr (1936a), pp. 164–80, especially p. 180. Elsewhere, Fehr interprets Dialectical Theology as a reaction against historicism: ibid (1938b), pp. 317–8, 322.

5.4.1 Barth and Thomism

To understand revelation as God's Word in the same way that Dialectical Theology does, implies, according to Fehr, not simply that the human person is able to *hear* what God says; this position assumes also that what is heard can be put into words. What the person has rationally apprehended must be a true, albeit inadequate expression of the divine Word which provides a way of knowing the God who reveals himself.[48] With this understanding of revelation in view, Fehr now has a basis from which he can depict Barth's position and, by contrast, that of Thomism. While Thomas Aquinas assumed a connexion between the Word of God and human words, Barth wants to strictly differentiate the two.[49] The real problem, therefore, is the concept of analogy.

For Fehr, it is important to recognize that the idea of analogy is not restricted to one particular denomination, but represents a systematic theological necessity, a point which Barth, incidentally, also recognized.[50] Analogy means neither absolute identity nor absolute difference, but instead a relative unity, a mutuality of different analogata in relationship to an analogon. It is, simply put, indispensible for theology.[51] Theology, as human talk about God, cannot manage without it. In Fehr's estimation, the representatives of Dialectical Theology do not have a consistent conception of what analogy means and miss its main purpose. Barth emphasizes the element of difference in such a way that the concept of analogy finally vanishes.[52] He vehemently denies any possibility of a natural knowledge of God, as he considers the *analogia entis* to be a dubious substitute for revelation. Additionally, he denies the possibility of gaining knowledge of God on the basis of the Scripture, for human concepts of God can never reproduce the reality of God. If God is known at all, it is only as he makes the sinful and chaotic human word his own through the Holy Spirit.[53] In contrast to Barth, who attaches too much importance to difference within the analogous relationship, Emil Brunner pushes the aspect of *identity* too far.[54] Brunner assumes that likeness to God constitutes humanity's true nature, and thus the person does not forfeit his supernatural connexion to God after the Fall, but merely possesses a diminished understanding of human nature until revelation manifests it once again. For this reason Brunner has

---

[48] Cf. Fehr (1937a), pp. 56, 61; ibid (1938a), pp. 15–6.
[49] Cf. Fehr (1937a), pp. 56–61 or pp. 61–4.
[50] Cf. Fehr (1937b), p. 291.
[51] This preconception can be reconstructed from Fehr (1937b), pp. 295, 298.
[52] Cf. Fehr (1937b), pp. 291–5, especially pp. 294–5.
[53] Cf. Fehr (1937b), p. 294 with reference to KD I/1 (1932), pp. 123, 252–3, 352–3.
[54] Cf. Fehr (1937b), pp. 295–7, especially p. 296.

to give up, for instance, the traditional doctrine of original sin, which for Fehr renders his theology unacceptable.

In contrast to the exponents of Dialectical Theology who cannot produce a consistent conception of analogy, Thomism offers a balanced conception. Here, as Fehr argues, the knowledge of God which comes from the *analogia entis* forms the prerequisite for the knowledge of God gained from the *analogia fidei*. In his opinion the true location of the *analogia entis* is 'natural metaphysics'.[55] The becoming which has become and is only partial in the beginning will become an absolutely unconditioned being, enclosed in its own ground. This being is identified as the Creator whose very essence includes his existence, for if the Creator did not exist he could not be the ground of all becoming. On the principle of such an *analogia entis* rests the possibility of a natural knowledge of God. As God, in an analogous way (but in a real sense), can be regarded as becoming, all the other ontological characteristics, which in themselves signify perfection, can be predicated of him, whether they are (only) fulfilled in a limited way or completely. In Fehr's view, however, the *analogia entis* not only enables the knowledge of God but at the same time limits it, most likely because it belongs to the realm of natural metaphysics. Certainly, one can recognize that in God perfections such as being, spirit and life exist, but not *how* they exist. God is not known in his own essence. This is why Barth's harsh accusations against the *analogia entis* are simply unfounded. The *analogia entis* neither allows us to move beyond God's revelation to some secret lying behind it nor to transform the indirectness of the knowledge of revelation into directness.[56] At best, the knowledge of God based on the *analogia entis* is and remains indirect, inadequate and vague. Although it is limited in its extent, it nevertheless remains anything other than superfluous. If a human being had no natural knowledge of God, he or she could neither be considered as responsible for this knowledge nor counted as a sinner, for he or she could only become such a being on the basis of knowledge of God.[57]

As Fehr stresses, as metaphysics is rational reflection which moves from the finite to the infinite, it cannot be a substitute for revelation, for reason can only abstract from what it encounters in the concrete, visible world. Consequently, the analogies it constructs are dependent upon this concrete, visible world. But God in his true inner essence is not a worldly object, and therefore cannot be known by reason. If God desires to reveal himself to humanity, a mere broadening of the objects humans can know within some formal basis of knowledge would be necessary. Yet beyond even this broadening, the human being must also be able to understand God's essence

---

[55] Cf. Fehr (1937b), pp. 297–302.
[56] Cf. Fehr (1937b), p. 300 with reference to KD I/1 (1932), pp. 175, 180.
[57] Cf. Fehr (1937b), p. 301.

through a new, higher ground of knowledge.[58] The ground of this knowledge is faith. To outline the knowledge of God which happens in faith more sharply, Fehr contrasts it with what would be granted to humans in their earlier blissful vision of God.[59] What will happen perfectly in the *visio beata* now takes place in a highly imperfect way: God makes himself the basis of humanity's ability to know. Thus neither the knowledge of God which comes from faith nor from natural metaphysics is direct. Both metaphysical and theological concepts are always and only analogous. There are, however, important differences between the two ways of obtaining knowledge of God.[60] First of all, the way of faith signifies a 'more' when compared with the way of natural metaphysics, yet is signifies a 'less' when compared with the way of the *visio beata*. Second, the analogies of faith, in contrast to those deduced in a reflective, natural way, always form part of revelation, for the *analogia entis* can reveal that God is perfect, but not that God is triune. In contrast to Barth and Brunner, in whom the idea of analogy disappears, Thomism represents a position that does justice to revelation.[61]

5.4.2 God's Word in the Human Word

The initial question as to how one can hear God's Word and talk about God in an appropriate way has only been partially answered; it remains to be answered how one can recognize God's words in particular human words.[62] It is taken for granted that only God has the power to make the cognition happen; one cannot do it by oneself. This raises the question of what significance is really given to faith, especially as this then determines the relationship between concept and reality. Since Barth sees no connection between the human word and that of God, and thus the analogy plays no part of this relationship, even faith cannot surmount the difference between words and the Word. True knowledge of God is rendered impossible for human beings.[63] Nevertheless, it is and remains the task of theology to talk about God, and for Fehr it is precisely here where the major problem of Dialectical Theology lies. If not only any natural knowledge of God is confused and untrue, but even the knowledge of God which comes from faith, then absolutely nothing can truly be said about God. But if there is talk about God, the only kind of 'knowledge' that seems to be left is existential experience. For Fehr, as much as Dialectical Theology may want to criticize and move beyond a liberal theology of experience, it hardly achieves as

---

[58] Cf. Fehr (1937b), p. 303.
[59] Cf. Fehr (1937b), pp. 304–6.
[60] For what follows see Fehr (1937b), pp. 306–7.
[61] Cf. the summary of the Thomist position in Fehr (1937b), p. 307.
[62] Cf. Fehr (1938a), p. 15.
[63] Cf. Fehr (1938a), p. 20.

much.[64] Furthermore, Dialectical Theology also fails to overcome historicism, whose supremacy in Protestant theology it initially set out to counter. For, instead of clarifying how Scripture and dogma could have absolute validity in spite of their limitations, Dialectical Theology declares both of them to be simply human words while then taking refuge in an account of revelation as a historically transcendent event.[65] If, however, one follows Thomas Aquinas and accepts the possibility of analogy, then Scripture and dogma become realities from which a person can gain knowledge of God.[66] Even so, the God recognized in revelation will not thereby be completely available to the human person. This is already ensured by the differentiation of the external and internal understanding of the revelation. Hearing the *Word* of God is initially an external act and the Holy Spirit must still enlighten the hearer of the Word so that it can become *God's* Word.[67]

When one understands Fehr's observations, the following picture comes to light: Dialectical Theology's account of revelation is completely implausible, particularly in comparison to Thomism. Barth and Brunner certainly make a lot of noise regarding revelation, but in the end it remains pure rhetoric, bluster and assertion. If there is an insurmountable gulf between God and humanity, as they maintain, then the human being can say nothing about God, or at least nothing which is actually true. As a result theology falls into a highly precarious position, for it cannot fulfil its actual task: talking about God.

Fehr clarifies how Dialectical Theology deals with this awkward situation in his review of *Church Dogmatics* I/1 and I/2.[68] While in his other articles he explores material topics, he now outlines the formal principles of Barth's line of thought. What takes up almost one thousand five hundred pages, to his mind, can be summarily expressed by two closely related ideas: *dialectics as theological method* and the *actualization of revelation*.

Although Barth argues that revelation is completely transcendent, he still talks about it in an incredibly verbose and eloquent way. The dialectical method he falls back upon so masterfully enables him to do so. While on the one hand he accepts and radicalizes the complete relativity of all that is human, rendering impossible humans talk about God, on the other hand he assumes that the work of the Holy Spirit makes such human talk about God, which is impossible in and of itself, possible after all. When Barth starts out from a factual self-visualization of revelation he can talk about it at length, despite its transcendence. Everything that humanity thinks it must say about God is in itself completely false, but if God makes the human word his own,

---

[64] Cf. Fehr (1938a), pp. 27–9.
[65] Cf. Fehr (1938b), pp. 317–22, especially p. 318.
[66] Cf. Fehr (1938a), p. 23 and also ibid (1938b), p. 322.
[67] Cf. Fehr (1938a), pp. 30–2.
[68] For what follows see Fehr (1939b).

then even what is false becomes true. For Fehr, however, this is anything but obvious. From a Catholic point of view, the fact that Dialectical Theology declares its lack of a system to be a system makes it finally unacceptable. In such an unrestrained qualification of all human speech about God, the result will not only be the disintegration of the idea of revelation, its character as a reality that demands a decision and obedience will also be annulled. If the human person cannot hear God's Word, he or she cannot be obedient to it in his or her thinking, speaking and action.[69]

After this full frontal assault, Fehr offers a few appreciative words at the very end of his review article regarding the seriousness and consistency with which Barth developed his theology.[70] These parting compliments still do not mitigate his fundamental reservations about Dialectical Theology. Despite these reservations, however, Fehr still sent Barth a copy of his monograph on Dialectical Theology's account of revelation.[71] Anticipating Barth's reaction, Fehr writes in the accompanying letter:

> What pains me most about my work is how far it gives the impression that I believe I have finished with your theology. That is much less the case than it may appear. One thing, admittedly, is true: there is something in your theology which is incomprehensible for me, and which I could not go along with. But there is so much in it which was and which will always remain a salutary unsettling.[72]

To be sure, Barth's reply reveals that he is in no way put off (although some of Fehr's statements seem rather bitter and malicious), but he still has critical questions about Fehr's interpretation, especially in relation to his heavy-handed emphasis upon dialectics.[73] Fehr immediately replied and protested against Barth's impression that his own statements bordered on being bitter, coldly malicious and a kind of verbal assault and battery. He readily and sincerely conceded the defects in his work and attributed them

---

[69] Cf. Fehr (1939b), pp. 106–7.

[70] Cf. Fehr (1939b), p. 107.

[71] According to the note in *Karl Barth – Eduard Thurneysen. Briefwechsel*, vol. 3, ed. Caren Algner, Gesamtausgabe V. Briefe (Zürich: Theologischer Verlag Zürich, 2000), p. 650 fn 30 (translated), the dedication read: 'Dedicated by the author to Professor Dr. Karl Barth in thankful recollection of my time of study in Bonn.'

[72] Cf. KBA 9339.403 (Jakob Fehr to Barth, letter dated 28 June 1939): 'An meiner Arbeit tut mir etwas am meisten leid: dass sie gar so sehr den Eindruck macht, dass ich glaube mit Ihrer Theologie fertig geworden zu sein. Das ist nicht der Fall, viel weniger als es scheinen mag. Das ist freilich richtig: Ihre Theologie ist mir im letzten etwas Unbegreifliches, das ich nicht mitmachen könnte. Aber es ist an ihr doch so vieles, das mir immer eine heilsame Beunruhigung war und bleiben wird.'

[73] Cf. KBA 9239.119 (Karl Barth to Jakob Fehr, letter dated 2 July 1939, copy).

to his own clumsy and inadequate knack for description.[74] Nevertheless, Barth's objections to the content of Fehr's presentation seemed not to make much of an impression on Fehr. At the celebratory assembly for St. Thomas in the theological faculty in Lucerne held in March 1941, Fehr had the opportunity tone down, if not exactly qualify, his harsh criticism of Dialectical Theology in a lecture he gave dealing with Barth's theological and intellectual significance.[75] Fehr simply repeated the interpretation already published, unaltered in content and style. Here Fehr and Barth seem to have completely parted way, for it appears as if contact between them broke off.

Barth's relationship to Gottlieb Söhngen, however, would prove to be completely different – friendlier on a personal level and more productive theologically. In fact, Söhngen came closer to Dialectical Theology than virtually any other Catholic.

5.5 Towards Salvation History: Gottlieb Söhngen

When Catholic theology attempted to guard the idea of God against atheism and agnosticism by putting strong emphasis on the *praeambula fidei*, it ironically took over the intellectualism of modern philosophy. It became uncertain whether and to what extent one could still posit any difference between the God of the philosophers and the God of Abraham, Isaac and Jacob. So strongly was Neo-Scholasticism concerned with metaphysics that at times it appeared as if there were only slight differences between the natural and the supernatural knowledge of God. In the first half of the twentieth century it was remembered that the God of the philosophers is not simply identical with the God of Scripture.[76] In this regard we must mention Gottlieb Söhngen, who in 1937 was a professor in East Prussian Braunsberg and then in Munich after World War II. Söhngen counts as one of the most important figures in Catholic theology at that time, for his methodological reflections regarding theology made a considerable contribution to the surmounting of Neo-Scholasticism and its principally metaphysical approach to theology. Although Söhngen did not flat out reject natural theology, he remained extremely sceptical about it,[77] and instead opted for theology oriented by salvation history ('Heilsgeschichte').[78]

---

[74] Cf. KBA 9339.416 (Jakob Fehr to Karl Barth, letter dated 4 July 1939).
[75] Cf. Jakob Fehr, 'Karl Barths theologische und geistesgeschichtliche Bedeutung', *Schweizerische Kirchenzeitung* 109 (1941), pp. 121–3, 133–6.
[76] Cf. Aidan Nichols, *Catholic Thought Since The Enlightment. A Survey* (Pretoria: Unisa Press and Leominster, UK: Gracewing, 1998), p. 107.
[77] Cf., for instance, Gottlieb Söhngen, 'Natürliche Theologie. I. Im katholischen Verständnis', *LTK*² 7 (1962), pp. 811–6, 812.
[78] Cf. Gottlieb Söhngen, 'Die Weisheit der Theologie durch den Weg der Wissenschaft', in *Mysterium Salutis. Grundriss heilsgeschichtlicher Dogmatik*, ed. Johannes Feiner and

Some initial indications of this future direction can be found at the beginning of his teaching career. A postdoctoral lecture that Söhngen delivered in July 1931 at the University of Bonn reveals a lively interest in theoretical theological questions which was soon combined with an intensive examination of Dialectical Theology.[79] As will be detailed further below, Robert Grosche provided the initial impetus for Söhngen's engagement with Dialectical Theology.[80] In 1934, two of Söhngen's articles which owe a great deal to his consideration of the *Church Dogmatics*[81] appeared in the periodical *Catholica*, then under Grosche's direction. In contrast to his contemporaries Bernhard Bartmann and Daniel Feuling, Söhngen was not at all surprised by Barth's rejection of the *analogia entis*; in fact, it sharpened his own perception of the Catholic theology of his time. Söhngen thought the theology of his contemporaries to be too heavily focused on the *analogia entis*, and thus on philosophy, instead of on the *analogia fidei*, and thus on theology.[82] In a letter addressed to Barth in November 1934, Söhngen identified Erich Przywara as his real opponent and described him as a principal representative of 'Neo-Catholicism'.[83] What Söhngen means by this term can be inferred from the *Church Dogmatics*, where Barth criticized 'Neo-Protestantism' for giving human self-understanding such

---

Magnus Löhrer, vol. 1 (Einsiedeln et al.: Benzinger, 1965), pp. 905–80. In particular, Söhngen criticized Neo-Scholasticism's unhistorical attitude, for example, in his article 'Neuscholastik', in *LTK*² 7 (1962), pp. 923–6, 924–5.

[79] Söhngen's lecture, held as a part of his 'Habilitation', appeared in the following year under the title 'Die katholische Theologie als Wissenschaft und als Weisheit', *Cath(M)* 1 (1932), pp. 49–69. Here, already, we find the first indications that Söhngen was looking into Dialectical Theology; cf. p. 49 fn 1 with reference to Heinrich Scholz, 'Wie ist eine evangelische Theologie als Wissenschaft möglich?', *Zwischen den Zeiten* 9 (1931), pp. 8–53.

[80] Cf. Joseph Ratzinger, 'Das Ganze im Fragment. Gottlieb Söhngen zum Gedächtnis', *Christ in der Gegenwart* 23 (1971), pp. 398–9, 398.

[81] Cf. Gottlieb Söhngen, 'Analogia entis: Gottähnlichkeit allein aus Glauben?', *Cath(M)* 3 (1934), pp. 113–36; ibid, 'Analogia entis: Die Einheit in der Glaubenswissenschaft', *Cath(M)* 3 (1934), pp. 176–208. After the *Church Dogmatics* appeared, Söhngen offered seminars for two semesters on the topic of analogy which, according to his own admission, were extremely important for the development of his own opinion on the matter. On this see Dahlke (2010), p. 119 fn 115.

[82] Cf. Söhngen (1934), pp. 113–4.

[83] Cf. KBA 9334.1071 (Gottlieb Söhngen to Karl Barth, letter dated 9 November 1934). As also emerges from this letter, Barth and Söhngen had already corresponded and exchanged publications. Barth had indeed in his polemic 'Nein!', dated October 1934, referred to an article by Söhngen – cf. Barth (1934), p. 27 in relation to Söhngen (1934), pp. 113–36. Söhngen's disapproval of Przywara can also be detected in the article 'Analogia entis oder analogia fidei?', *Wissenschaft und Weisheit* 9 (1942), pp. 91–100: Looking back at the development of Catholic theology since the end of World War I, he writes (p. 91, translated): 'In Catholic theology the *analogia entis* has become as it were

a prominent position in its account of revelation.[84] On the Catholic side, according to Söhngen, the position represented by Przywara does something similar when it grants natural theology such a central place in its theology, so much, in fact, that the knowledge of God gained on the basis of revelation risks becoming a mere appendage to the natural knowledge of God.

This letter could suggest that Söhngen had developed his own line of thought solely by a critical dissociation from Przywara's thought. However, his study and analysis of the *Church Dogmatics* proved to be just as important. In addition to his implicit criticisms of Przywara, Söhngen also finds fault with Barth's ontology and its subsequent effects within Barth's theology. Since thought follows existence, understanding the latter is of the utmost importance.[85] If Söhngen found in Przywara a univocal ontology, which basically amounts to an ontological monism that envelops both the existence of God and that of humanity, he sees in Barth an equivocal ontology. Barth's rejection of the *analogia entis*, in principle, and his granting of validity to only the *analogia fidei* can be explained against the background of the ontological dualism characteristic of Protestantism as a whole.[86] For Protestantism, a relationship between God and humanity only exists through faith, as the being of God and the being of humanity are and will always remain completely different from each other. Thus Barth's doctrine of analogy can be summed up in one sentence: 'The *analogia fidei* is placed fiercely against the *analogia entis* (in the logical consistency of the Reformation's sola fide and *simul iustus et peccator*).'[87]

Brunner's stress, in contrast to Barth, on the necessity of a natural theology, with philosophy playing a leading role, certainly may be more fitting, but it is also less Protestant.[88] For example, humanity is, for Luther, totally corrupted by sin and thus has no similarity whatsoever with God.[89] Söhngen's objection

---

the battle-cry in which Catholic confidence of victory was revealed; and the slogan of the *analogia entis* was brought into the so-called lay theology, i.e. into the theological literature for Catholic academics.' Söhngen refers to Przywara's writings explicitly (p. 91 fn 1).

[84] Cf. KD I/1 (1932), pp. 35–9 [English translation: CD I/1, pp. 36–40].

[85] Cf. Söhngen (1934), p. 114. Söhngen completely follows scholasticism in his distinction between the *ordo cognoscendi* and the *ordo essendi*.

[86] Cf. Söhngen (1934), pp. 115–7, with reference to KD I/1 (1932), pp. VIII–IX, 250–61, 352–67.

[87] Söhngen (1934), p. 117 (translated); also pp. 120, 123.

[88] Cf. Söhngen (1934), pp. 117–20, with reference to Emil Brunner, *Natur und Gnade. Zum Gespräch mit Karl Barth* (Tübingen: Mohr, 1934). Söhngen participated in the debate about natural theology which had developed between Barth and Brunner with his article 'Natürliche Theologie und Heilsgeschichte. Antwort an Emil Brunner', *Cath(M)* 4 (1935), pp. 97–114.

[89] Cf. Söhngen (1934), pp. 121–36. There has been little agreement in Catholic theology since the 1930s about how the *simul* of the *iustus et peccator* should be interpreted.

against this position, which appeared to him to constitute an ontological dualism, is that the reality of human participation in God could no longer be account for or explained. God, in Jesus Christ, had participated in human existence, and thus the human being can also have communion with God through Christ.[90]

Yet this soteriological objection is not yet the central issue for Söhngen. Contrary to Barth, he stresses that a theology appropriate to revelation necessarily includes natural theology, for God has revealed himself in nature as well as in history. On the basis of the relationship which exists between creation and its Creator and preserver, human reason can very well infer that God exists. In this regard, Söhngen quotes Rom 1.20, the classical prooftext for natural theology.[91] Although the knowledge of God obtained in this way is extremely weak, it is real knowledge, for the claim that God is the Creator is true. Yet even if creation is a revelation of God as Creator, it still does not reveal how God is in himself; that God is triune must be specifically revealed.[92] That the latter does not necessarily follow from the former is due to the fact that while existence logically precedes action, noetically speaking the opposite is the case.[93] God allows himself to be known by his outward creative action, above all by his actions in history. The human being can only suspect *that* God reveals himself or *as what* he turns out to be, and so Söhngen pointedly declares that the self-disclosure of God can only be known in this divine self-disclosure.[94] Without developing this thought further, one can still see that he is very close to Barth, who in the *Church Dogmatics* argued that the Word of God becomes knowable by making itself known.[95]

That being said, Söhngen hardly rejects natural theology lock, stock and barrel. Not every human statement about God is hopelessly false, but neither can each claim to automatically count as true. Salvation history remains the criterion which judges the claims of metaphysics; what can be said about God on the basis of historical revelation acts as a counter-balance to the natural knowledge of God possible from his self-revelation in creation. In Söhngen's view the salvation history limits and restricts metaphysics, but does not make it superfluous.[96] Hence the *analogia entis* is both independent

---

Such can be seen in exemplary form in a piece by Robert Grosche, possibly written as a reaction to Söhngen; Robert Grosche, 'Simul peccator et iustus. Bemerkungen zu einer theologischen Formel', *Cath(M)* 4 (1935), pp. 132–9.

[90] Cf. Söhngen (1934), pp. 134–5.
[91] Cf. Söhngen (1934), pp. 198–9.
[92] Cf. Söhngen (1934), pp. 204–5. This is why Söhngen (p. 205 with fn 39) is very sceptical about the doctrine of the *vestigia trinitatis*.
[93] Cf. Söhngen (1934), p. 198.
[94] Cf. Söhngen (1934), p. 204.
[95] Cf. KD I/1 (1932), p. 260 [English translation: CD I/1, p. 246].
[96] Cf. Söhngen (1934), p. 204.

of the *analogia fidei*, and yet finally coincides and 'fits into it' as well. The final reason for this claim is God's revelation in Jesus Christ.

What exactly Söhngen meant by this remains on the whole very vague. In general, it appears that in his two 1934 articles he is naming the problem rather than offering a definitive solution. He is suggesting a theological change in theology. Instead of starting from an abstract, philosophically derived concept of God as was typical in Neo-Scholasticism, he is advancing a theology which is derived from the historical concreteness and positivity of revelation. This position implies an account of the relationship between philosophy and theology that is different from what was customarily offered by Neo-Scholasticism. Appropriately, then, in his subsequent work Söhngen attempts to relativize metaphysics before the contingency and non-deducibility of revelation.[97] He returns to the branch of Catholic theology which follows Augustine and sees in Bonaventura a philosopher of the *analogia fidei*.[98] Söhngen's work on the *Church Dogmatics* at the beginning of the 1930s was a decided influence upon these attempts to replace a Neo-Scholastic theology focused on metaphysics with a theology oriented by salvation history.

Barth was heavily in favour of this project from the beginning. In his 1940 doctrine of God he reviewed the two articles which Söhngen had published in *Catholica* and expressed his approval.[99] Even so, he immediately added that Söhngen's position scarcely reflected *the* Catholic understanding of the *analogia entis*, which for Barth was best represented by figures such as Daniel Feuling and Jakob Fehr.[100] Yet Barth had much sympathy for Söhngen's project, for he saw in him the precursor of a new form of Catholic theology.[101]

5.6 Analogia Entis *is not* analogia entis: *Erich Przywara*

While Barth was positively disposed to theologies centred on salvation history, such as that of Gottlieb Söhngen, he completely rejected any form of natural theology. It can hardly be doubted that the *analogia entis* was, for

---

[97] Gottlieb Söhngen, 'Wunderzeichen und Glaube. Biblische Grundlegung der katholischen Apologetik', *Cath(M)* 4 (1935), pp. 145–64, 145–6; ibid, 'Philosophie', in *LTK* 8 (1936), pp. 244–7, 246.

[98] Gottlieb Söhngen, 'Bonaventura als Klassiker der analogia fidei', *Wissenschaft und Weisheit* 2 (1935), pp. 97–111, especially pp. 99–100.

[99] Cf. KD II/1 (1940), pp. 89–91 with reference to Söhngen (1934) [English translation: CD II/1, pp. 81–2].

[100] Cf. KD II/1 (1940), p. 89 with reference to Feuling (1934) and Fehr (1937b) [English translation: CD II/1, pp. 82–3].

[101] Cf. Eberhard Busch, *Karl Barths Lebenslauf. Nach seinen Briefen und autobiographischen Texten* (Munich: Kaiser, 1975), p. 444 with p. 540 fn 74. Söhngen contributed an

Barth, a Catholic variety of natural theology.[102] Humanity has no relationship to God outside of revelation through which faith could lose its absolute seriousness.[103] Barth understands the *analogia entis* as an ontological concept which corresponds to a particular account of knowledge of God. Starting from the knowledge that God *is*, one infers *what God is like*. At this point, however, metaphysics is encroaching upon revelation's territory and unacceptably begins to qualify and determine revelation as well.

There is no doubt that Barth borrowed the term *analogia entis* from Erich Przywara. It is, however, still worth discussing whether he is really aiming at the Jesuit in Munich in the main part of the *Church Dogmatics*. Przywara was, in fact, not simply interested in natural theology, as can already be seen in his 1927 *Religionsphilosophie katholischer Theologie*, which Barth studied intensely.[104] In this work Przywara understands the *analogia entis* as an ontological structure but not as a noetic principle.[105] Przywara sees the human person as marked by the tension between essence and existence. By virtue of this tension, the human person is open for something which lies outside and beyond. The tension existing in the creature points to the one in whom existence and essence constitute an intrinsic unity, namely God, who still does not become merely a function of human striving. This relationship between God and humanity, which Przywara labels the *analogia entis*, should preserve a positive view of revelation. If the human being meets God in revelation, he or she does not meet God as something completely alien, but as something foreign towards which he or she has nevertheless always been oriented, and to that extent (but only to that extent) as something which has always been his or her very own. Przywara also stresses that this structure only appears when they meet and can in no way be acquired independently of this meeting. The necessary relationship of the human being to God only becomes clear in God's free relationship to that person. Przywara expressly opposes the view that posits any direct path leading

---

article to the Festschrift honouring Barth's seventieth birthday, 'Analogia entis in analogia fidei', in Ernst Wolf et al.: *Antwort*, Festschrift Karl Barth (Zollikon and Zürich: Evangelischer Verlag, 1956), pp. 266–71.

[102] The clearest evidence of this is probably KD I/1 (1932), p. 527 (Register) [CD I/1, p. 503 (Index)], where we find the following order of classification: 'Theology' > 'Natural Theology' > '*analogia entis*'. Also striking is also a section in *Credo* [. . .] (Munich: Kaiser, 1935), p. 77, in which Barth mentions the *analogia entis* in the same breath as Brunner's anthropological link.

[103] Cf. KD I/1 (1932), p. 40 [English translation: CD I/1, pp. 40–1].

[104] Erich Przywara, *Religionsphilosophie katholischer Theologie* (Munich and Berlin: Oldenbourg, 1927).

[105] For what follows see Przywara (1927), pp. 3–25; the central statements can be found on pp. 24–5.

THE INVENTION OF THE ANTICHRIST?

from the natural knowledge of God to revelation and, accordingly, stresses the difference between philosophy and theology.[106]

It is, then, rather surprising that Przywara assumed Barth had developed the theology of *Church Dogmatics* in a critical dissociation from him.[107] That Przywara could come to such an idea can be explained by other events. In April 1932 he had contacted Barth to ask him to review his book which was just about to appear, preferably for the periodical *Zwischen den Zeiten*.[108] Barth turned down the offer and explained that writing reviews did not particularly interest him, even though he found the book quite interesting.[109] Przywara was disappointed by Barth's refusal, but completely understood. What is more, Przywara promised to send Barth a copy directly.[110] The *Analogia Entis* appeared that summer.[111] Although a copy of the book can be found in Barth's private library, it is more than doubtful whether he actually read it at all. There are certainly some signs, such as marks and marginal notes, that the book had been read, but these were made neither by Barth himself nor by his secretary, Charlotte von Kirschbaum (1899–1975), but presumably by a student who lived in the house during the winter of 1948/1949.[112] Thus Barth probably did not look at the book at all, although this fact remained unknown to Przywara. When the *Church Dogmatics* appeared at the end of 1932 Przywara must have had the impression that Barth was thinking of the book *Analogia Entis* when he described the *analogia entis* as the invention of the Antichrist. Twenty years later Przywara was still firmly convinced of this connexion,[113] although it was also slowly dawning upon him that

---

[106] Cf. Przywara (1927), pp. 58, 61–2.

[107] Cf. Erich Przywara, 'Die Reichweite der Analogie als katholischer Grundform', *Scholastik* 25 (1940), pp. 339–62, 508–32, 340; ibid, 'Um die analogia entis' [1952/1955], in *In und gegen. Stellungnahmen zur Zeit* (Nürnberg: Glock und Lutz, 1955), pp. 277–81, 279.

[108] Cf. KBA 9332.210 (Erich Przywara to Karl Barth, letter dated 26 April 1932).

[109] Cf. KBA 9232.150 (Karl Barth to Erich Przywara, letter dated 6 May 1932, copy).

[110] Cf. KBA 9332.257 (Erich Przywara to Karl Barth, letter dated 9 May 1932).

[111] Cf. Erich Przywara, *Analogia Entis. Metaphysik*, vol. 1 (Munich: Kösel and Pustet, 1932). The 'Imprimatur' (p. IV) dates from 2 June 1932.

[112] I am grateful to Hans-Anton Drewes (Basle) for this information. Also informative is a remark by Barth regarding his way of working: 'It will certainly not have escaped your notice that I come out with a review of a book barely every few years. This is because I can only ever give an opinion on things slowly and little by little, and often can only become clear years later of what my opinion of a book actually is [. . .].' Cf. KBA 9232.150 (Karl Barth to Erich Przywara, letter dated 6 May 1932, copy): 'Es wird Ihnen ja kaum entgangen sein, dass ich kaum alle paar Jahre einmal mit einer Besprechung eines Buches herausrücke. Es hängt damit zusammen, dass ich eigentlich immer nur langsam und nach und nach zu den Dingen Stellung nehmen kann und mir oft erst nach Jahren klar darüber werde, wie ich zu einem Buch nun eigentlich stehe [. . .].'

[113] Cf. KBA 9352.181 (Erich Przywara to Karl Barth, letter dated 30 March 1952).

Barth's remark had been intended with a wink.[114] Indeed, Przywara would have already had reason to be suspicious when his book, which appeared in the summer of 1932, was actually not even mentioned at any point in the *Church Dogmatics*. Why Przywara made no effort to have this explained seems puzzling. It is also strange that he did not immediately react. Only at the end of 1933 did Przywara finally turn his attention to the *Church Dogmatics*, and then only in passing.[115] Barth was completely satisfied with the article which appeared in the *Stimmen der Zeit*.[116]

To make the spiritual life of the present age understandable, Przywara turned to the concept of dynamism. In Przywara's opinion, dynamism is the characteristic of the present. The human being experiences that she is insecure, rootless and restless in a modern world controlled by the economic laws and realities. For this reason she searches for the absolute and for an intelligible task to which she can devote herself.[117] Przywara understands this search as a call for Christianity to provide an answer to the questions of the present. Why at least Protestantism does not take up such a call can be seen, according to Przywara, in the *Church Dogmatics* itself. He argues that Barth's basic presupposition is that of actualism, meaning that God's revelation is an irreducible event which is never simply available.[118] Theology must, therefore, adopt a middle position between Roman Catholicism and modern Protestantism as both consider God to be simply at humanity's disposal,[119] as if Christ's powers can be transmitted to humans. Catholicism, for example, understands apostolic succession in a purely mechanical rather than a spiritual way, as if Christ's power could be given over to humans. In this way, however, Christ is not only dethroned as the true Lord of the Church, but the dynamism of God is rendered a static possession of humanity. Protestant modernism is no less objectionable for God in its emphasis upon the human person as theology's true area of interest and concentration, while in the process omitting God.

What Przywara emphasizes in particular is the insurmountable contradiction between God and humanity which Barth's thought implies. God and humanity remain unconnected even in faith, ruling out any

---

[114] Cf. Przywara (1952/1955), p. 279.

[115] Cf. Erich Przywara, 'Dynamismus', *StZ* vol. 126 (1933/1934), pp. 155–68, 162–5 with reference to KD I/1 (1932).

[116] Cf. *Karl Barth – Eduard Thurneysen. Briefwechsel*, vol. 3, ed. Caren Algner, Gesamtausgabe V. Briefe (Zürich: Theologischer Verlag Zürich, 2000), pp. 553–6 (Karl Barth to Eduard Thurneysen, letter dated 29 November 1933), 556; reprinted in ibid, *Briefe des Jahres 1933*, ed. Eberhard Busch (Zürich: Theologischer Verlag Zürich, 2004), pp. 559–60.

[117] Cf. Przywara (1933/1934), pp. 155–62.

[118] Cf. Przywara (1933/1934), pp. 163–4.

[119] For what follows see Przywara (1933/1934), p. 163 with particular reference to KD I/1 (1932), pp. 23–43 (§ 2. Die Aufgabe der Prolegomena zur Dogmatik).

possibility of an *analogia fidei*.[120] Przywara only mentions in passing the condemnation of the *analogia entis* and does not explore it in any more detail.[121] More important for Przywara is the conclusion that Barth's theology leaves humanity in the rootlessness and insecurity bewailed on all sides. Przywara thus reaches a determinedly negative verdict of Barth's theology.[122] This judgement allows Przywara to proceed to his real aim: presenting Catholicism as the answer to a widely felt existential need. He finally puts forward Ignatian spirituality as the key to this situation, for such a spirituality allows humanity a real significance and place in the divine salvific plan and also allows human life, as such, to begin to make sense.[123]

Przywara apparently made no further comment on the *Church Dogmatics* in the following period. Only in 1940 did he publish an article in which he expounded analogy as the basic form of Catholicism.[124] Unable to understand how this could have happened, he noted that both philosophy and theology had adopted ways which were not acceptable to him. Przywara stood largely alone in his attempt to use analogy to solve the problems of the present. Even his protégé, Hans Urs von Balthasar, seemed to have distanced himself from his former mentor.[125] Within such a context, Przywara developed his concept of analogy anew. Here he casually referenced the absurd attempts of Barth and Söhngen to develop an *analogia fidei* contrary to the *analogia entis*.[126] It simply could not be otherwise than what Przywara himself had argued, and so in the 1950s he bitterly noted that instead of being the starting-point of a productive discussion, his concept of the *analogia entis* had become a grotesque distortion.[127] Why his revised version remained ineffective could be explained, in his own view, by the fact that the discourse of that time required someone who stood for an extreme and yet ultimately nonsensical position.[128]

This diagnosis is not entirely unfounded. The *analogia entis* had quickly become the catchword for a style of natural theology which opposed

---

[120] Cf. Przywara (1933/1934), p. 164.
[121] Cf. Przywara (1933/1934), p. 163 with reference to KD I/1 (1932), p. VIII.
[122] Przywara (1933/1934), p. 165.
[123] Cf. Przywara (1933/1934), pp. 165–8.
[124] Erich Przywara, 'Die Reichweite der Analogie als katholischer Grundform', *Scholastik* 25 (1940), pp. 339–62, 508–32.
[125] Cf. Przywara (1940), p. 341 with reference to Hans Urs von Balthasar, *Apokalypse der deutschen Seele. Studien zu einer Lehre von letzten Haltungen*, 3 vols (Salzburg and Leipzig: Pustet, 1937–1939).
[126] Cf. Przywara (1940), p. 530 fn 24.
[127] Cf. Przywara (1952/1955), p. 278.
[128] Cf. Przywara (1952/1955), p. 278 with reference to ibid (1940): 'Hätte man diese Klärung angenommen, so wäre freilich die "Lieblings-Karnevals-Puppe" verloren gewesen.' Translated: 'If this clarification had been accepted, then the "favourite carnival marionette" would obviously have been lost.'

revelation: with references to Przywara, Protestant theologians took it to be a teaching that divides the Church.[129] As a result of these events, Catholic acceptance of Barth, which was slight anyway, was in danger of fading away completely. Scarcely three years after the appearance of the *Church Dogmatics*, Robert Grosche, who had been quite attached to Barth for some time, made an almost desperate attempt to rescue him for Protestant-Catholic discussions.

5.7 The Rescue Attempt: Robert Grosche

In addition to his work as a parish priest, Robert Grosche (1888–1967) was also responsible for the periodical *Catholica*.[130] In 1935 he published a short article dealing with Barth's condemnation of the *analogia entis*.[131] What we read in the preface to the *Church Dogmatics* should actually be qualified by Barth's more recent work *Das Evangelium in der Gegenwart*, originally a lecture Barth delivered in Bern and Basle at the beginning of June 1935.[132] This lecture had essentially nothing to do with the debate about the *analogia entis*; indeed, the concept is not even mentioned once. Barth is more concerned here with the (even then conspicuous) phenomenon of secularization. He comes to a shattering conclusion: even in the circles in which Christianity can be found at all, it has lost all sense of certainty. He then reminds us that the Gospel is not identical with Christianity. The former is the powerful message which Christianity attempts to speak, upon which it always bases itself and to which it must always relate itself.[133] The dissolving of the covenant formed between the Gospel and Western culture, a covenant which has endured over centuries, in no way signifies the end of Christianity, but a change in its form. At the end of an age which Barth describes as 'bourgeois-Christian', he writes:

> It should be the time of synthesis – a single great vision as it were, a human, all too human reflection and echo of the incarnation – a sign to tell all ages where they come from and where they are going. It was a passing sign, a transitory allegory, set up amidst the frailness of all things human and itself part of this frailness, doomed to termination and ruin long before it had reached perfection even at a distance. Yet

---

[129] Cf. Dahlke (2010), pp. 128–9.
[130] Cf. Chapter 3.
[131] Robert Grosche, 'Karl Barth und die Analogia entis', *Cath(M)* 4 (1935), pp. 185–6.
[132] Cf. Grosche (1935) with reference to Karl Barth, 'Das Evangelium in der Gegenwart', in *Das Evangelium in der Gegenwart* (Munich: Kaiser, 1935), pp. 18–36.
[133] Cf. Barth (1935), pp. 22–3.

THE INVENTION OF THE ANTICHRIST?

it was a sign and allegory of things eternal, a pleasant provision of providence for the survival of the Gospel.[134]

Grosche draws attention to just this section, even quoting it verbatim.[135] What Grosche finds worthy of consideration is the thought that the Gospel is essentially free as regards any and all cultures. Freedom *from* culture is not the issue here, as the two never ought to become one. There is, however, a freedom of the Gospel *for* a particular culture insofar as the Gospel as such, an 'unadorned' Gospel, is never given, but always stands within a context. The truly decisive question, then, is to what extent the freedom of the Gospel is guaranteed *within* its connexion to a particular culture. It is with these remarks in mind that Grosche wishes to understand the *analogia entis*. Barth's admission that the covenant which existed between the Gospel and Western culture was neither reprehensible in principle nor threw the integrity of what is Christian into question would also be true of the *analogia entis*. Instead of describing it as 'the invention of the Antichrist' (and surely there are other things more deserving of such a title), one should ask how far it helps to articulate the Gospel.[136] For Grosche the *analogia entis* represents one possible way of thinking, and in no way an essential metaphysical concept.

Grosche's argument for how Barth could not really have intended to condemn the *analogia entis* in the *Church Dogmatics* seems rather contrived. Additionally, he does not take into consideration the reasons offered there for its rejection. Instead of entering into a discussion of its material content, he points to a basically irrelevant lecture which also has little or no relation to the *Church Dogmatics*. Clearly, he wished to counter the picture of Barth which was beginning to become an established fact in Catholic theology. Such a project is completely understandable in the light of the reviews and judgements of Catholic theologians which had already appeared. Catholic theologians such as Erich Przywara, Bernhard Bartmann, Daniel Feuling and Heinrich Weisweiler could make very little of Barth's *Church Dogmatics*. Barth's thought appeared to them to be the perfect expression

---

[134] Barth (1935), p. 33: 'Es sollte diese Zeit der Synthese – ein einziges großes Traumgesicht sozusagen, ein menschlicher, allzu menschlicher Abglanz und Widerhall der Inkarnation – ein Zeichen sein, um allen Zeiten zu sagen, wo sie herkommen, wo sie hingehen. Sie war ein vorübergehendes Zeichen, ein vergängliches Gleichnis, aufgerichtet inmitten der Hinfälligkeit aller menschlichen Dinge und selber dieser Hinfälligkeit teilhaftig, dem Stillstand und Verderben geweiht, lange bevor es auch nur von fern Vollkommenheit gewonnen hätte. Sie war dennoch und gerade so ein Zeichen und Gleichnis ewiger Dinge, eine freundliche Veranstaltung der Vorsehung zur Überwinterung des Evangeliums.'

[135] Cf. Grosche (1935), p. 186, quoting Barth (1935), p. 33.

[136] Cf. Grosche (1935), p. 186.

of Protestant intransigence. At almost the same time of Grosche's rescue attempt, the Jesuit Max Pribilla (1874–1956), an editor of the *Stimmen der Zeit* and a vigilant observer of the ecumenical movement, noted that there was an intensification of Protestant-Catholic differences. As proof for such an anecdotal judgement, he referred specifically to Barth's condemnation of the *analogia entis*.[137]

5.8 Results

If God is that than which nothing greater can be thought, then it is easier to establish what God is not rather than what God is. Knowledge of God is thus aware of its own limits: every attempt to say something about God remains inevitably inadequate. But as acts of definition are in some way also acts of control, there is always a chance for God's freedom to become restricted and subjected to the human person. Worries such as these contribute to recent attempts in theology to understand God as *event* rather than as being, especially in the sense of much-reviled ontotheology.[138]

If Neo-Scholastic theology decides to work in an ontological register, it certainly has its reason for doing so. If one truly can infer an infinite unconditioned being from a finite conditioned being, then the idea of God is secured insofar as there must be a Creator. Then, in a second phase of the argument, one demonstrates that this Creator-God has clearly revealed himself to also be Redeemer. The concept of being is thought to be remarkably useful for the idea of God following the theoretical and practical atheism and agnosticism which became *en vogue* during and after the Enlightenment. Such a strategy is, nevertheless, highly ambivalent. It may be able to support rationally the claims of validity put forward by Christian faith, and thus militate against any revelatory positivism, but there still remains a tendency towards rationalism. If God can also be known through reason, then there remains only a difference in degree from the knowledge gained through faith.

Barth definitely touches a sore point when he condemns natural theology as a perversion of revelation. His criticism of the *analogia entis*, at least in the main sections of the *Church Dogmatics*, fits into this more general condemnation. Barth wants to develop his own theology and he uses a methodological process which consists of claiming that both Catholicism and Neo-Protestantism conflict with genuine Protestant faith. Thus his

---

[137] Cf. Max Pribilla, 'Nach vierhundert Jahren', *StZ* vol. 129 (1935), pp. 155–68, 164 quoting KD I/1 (1932), pp. VIII–IX.

[138] See, for instance, Colin Gunton, *Act and Being* (London: SCM Press, 2002); Jean-Luc Marion, *Dieu sans l'être* (Paris: Presses Universitaires de France, ²2002); Fergus Kerr, 'God in the *Summa Theologiae*', in *After Aquinas. Versions of Thomism* (Oxford et al.: Blackwell, 2002), pp. 181–206.

THE INVENTION OF THE ANTICHRIST?

dissociation from the *analogia entis* fulfils a quite specific function: it serves to identify the true Protestant theology which has its place in between Catholicism and Neo-Protestantism.

Barth was perfectly aware that the position of Roman Catholic theology on this issue was far more complex. His recognition of this complexity can be seen in his 1934 piece, *Nein!*, which marks his explicit break with Emil Brunner. Barth described his former confrere's ascription to Catholic theology a natural theology seemingly unaffected by sin and completely dependent on reason as a terrible misrepresentation which missed the real point: 'The way in which Brunner and many others present the Catholic *theologia naturalis* certainly does not exist in today's authoritative Catholic theology.'[139] In spite of this admission, Barth remained undeterred in his methodology in the following years.[140] When he had finally found the starting-point for his own theology, his methodology changed abruptly. In no volume of the *Church Dogmatics* following the publication of his doctrine of election in 1942 does Barth treat the *analogia entis* in detail. From that time onwards he was busy developing his theology in the light of the fact that God chose humanity for himself in Jesus Christ and at the same time made himself the God of humanity.[141] He no longer seemed interested in discussing the question further, even though it was taking on a life of its own. That Barth did not explain himself and elaborate upon what he meant to do by condemning the *analogia entis*, which was basically to contradict the sneaking suspicion that Barth's theology made Protestants become Catholics, proved to be fatal. Party lines were increasingly adopted, and not only on the part of Protestant theology.

It was Oskar Bauhofer, of all people, whose conversion to Catholicism probably led to Barth's polemic in the first place, who declared the *analogia*

---

[139] Cf. Barth (1934), p. 34: 'So wie Brunner und manche Andere die katholische theologia naturalis sich vorstellen, existiert sie in der heute maßgebenden katholischen Theologie sicher nicht'; also see pp. 37–40. Barth, in addition, found fault with the fact that Brunner caricatured Thomism in KBA 9234.228 (Karl Barth to Damasus Winzen, letter dated 3 July 1934, copy).

[140] Cf. Karl Barth, *Gotteserkenntnis und Gottesdienst nach reformatorischer Lehre* [. . .] (Zollikon: Verlag der Evangelischen Buchhandlung Zollikon, 1938), pp. 45–6 [English translation: *The Knowledge of God and the Service of God according to the Teaching of the Reformation* (London: Hodder and Stoughton, ³1955), pp. 8–9]. How little Barth could claim to represent the Protestantism of the time can be seen by a glance at Louis Berkhof, *Reformed Dogmatics*, vol. 1 (Grand Rapids, MI: Eerdmans, 1932), pp. 13–21, where a very different position on Natural Theology is adopted. The same can be said of Dietrich Bonhoeffer, *Akt und Sein. Transzendentalphilosophie und Ontologie in der systematischen Theologie* (Gütersloh: Bertelsmann, 1931), pp. 56–60 with reference to Przywara (1927). Also instructive are the remarks of Michael Sudduth, *The Reformed Objection to Natural Theology* (Farnham, UK: Ashgate, 2009), pp. 9–54.

[141] See KD II/2 (1942). For background see Matthias Gockel, *Barth and Schleiermacher on the Doctrine of Election. A Systematic-Theological Comparison* (Oxford et al.: Oxford University Press, 2006), pp. 158–97.

entis to be a 'cardinal proposition' in an article highly critical of Dialectical Theology.[142] To crown it all off, the essayist Theodor Haecker (1879–1945), himself a convert, had to speak up for Przywara. In a contribution which appeared simultaneously in the widely distributed magazine *Hochland* and as a part-chapter in a much-read book, he sharply attacked Barth and spoke of an *analogia Trinitatis* which went beyond the *analogia entis*.[143] In so doing, Haecker did not grasp the complexity of Przywara's reflections, nor did he really do Barth justice. He did, however, contribute to reinforcing the Catholic impression that Barth was the personification of Protestant intransigence with his attempt to tear God and humanity as far apart as possible. One can conclude how deeply this impression had taken root when Hans Urs von Balthasar had to combat it, and not only in his 1951 *Darstellung und Deutung* of Barth's theology.[144] He certainly succeeded in initiating a debate on the problem of analogy which was to last into the 1960s and in which many of today's leading Protestant theologians participated.[145] Yet his efforts scarcely made any difference to the bad reputation that Barth had gained in the meantime. Even until the present the remark that the *analogia entis* is *the* invention of the Antichrist has had a strong influence on the perception of Barth.[146] There is even talk of a 'new Reformation-Catholic controversy'.[147]

---

[142] Cf. Oskar Bauhofer, 'Dialektik oder Theologie', *Cath(M)* 2 (1933), pp. 49–60, 58: 'Die analogia entis ist aus katholischer Lehre nicht wegzudenken: die ganze Metaphysik schwingt um diesen Kardinalsatz – aber nicht weniger fordert die Theologie den durch ihn metaphysisch festgelegten und geklärten ontologischen Tatbestand.' Translated: 'The *analogia entis* cannot be removed from Catholic doctrine; the whole of metaphysics rotates around this cardinal proposition – but no less does theology demand the ontological facts which are metaphysically established and clarified by it.'

[143] Cf. Theodor Haecker, 'Analogia trinitatis', *Hochland* 31/2 (1934), pp. 499–510 = ibid, *Schöpfer und Schöpfung* (Leipzig: Hegner, 1934), pp. 135–68.

[144] Hans Urs von Balthasar, *Karl Barth. Darstellung und Deutung seiner Theologie* (Cologne: Hegner, 1951). We will look at this work in detail later.

[145] Cf. Dahlke (2010), p. 134 fn 191.

[146] See Maurus Heinrichs, *Theses Dogmaticae*, vol. 2 (Hong Kong: Studium Biblicum O.F.M., ²1954), pp. 35–42 (§ 8. *De praerequisitis ad fidem theologicam*), pp. 37–8; Walter Brugger, *Theologia Naturalis* (Pullach: Berchmanskolleg Verlag, 1959), pp. 209–10; Michael Schmaus, *Katholische Dogmatik*, vol. 1 (Munich: Hueber, ⁶1960), pp. 216–44 (§ 30. Die natürliche Erkennbarkeit Gottes), p. 219; Josef Schmidt, *Philosophische Theologie* (Stuttgart: Kohlhammer, 2003), p. 31 with reference to KD I/1 (1932/⁵1947), p. VIII. The Orthodox theologian David Bentley Hart went much further recently in: *The Beauty of the Infinite. The Aesthetics of Christian Truth* (Grand Rapids, MI and Cambridge: Eerdmans, 2003), pp. 241–9, especially p. 242: 'If the rejection of the *analogia entis* were in some sense the very core of Protestant theology, as Barth believed, one would still be obliged to observe that it is also the invention of antichrist, and so would have to be accounted the most compelling reason for not becoming a Protestant.'

[147] Thus Gerhard Ludwig Müller, 'Analogie. II. Theologisch', *LTK*³ 1 (1993), pp. 579–82, 581.

THE INVENTION OF THE ANTICHRIST?

In the face of the polarization the *analogia entis* has caused, we should note that it is a matter of two fundamental problems in systematic theology: how human talk of God relates to the reality of God himself, and the relationship between the being of the world and the being of God.[148] Even if one distinguishes between the *analogia nominum* and the *analogia entis*, both forms of analogy are related to and indwell each other. Making statements and judgements about some reality requires at least some awareness of its ontological status, and thus talk about God is not possible without ontology. It is not a matter of metaphysical hair-splitting. Insofar as anthropology is the horizon of theology, the question arises whether talk of God should begin from the side of humanity and its self-understanding or with God and his self-communication.[149] This question has been debated for decades within both Protestantism and Catholicism.[150] In the face of an anthropological reduction of revelation, one can certainly stress the positivity of revelation, but such a stress risks riding revelation of any relevance for humanity. It was the irrelevance of God that Neo-Scholasticism wanted to avoid in its tactic of emphazing and developing natural theology. Barth, however, thought a very different task was put before him. He saw the anthropomorphization of revelation growing in both Protestant theology since the Enlightenment and also in contemporary Catholic theology. In the face of both 'heresies' he stressed that God can only be known through God, which means only through Jesus Christ in the Holy Spirit.[151]

The *analogia entis*, then, deals with a fundamental question within systematic theology; it is not simply an interesting topic for debate between Catholics and Protestants. Seen in this light, the debate proceeded unfavourably from the start. Barth confirmed this judgement to those students from Wuppertal who visited him in 1968.

---

[148] Cf. Jüngel (1977), pp. 357–83 (§ 17. Das Problem analoger Rede von Gott); Philip A. Rolnick, 'Realist Reference to God: Analogy or Univocity?', in *Realism and Antirealism*, ed. William P. Alston (Ithaca, NY and London: Cornell University Press, 2002), pp. 211–37; William P. Alston, 'Religious Language', in *The Oxford Handbook of Philosophy of Religion*, ed. William J. Wainwright (Oxford et al.: Oxford University Press, 2005), pp. 220–44, especially pp. 239–41; *Reason and the Reasons of Faith*, ed. Paul J. Griffiths and Reinhard Hütter (London and New York: T&T Clark, 2005).

[149] Cf. Louis Dupré, 'Philosophy and the Natural Desire for God. An Historical Reflection', *International Philosophical Quarterly* 40 (2000), pp. 141–8, especially pp. 146–7.

[150] Cf. Jüngel (1977), pp. 16–44 (§ 2. Ist Gott notwendig?), especially pp. 19–20 fn 6 with reference to Wolfhart Pannenberg, 'Anthropologie und Gottesfrage', in *Gottesgedanke und menschliche Freiheit* (Göttingen: Vandenhoeck und Ruprecht, 1972), pp. 9–28, or Hans Urs von Balthasar, *Cordula oder der Ernstfall* (Einsiedeln: Johannes, 1966), pp. 85–97 with reference to Karl Rahner, *Schriften zur Theologie*.

[151] Cf. KD II/1 (1940), pp. 67–200 (§ 26. Die Erkennbarkeit Gottes), pp. 78–9 ('modernistischer Protestantismus') or pp. 86–92 ('römischer Katholizismus') [English translation: CD II/1, pp. 63–178 (§ 26. The Knowability of God)].

It was rather pedantic the way I dashed it off. And when I heard how it had raised a thousandfold echo in the theological world and all were racking their brains; *analogia entis, analogia fidei* etc., I said; 'Well, prattle on about the nonsense! I did not mean it in that sense. [. . .]' Of course we had other quite different things to do than to fight against Catholicism.[152]

But the state of affairs was not so simple then. As a result of the condemnation of the *analogia entis*, Barth's thought was interpreted by Catholics as decisively and narrowly Protestant. Catholics who devoted time and attention to Barth had many different prejudices working against them. Hans Urs von Balthasar, however, was one of those Catholics who decided to work on the *Church Dogmatics* anyway. He also numbers among the protagonists of the renewal of Catholic Theology in the run-up to Vatican II.

---

[152] Barth (1997), pp. 484–5.

6

HANS URS VON BALTHASAR'S CONTRIBUTION TO THE RENEWAL OF CATHOLIC THEOLOGY

6.1 *The Problem of Neo-Scholasticism*

The high opinion that the Vatican had of Hans Urs von Balthasar (1905–1988) can be seen in his being nominated a cardinal in 1988. One should say, however, 'the high opinion the Vatican *eventually* had', as a few decades earlier Balthasar was anything but the measure of Roman orthodoxy. He was considered to be an uncomfortable thinker and an intellectual revolutionary, not least because of his critical objections to traditional Catholic theology. At the beginning of the 1950s, for example, he published a treatise whose revealing and programmatic title was 'Razing the Bastions' and in which he defended a more liberal-minded Church.[1] In the turbulent time after Vatican II, however, he criticized what had become the proverbially 'anti-Roman attitude' of many Catholics.[2] Balthasar's elevation to the position of cardinal, however, is explained less by his loyalty to church polity than by his immense contribution to the renewal of Catholic theology. In this connexion, we should mention in particular his theological trilogy published between 1961 and 1988. Balthasar's trilogy truly is a massive and breathtaking project. It consist of three 'parts' dealing with aesthetics (*The Glory of the Lord*), drama (*Theo-Drama*) and logic (*Theo-Logic*), each 'part' in turn is composed of several volumes; the trilogy is also accompanied by several

---

[1] Hans Urs von Balthasar, *Schleifung der Bastionen. Von der Kirche in dieser Zeit* (Einsiedeln: Johannes, 1952) [English translation: *Razing the Bastions. On the Church in this Age*, trans. Brian McNeil (San Francisco: Ignatius Press, 1993)].
[2] Hans Urs von Balthasar, *Der antirömische Affekt* (Freiburg i.Br. et al.: Herder, 1974); also ibid, 'The anti-Roman attitude', *Communio: International Catholic Review* 8 (1981), 307–21.

volumes of articles (*Explorations in Theology*) and is finally summarized in a slim, capstone volume (*Epilogue*).[3]

If the theological world for a long time took only casual notice of Balthasar's ceaselessly expanding work, the secondary literature can scarcely be surveyed in one sweep and virtually every aspect of his work has undergone at least some kind of initial scrutiny. Indeed, even the high value and respect Balthasar had for Protestant theology has been explored.[4] How intensively and extensively Balthasar looked at Protestant theology can be surmised by a quick glance at any volume of his monumental trilogy. Of central important in this regard, of course, was Karl Barth, whom Balthasar quoted most frequently and by quite a wide margin.[5] It is thus with good reason that the literature maintains that Barth represented for Balthasar the leading theological figure who had to be taken into account and dealt with.[6] Why Balthasar looked at Barth in the first place, and in particular why he studied the *Church Dogmatics*, has not, however, been sufficiently researched yet. In the secondary literature, for the most part, it is established *that* Balthasar took up such an attitude to Barth's work, but it has not yet been explained *why*. Balthasar's motivation becomes clearer, however, if one taken into account the current form of Catholic theology at that time: even though Neo-Scholasticism acted as if it only gave answers to the questions of the Enlightenment, it was, in fact, substantially determined by the

---

[3] Hans Urs von Balthasar explains the structure of his work in 'Versuch eines Durchblicks durch mein Denken', *Internationale katholische Zeitschrift Communio* 18 (1989), pp. 289–93. Also see Stephen M. Garrett, 'Glancing into the Cathedral of Hans Urs von Balthasar's Theology – A Review Essay', *Christian Scholar's Review* 39 (2009), pp. 91–105.

[4] Cf., for instance, Steffen Lösel, *Kreuzwege. Ein ökumenisches Gespräch mit Hans Urs von Balthasar* (Paderborn et al.: Schöningh, 2001); Rodney Howsare, *Hans Urs von Balthasar and Protestantism. The Ecumenical Implications of his Theological Style* (London and New York: T&T Clark, 2005).

[5] Cf. John Thompson, 'Barth and Balthasar. An Ecumenical Dialogue', in *The Beauty of Christ. An Introduction to the Theology of Hans Urs von Balthasar*, ed. Bede McGregor and Thomas Norris (Edinburgh: T&T Clark, 1994), pp. 171–92; Ben Quash, 'Von Balthasar and the Dialogue with Karl Barth', *New Blackfriars* 79 (1998), pp. 45–55; ibid, 'Exile, Freedom and Thanksgiving: Barth and Hans Urs von Balthasar', in *Conversing with Barth*, ed. Mike Higton and John C. McDowell (Aldershot, UK and Burlington, VT: Ashgate, 2004), pp. 90–119; Aidan Nichols, *Divine Fruitfulness. A Guide through Balthasar's Theology beyond the Trilogy* (London and New York: T&T Clark, 2007), pp. 75–107; Stephen D. Wigley, *Karl Barth and Hans Urs von Balthasar. A Critical Engagement* (London and New York: T&T Clark, 2007).

[6] Cf. Martin Bieler, 'Die kleine Drehung. Hans Urs von Balthasar und Karl Barth im Gespräch', in *Logik der Liebe und Herrlichkeit Gottes. Hans Urs von Balthasar im Gespräch*, Festschrift Karl Lehmann, ed. Walter Kasper (Mainz: Grünewald, 2006), pp. 318–38, 319; Wigley (2007), pp. 156–62.

Enlightenment as well.[7] Neo-Scholasticism obviously shared, for example, the Enlightenment's central premise that reason is a universal faculty, not dependent on the historical circumstances in which it reasons. While there is assumed to be an autonomous area of 'the natural', grace and revelation can only be defined by the supernatural which is still to come.[8] There was, then, a strict differentiation between the knowledge of God based on revelation and that deriving from rational inquiry. Apologetics then tried to prove that the natural knowledge of God was, in fact, inadequate and that the Christian religion was divinely revealed, its authentication being miracles and the fulfilment of various prophetic promises. The doctrine of grace was also characterized by a rigid differentiation between nature and the supernatural, although for slightly different reasons. The decisive factor here is the conflict-laden history and reception of a religious tract from the end of the sixteenth century linked to the name of the Leiden theologian, Michael Baius (1513–1589). He maintained the thesis, which was later condemned, that the paradisiacal primordial state necessarily included both Adam's being destined for salvation and his original righteousness.[9] This position, however, seems to question the absolute freedom of the gift of grace. To protect the freedom and gracious nature of grace, Catholic theology fell back upon the concept of *natura pura*, according to which humanity, at least hypothetically, did not need grace. At the same time, however, the traditional idea that a person only becomes perfect through participation in the supernatural reality of God was still maintained.

Making distinctions and pointing out differences is one thing, but it is quite another thing to reunite what has been differentiated. Such was precisely the problem of Neo-Scholasticism. The way in which the relationship of the natural and the supernatural was defined could scarcely fail to give the impression that it is a question of realities not simply logically but ontically differentiated. If grace and revelation do not have any inner relationship to the human being, then they remain external and extrinsic realities. It was precisely this fundamental inadequacy which would finally be the downfall of the Neo-Scholastic system.[10]

---

[7] Cf. Aidan Nichols, *Catholic Thought Since The Enlightment. A Survey* (Pretoria: Unisa Press and Leominster, UK: Gracewing, 1998), p. 107. On what follows see Guido Pozzo, 'La Manualistica', in *Storia della teologia*, ed. Rino Fisichella, vol. 3 (Rom and Bologna: Edizioni Dehoniane, 1996), pp. 309–36.

[8] Cf., for instance, Johannes Brinktrine, *Offenbarung und Kirche. Fundamental-theologische Vorlesungen*, vol. 1 (Paderborn: Schöningh, 1938), pp. 78–96; Karl Feckes, 'Übernatürlich', in *LTK* 10 (1938), pp. 354–6; A. Michel, 'Surnaturel', in *Dictionnaire de théologie catholique* 14 (1941), pp. 2849–59.

[9] Cf. Luis F. Ladaria, 'Nature et surnaturel', in *Histoire des dogmes*, vol. 2, ed. Bernard Sesboüé (Paris: Desclée, 1996), pp. 375–413, 392–407.

[10] Cf. Fergus Kerr, 'Quarrels about grace', in *After Aquinas. Versions of Thomism* (Oxford et al.: Blackwell, 2002), pp. 134–48.

6.2 Balthasar's Attempt to find a Solution

Hans Urs von Balthasar provided a key contribution, and in a rather surprising way, to the formulation of what is thought to be genuinely Catholic. After studying German and philosophy in Zürich, Berlin and Vienna, he became a Jesuit in 1929 and completed the customary training in Munich-Pullach and Lyons.[11] At first he worked in Munich as an editor of the Jesuit periodical *Stimmen der Zeit*, but he returned to his native Switzerland because of the war. In the following decades he created a prodigious work at whose centre was the aforementioned trilogy. Yet Balthasar's endeavour to put forward a novel understanding of what is Catholic can already been seen in his earlier writings. Barth's thought proved to be a significant stimulus for Balthasar even in these early works. He had already given attention to Dialectical Theology in his doctoral thesis and after his entry into the Society of Jesus continued to deal with it.[12] He closely followed Barth's theological development in particular.[13] What especially fascinated him about Barth's theology can be seen in a letter he sent to Barth in May 1940:

> Certainly the outrageous element of truth which has become Christian through Protestantism has not been truly and fully assimilated in Catholic theology; the Counter-Reformation was too strongly a *Counter*-Reformation; the burden of medieval theology is enormous; for this theology was relatively justifiable in the situation at that time, but it remains as such a level upon which one cannot remain with impunity. I hope that your great work will help to foster this

---

[11] On the line of thought which characterized the Jesuit training institutions prior to Vatican II cf. Karl Heinz Neufeld, 'Jesuitentheologie im 19. und 20. Jahrhundert', in *Ignatianisch. Eigenart und Methode der Gesellschaft Jesu*, ed. Michael Sievernich and Günter Switek (Freiburg i. Br. u.a.: Herder, 1990), pp. 425–43. Regarding, in particular, the seminaries just mentioned cf. *Schule des Denkens. 75 Jahre Philosophische Fakultät der Jesuiten in München und Pullach*, ed. Julius Oswald (Stuttgart: Kohlhammer, 2000) and *Les jesuites à Lyon*, ed. Étienne Fouilloux and Bernard Hours (Lyons: ENS Editions, 2005), respectively.

[12] Cf. Hans Urs von Balthasar, *Geschichte des eschatologischen Problems in der modernen deutschen Literatur. Abhandlung zur Erlangung der Doktorwürde der Philosophischen Fakultät I der Universität Zürich* (Zürich 1930). The dissertation is readily available under the title *Geschichte des eschatologischen Problems in der modernen deutschen Literatur* (Freiburg i.Br.: Johannes, ²1998). Based on this work, Balthasar wrote his *Apokalypse der deutschen Seele. Studien zu einer Lehre von letzten Haltungen*, 3 vols (Salzburg and Leipzig: Pustet, 1937–1939). On the Barth-interpretation put forward in these books cf. Dahlke (2010), pp. 137–57.

[13] Instructive are the articles: 'Die Krisis der protestantischen Theologie', *StZ* vol. 134 (1938), pp. 200–1 and 'Karl Barth und der Katholizismus', *Der Seelsorger – Beiheft* 3 (1938; F. 2, 1939), pp. 126–32.

self-reflection in Catholic theology too; and that it likewise achieves the same courageous distance from its stages of development as you yourself have taken from the whole history of theology.[14]

When Balthasar wrote these lines he clearly already had in mind a desire to move Catholic theology beyond scholasticism, whether medieval or modern. Balthasar attached considerable importance to Barth in this regard. Although he did not develop in detail this 'outrageous element of truth' which has gained entry into Christianity through Protestantism, it is nevertheless clear that he found it in Barth's *Church Dogmatics*. At least two years earlier, in a short contribution in *Stimmen der Zeit*, Balthasar noted that with CD I/2 a change had taken place in Barth's thought.[15] The cause of this change was the insight that revelation does not take place through an *abstract principle* like that of dialectics, but has already taken place in a *concrete person*, namely, in Jesus Christ. As Balthasar sees it, if God and the world had stood over and against each other as two completely contradictory realities in the first phase of Barth's theological development, in his second phase they are connected by Jesus Christ. While as eternal Son of the Father, Jesus Christ stands on the side of God, as a human being he takes the world unto himself. Thus what is 'over and against' is realized within its revelatory Trinitarian 'over and against'. The intellectual progress made by recasting the event of revelation within a theology of the Trinity means that it is now possible for Barth to view the reality of the finite – which until then had been regarded as negative – in a positive light. A kind of independence can now be granted to the world; God is no longer entirely set over and against it. Barth therefore has reached a point where he can think that God meets a genuine other in creation and thus can recognize a true likeness between God and creature (in the ever greater dissimilarity). God's action provides the framework in which one should think of humanity, which also holds true for how one

---

[14] KBA 9340.234 (Hans Urs von Balthasar to Karl Barth, letter dated 4 May 1940): 'Gewiss ist in der katholischen Theologie das ungeheure Wahrheitsmoment, das durch den Protestantismus ins Christliche gekommen ist, noch nicht wirklich und voll assimiliert; die Gegenreformation war dazu zu stark Gegenreformation; die Belastung durch die mittelalterliche Theologie ist eine ungeheure; denn diese Theologie hatte in der damaligen Situation zwar ihre relative Berechtigung, sie bleibt aber als solche eine Stufe, auf der man nicht ungestraft verbleiben kann. Ich hoffe, dass Ihr grosses Werk diese Selbstbesinnung auch der katholischen Theologie fördern helfen wird; und dass diese ebenso mutig Distanz gewinnt zu ihren Entwicklungsstufen, wie Sie selbst Distanz genommen haben von der ganzen Geschichte der Theologie.'

[15] On what follows see Hans Urs von Balthasar, 'Die Krisis der protestantischen Theologie', *StZ* vol. 134 (1938), pp. 200–1 with reference to KD I/2 (1938), pp. 400, 405–6, 411, 435. The reference's context is CD I/1, 362–454 (§ 18. The Life of the Children of God).

should think about grace. According to Balthasar, the truest Augustinianism maintains that grace is no more likely to be bestowed on the 'good works' of the heathen than on their darkest sins. Grace can enter everywhere, and if sanctifying grace (*gratia sanctificans*) does join the preceding supporting grace (*gratia adiuvans*), then there are the greatest relative separations within God's one act of grace.

With these slightly cryptic comments Balthasar concludes his contribution. It is unfortunate that this piece has been largely ignored in the secondary literature, as it allows us to see that he began to read the *Church Dogmatics* in the light of the doctrine of grace. Remarkably, there is also a section of this doctrinal locus in a work whose main theme is actually quite different: the 1939 *Apokalypse der deutschen Seele*.[16] As will be ascertained later, in the following period Balthasar intensely desired and worked for not only change within the doctrine of grace then prevalent within Catholicism, but also for a fundamental renewal of dogmatics itself.

In a letter from May 1940, we can clearly and brightly see expressed Balthasar's hope that Barth's work might inspire Catholic theology to undertake a critical self-reflection. The way Barth approached his own confessional tradition with both great respect and constructive freedom appealed to Balthasar in particular. Barth truly returns to and grapples with the decisions of the early church councils and the confessional creeds of the Reformers, but he remains quite free in relation to them. He realizes that they form a confession he must heed and give attention to, but also that he is in no way entirely bound to them. It is not the historically contingent formula which is binding for him, but that to which the formula witnesses: God's incomprehensible revelation in Jesus Christ.[17] In any case, Balthasar's letter from May 1940 (the second piece of their correspondence that has come down to us) stands at the beginning of an intense material and personal exchange between the two extended over almost three decades.[18]

Balthasar lived in Basle from the spring of 1940 onwards. His Jesuit superiors gave him the choice of becoming a professor at the Gregorian

---

[16] Cf. Hans Urs von Balthasar, *Apokalypse der deutschen Seele. Studien zu einer Lehre von letzten Haltungen*, vol. 3 (Salzburg and Leipzig: Pustet, 1939), pp. 333–8.

[17] Cf. Georg Plasger, *Die relative Autonomie des Bekenntnisses bei Karl Barth* (Neukirchen-Vluyn: Neukirchener, 2000); Robert Jan Peeters, *Teken van de levende Christus. De openbaringsdynamische traditieopvatting van Karl Barth* (Zoetermeer: Boekencentrum, 2002).

[18] Cf. Hans-Anton Drewes, 'Karl Barth und Hans Urs von Balthasar – ein Basler Zwiegespräch', in *Die Kunst Gottes verstehen. Hans Urs von Balthasars theologische Provokationen*, ed. Magnus Striet and Jan-Heiner Tück (Freiburg i.Br. et al.: Herder, 2005), pp. 367–383 and Manfred Lochbrunner, 'Karl Barth und Hans Urs von Balthasar', in *Hans Urs von Balthasar und seine Theologenkollegen. Sechs Beziehungsgeschichten* (Würzburg: Echter, 2009), pp. 259–403.

University and setting up an Ecumenical Institute there, or moving to Switzerland and becoming a university chaplain. Balthasar opted for the latter. He explained to Barth himself why he turned down such an attractive offer of working and teaching in Rome:

> I want to tell you straight away that in Munich I was terribly jealous of Erich Przywara. Then when I read the '*Epistle to the Romans*' and then the rest, such a desire took hold of me to get to know you. I had developed such a liking for you (I knew that something definite had taken place here) and at the same time I wanted to debate with you, so that I welcomed it as an act of providence when Basle came in sight.[19]

Balthasar is here referring to the time of his philosophical studies in Pullach during which Erich Przywara was his mentor.[20] Balthasar was generally unsatisfied with what he was supposed to learn during the course of these studies, and his much older fellow brother provided him with important guidance, so much so that Balthasar wrote his philosophical licentiate paper on Przywara's metaphysics.[21] We have now mentioned a topic which was to play an important role in Balthasar's discussions with Barth. Balthasar clearly felt himself to be the trustee of Przywara, whose relationship to Barth had been very strained after Barth had described the *analogia entis* as *the* invention of the Antichrist and had apparently turned against the Jesuit. We must also note that from 1941 Przywara was increasingly hampered by a nervous disorder and was no longer at the height of his potential. But Balthasar was not primarily concerned with reconciling the two theologians. The way in which the debate had developed made it look as if there was an insurmountable confessional disagreement between the two, and so he turned his attention to this disagreement at the beginning of the 1940s. Moreover, there was another, equally pressing problem which motivated him to engage with and debate Barth. While his earlier publications were already concerned with the relationship between nature and grace, understanding this relationship became central in his 1951 exposition and interpretation of

---

[19] KBA 9342.305 (Hans Urs von Balthasar to Karl Barth, letter dated 30 August 1942): 'Daß ich in München schrecklich eifersüchtig auf P. Przywara war, das will ich Ihnen gleich auch noch verraten, denn als ich den "Römerbrief" und dann den Rest gelesen habe, erfaßte mich eine solche Lust, Sie zu kennen, ich hatte Sie so lieb gewonnen (ich wußte, daß hier etwas Definitives passiert war) und zugleich hatte ich solche Lust mit Ihnen zu zanken, daß ichs als eine Fügung begrüßte, als Basel in Sicht kam.'

[20] For an account of their relationship see Eva-Maria Faber, 'Künder der lebendigen Nähe des unbegreiflichen Gottes. Hans Urs von Balthasar und Erich Przywara', in Striet and Tück (2005), pp. 384–409 and Manfred Lochbrunner, 'Erich Przywara und Hans Urs von Balthasar', ibid (2009), pp. 17–146.

[21] Cf. Hans Urs von Balthasar, 'Die Metaphysik Erich Przywaras', *Schweizerische Rundschau* 33 (1933), pp. 489–99.

Barth's theology.[22] His theological studies in Lyons had prepared him well for this question, as his mentor and, in some sense, teacher in Lyons was none other than the Jesuit Henri de Lubac (1895–1991).[23]

Balthasar's discontent with Neo-Scholasticism had only increased during his student days. His aim was to move beyond the dominant type of theology and replace it with a different form. Balthasar was concerned with a *theological change in theology*, with a turn towards its true foundation and basis. Yet before this thesis is developed in more detail, we must point out an unusual feature in his publications which will then be analysed below.

As can be seen, especially when we look at his theological trilogy, Balthasar had developed his own line of thought, breaking away from Hegel's project of reshaping theological contents into a self-contained philosophical system.[24] Yet Balthasar thought *with* Hegel and by no means only *against* him, as when Balthasar uses Hegel's concepts and definitions. Although it is difficult to prove specific connexions, many of Balthasar's reflections only make sense in the light of the idealistic philosopher. Such is particularly true in the case of dialectics. Even if Hegel himself never formulated a simple three-step model of thesis, antithesis and synthesis, the triadic structure of his thinking can be schematized in this way. According to this way of thinking, the thesis always holds within itself its own contradiction, which consciousness then has to appropriate in order to reach a more comprehensive conception of itself.[25] Hegel calls the process in which this takes place the 'resolution' ('Aufhebung'), a movement which includes a positive aspect of preserving and a negative aspect of cancelling or terminating. Balthasar falls back upon dialectics in order to grasp Barth's theological development and gain a new understanding of Catholic theology – the synthesis in Hegel's sense.

---

[22] Cf. Hans Urs von Balthasar, *Karl Barth. Darstellung und Deutung seiner Theologie* (Cologne: Hegner, 1951) [English translation: *The Theology of Karl Barth. Exposition and Interpretation*, trans. Edward T. Oakes (San Francisco: Ignatius Press, 1992)].

[23] On their relationship cf. Michael Figura, 'Das Geheimnis des Übernatürlichen. Hans Urs von Balthasar und Henri de Lubac', in Striet and Tück (2005), pp. 349–66 and John Milbank, *The Suspended Middle. Henri de Lubac and the Debate concerning the Supernatural* (London: SCM Press, 2005), pp. 62–78.

[24] Cf. Michael Schulz, 'Die Logik der Liebe und die List der Vernunft. Hans Urs von Balthasar und Georg Wilhelm Friedrich Hegel', in Kasper (2006), pp. 111–33.

[25] Cf. Michael Forster, 'Hegel's dialectical method', in *The Cambridge Companion to Hegel*, ed. Frederick C. Beiser (Cambridge et al.: Cambridge University Press, 1993), pp. 130–70, 131–3.

7

BALTHASAR'S PERCEPTION OF BARTH'S LINE OF THOUGHT

7.1 Balthasar's Dissatisfaction with the School Theology

Balthasar sought personal contact with Barth soon after his arrival in Basle.[1] On 25 April 1940 Balthasar wrote to him, declaring that he was unhappy with Barth's treatment of the *analogia entis* and offering to have a discussion.[2] As is documented in a letter almost five pages long which he subsequently wrote to Barth, the meeting made a lasting impression upon him.[3] This letter, dated 4 May, is informative, not least because Balthasar freely expresses his dissatisfaction with the theology which he had to learn as a student: he always longed for a style of dogmatics which would give prominence to the unavailability of revelation instead of trying to encapsulate it in all sorts of theses. He finds such a type of dogmatics in Barth:

> A discussion with you has been on my mind for years, for the 'conversations' I have had with you are innumerable. I have already told you how much I have been frustrated by what is taught and in which I had to participate in seminars although I realized that not

---

[1] Cf. Hans-Anton Drewes, 'Karl Barth und Hans Urs von Balthasar – ein Basler Zwiegespräch', in *Die Kunst Gottes verstehen. Hans Urs von Balthasars theologische Provokationen*, ed. Magnus Striet and Jan-Heiner Tück (Freiburg i.Br. et al.: Herder, 2005), pp. 367–83, 368–9.
[2] KBA 9340.216 (Hans Urs von Balthasar to Karl Barth, letter dated 25 April 1940).
[3] The whole letter is printed in Manfred Lochbrunner, 'Karl Barth und Hans Urs von Balthasar', in *Hans Urs von Balthasar und seine Theologenkollegen. Sechs Beziehungsgeschichten* (Würzburg: Echter, 2009), pp. 259–403, 269–79. But this is not a critical edition. We can also detect slight grammatical and stylistic corrections. In consequence the original document will be quoted in what follows.

much could be changed under the prevailing conditions. I was always looking out for a form of dogmatics which contained not simply a banal schema and a collection of rationalized theses but one which in form and tone allowed a person to sense something of the form and tone of revelation itself. On our side there exists the temporary irreparable disgrace that theological instruction wishes to be at one and the same time a practical preparatory course and serious theology; that this – actually from the time of scholasticism – represents a compromise between science and 'school' and in the course of this the former necessarily comes off badly. Your colossal work has been a source of great joy for me because it has fulfilled the ideal which I had in mind. I had myself thought of writing a larger Catholic dogmatics, and all my publications were intended as a preliminary exercise for this. But the immense service which you have provided for us makes a great deal of what I wanted to produce already superfluous.[4]

In fact, Balthasar had, in the late summer of 1939, met with his fellow Jesuit, Karl Rahner, in Innsbruck to plan a new handbook of dogmatics which would offer an alternative to the other textbooks then in use.[5] Although a detailed plan had been outlined and a publisher found, the project was never realized.[6] Balthasar himself was responsible for the halting of the project when, in the late autumn of 1941, he finally decided against taking part in it,

---

[4] KBA 9340.234 (Hans Urs von Balthasar to Karl Barth, letter dated 4 May 1940): 'Es hat mir seit Jahren eine Aussprache mit Ihnen vorgeschwebt, denn der "Gespräche", die ich mit Ihnen gehalten habe, sind unzählige. Ich sagte Ihnen schon, wie sehr ich von dem Schulbetrieb, den ich in Seminarien mitmachen musste, abgestossen worden bin, obwohl ich mir klar machte, dass unter den gegebenen Umständen hier nicht viel zu ändern sei. Immer hatte ich ausgeblickt nach einer Dogmatik, die nicht nur ein ödes Schema und eine Sammlung rationalisierter Thesen enthielte, sondern auch in der Form und im Ton etwas von der Form und dem Ton der Offenbarung selbst spüren liesse. Es ist eben bei uns der vorläufig unbehebbare Misstand [sic] vorhanden, dass die theologische Ausbildung zugleich eine praktische Propädeutik und eine ernsthafte Theologie sein will; dass sie – eigentlich seit der Scholastik – einen Kompromiss darstellt zwischen Wissenschaft und "Schule" und die erstere dabei notwendig sehr zu kurz kommt. Ihr gewaltiges Werk ist für mich eine Quelle grösster Freude gewesen, weil sie [sic] zum erstenmal das Ideal verwirklicht, das mir vorschwebte. Ich hatte selbst im Sinn, eine grössere katholische Dogmatik zu schreiben und alle meine Publikationen waren als eine Vorübung zu dieser gemeint. Aber die gewaltige Leistung, die Sie uns geschenkt haben, macht sehr vieles, das ich darstellen wollte, eigentlich schon überflüssig.'

[5] For what follows see Andreas R. Batlogg, 'Hans Urs von Balthasar und Karl Rahner: zwei Schüler des Ignatius', in Striet and Tück (2005), pp. 410–46, 424–30.

[6] The plan outlined at that time was later published by Karl Rahner, 'Über den Versuch eines Aufrisses einer Dogmatik', in *Schriften zur Theologie*, vol. 1 (Einsiedeln et al.: Benziger, 1954), pp. 9–47 [English translation: 'The Prospects for Dogmatic

citing overwork and the inclusion of collaborators who were not acceptable to him. But as the letter just quoted shows, he could not in the meantime have laid much comparative worth on the project: in a certain way the *Church Dogmatics* had made a new Catholic dogmatics superfluous.

Balthasar appeared to be thinking in particular of CD II/1, published in 1940. Here Barth develops a lengthy theology of the attributes or 'perfections' of God.[7] In that letter, dated 4 May, he struck up a virtual paean of praise to it. Particularly remarkable was the fact that the idea of the personality and thus the freedom of God was made central, which is why he also called it the first consistent systematic doctrine of God with a Scotist character.[8] What is remarkable in this assessment is that Scotism was understood as taking an opposite direction to Thomism and thus to the then current Neo-Scholastic theology. Balthasar apparently valued that volume of the *Church Dogmatics* so much that he almost continually had it with him.[9]

At that time (the summer semester of 1941), Balthasar also took part in Barth's seminar on the Council of Trent's teachings on the sacraments. Judging by the minutes of the meetings Balthasar played an important part in this seminar,[10] and not simply because he could explain the Catholic position to the Protestant students. As he wrote to Barth after the end of the seminar, he had been able to gain a completely new theological perspective by learning to perceive Catholicism through Protestant eyes.[11]

Theology' or 'A Scheme for a Treatise of Dogmatic Theology' in *Theological Investigations*, vol. 1, trans. Cornelius Ernst (Baltimore, MD: Helicon Press, 1961), pp. 1–18 or pp. 19–38]. The editors of *Mysterium Salutis*, a dogmatic collection marked by an emphasis upon salvation history ('Heilsgeschichte'), worked with this original outline. Incidentally, the first volume of the dogmatics, published in 1965, was dedicated to Balthasar.

[7] Cf. KD II/1 (1940), pp. 495–764 (§ 31. Die Vollkommenheiten der göttlichen Freiheit) [English translation: CD II/1, pp. 440–677 (§ 31. The Perfections of the Divine Freedom)]. This section made a deep impression on Balthasar according to Werner Löser, 'Der herrliche Gott. Hans Urs von Balthasars "theologische Ästhetik"', in *Herrlichkeit. Zur Deutung einer theologischen Kategorie*, ed. Rainer Kampling (Paderborn et al.: Schöningh, 2008), pp. 269–93, 272–4.

[8] KBA 9340.234 (Hans Urs von Balthasar to Karl Barth, letter dated 4 May 1940).

[9] Cf. Busch (1975), p. 316.

[10] Cf. Drewes (2005), p. 370.

[11] KBA 9341.373 (Hans Urs von Balthasar to Karl Barth, undated letter, translated): 'There are *so* many misunderstandings between the denominations. For me, the most instructive in this seminar was this: How Catholicism looks seen through Protestant lens. One sees a totally new, completely changed landscape. Much may be attributed to the simple-minded modern textbook-theology, which admittedly could not remain entirely without influence on the practice. And yet the abuse here too does not meet the substance of the use.' According to Drewes (2005), p. 370, the letter presumably dates from July 1941.

Balthasar took this experience as the occasion, still in the summer of 1941, to write a treatise entitled *Analogia. Gespräch mit Karl Barth*.[12] The basis of this piece was an article Erich Przywara published the previous year elucidating his understanding of the *analogia entis*.[13] In addition to Przywara's piece, Balthasar used and dealt with *Church Dogmatics* II/1, the volume on the doctrine of God, which had in turn made such a strong impression on him.[14] In November the manuscript was finished and a publishing house had been found. The only thing lacking was permission to publish the work from his superiors. Even when Balthasar pressed for a speedy granting of this permission, the internal censorship of the Society of Jesus dragged on until January 1942. Their decision was, moreover, negative. Balthasar then revised the manuscript and submitted it again for examination. When the censors registered reservations about this version too, the manuscript was sent to Rome, in all probability in May of the same year. The leaders of the Order chose a censor of their own whose report was submitted in September. Although the possibility of publishing the book after a renewed revision had been left open, the Provincial Counsel of the Swiss Jesuits dispensed with the possibility of granting further rounds of revision. A short time before, several theological publications had been put on the Index, including the plea by the French Dominican, Marie-Dominique Chenu (1895–1990) for a historically informed interpretation of Thomas. The same, so it was feared, could also happen to Balthasar's *Analogia. Gespräch mit Karl Barth*.

At the end of 1943 there was a renewed interest and movement in the matter. In spite of the decision of the Counsel, the Provincial suggested to Balthasar that he publish the manuscript, if not in the form of a monograph, then at least in the form of several articles. Although Balthasar was initially sceptical, he finally agreed and contacted the editor of the Fribourg periodical *Divus Thomas*. Nevertheless, some time would again pass before the articles into which he broke up the manuscript could finally be printed: a first article appeared in 1944; a second in the following year;[15] a third, which intended to deal with the question of the natural knowledge of God, was not published,

---

[12] For what follows cf. Drewes (2005), pp. 370–1; Manfred Lochbrunner, 'Die schwere Geburt des Barth-Buches von Hans Urs von Balthasar. Ein Beitrag zur Werkgenese', in *Die göttliche Vernunft und die inkarnierte Liebe*, Festschrift Joseph Ratzinger, ed. Albrecht Graf von Brandenstein-Zepplin et al. (Weilheim-Bierbronnen: Gustav-Sieverth-Akademie, 2007), pp. 631–64, 635–47. Lochbrunner's contribution was reprinted with the same title in ibid (2009), pp. 405–47.

[13] Przywara (1940).

[14] KD II/1 (1940).

[15] Hans Urs von Balthasar, 'Analogie und Dialektik. Zur Klärung der theologischen Prinzipienlehre Karl Barths', *DT* 22 (1944), pp. 171–216; ibid, 'Analogie und Natur. Zur Klärung der theologischen Prinzipienlehre Karl Barths', *DT* 23 (1945), pp. 3–56.

probably at the behest of the Superiors.[16] Due to the state of the sources, it currently remains unclear whether further articles were to follow, as well as how large the original manuscript was.[17]

Balthasar's difficulties with the censors, however, were more than merely political. Both his Provincial and the different censors almost unanimously found that he represented the prevailing Catholic theology far too disparagingly and bitterly.[18] Moreover, he significantly deviated from the customary Neo-Scholastic teaching in his interpretation of the natural knowledge of God. While the traditional doctrine suggested that there existed a self-standing natural order to which a supernatural one was joined, Balthasar maintained that both were actually and universally unified while also attempting to preserve their material dissimilarity. He explained that if God can be known by means of reason, this is only because of its real elevation by grace.[19]

Barth was, in some regards, a factor within these reflections, as Balthasar seems to have been made aware of the weak points in Neo-Scholastic theology through his engagement with Barth's theology and thought he could discover concrete strategies to deal with these soft spots. He follows Barth in making Jesus Christ the starting-point of theology, and not an abstract philosophical reflection on the natural as was the case in Neo-Scholasticism. He is clearly interested in initiating a *theological change in theology* within Catholicism and using Barth to bring about this change.

The direct occasion, however, for his analysis of Barth was Barth's controversy with Przywara. In Balthasar's estimation this debate went far beyond a quarrel between two individual theologians. In his article '*Analogie und Dialektik*', which will be discussed below, Balthasar thought the controversy had important ecumenical import. Generally speaking, ecumenics played a considerable role in the numerous conversations he had with Barth. This aspect of their correspondence can be seen clearly in a letter from the autumn of 1942 in which Balthasar opined that they actually conversed with each other as if they were 'theologians of union'.[20] The clear

---

[16] Everything suggests this article later found its way into Balthasar's *Karl Barth. Darstellung und Deutung seiner Theologie* (Cologne: Hegner, 1951). There one can find a section, namely pp. 314–35, in which the theme in question is treated [English translation: *The Theology of Karl Barth. Exposition and Interpretation*, trans. Edward T. Oakes (San Francisco: Ignatius Press, 1992), pp. 302–25 (Nature in the Decrees of Vatican I)].

[17] While Drewes (2005), p. 371, assumes it was 160 pages, Lochbrunner (2007), p. 643, conjectures that it was about 300 or 400. On this see Lochbrunner's review of Dahlke (2010), published in *TP* 86 (2011), pp. 297–9.

[18] Cf. Lochbrunner (2007), p. 636.

[19] Cf. Lochbrunner (2007), p. 637.

[20] Cf. KBA 9342.382 (Hans Urs von Balthasar to Karl Barth, letter dated 28 October 1942, translated): 'Basically we always talk with one another – and must do so if one

allusion here is to the religious colloquies which were held once and again after the Reformation in an attempt to overcome the schism.

7.2 Analogie und Dialektik (1944)

When Balthasar returned to the controversy between Erich Przywara and Karl Barth it was not because he merely wanted to reconcile two theologians who disagreed with each other about something. He is not concerned with settling personal animosities, but with clarifying factual questions. Just as Barth's theology seemed to him the first and perhaps only consistent form of Protestant thinking, so Przywara's appeared to be the genuine Catholic form.[21] The issue is not simply the encounter and debate between two individual theologians, but between two confessions. Balthasar thought that a fundamental confessional disagreement was at stake inasmuch as he considered Barth's condemnation of this account of analogy to be the condemnation of the very principle of what was Catholic as well as being revelatory of what forms the basis of Protestantism. If this were the case then any attempt to reach an ecumenical agreement would be senseless and necessarily doomed to failure. Although Balthasar at no point draws this conclusion, such a sentiment forms the context in which his remarks can be understood. It also explains why, as the identical subtitle of both articles suggests, it is a matter of the principles of Barth's theology. A productive confessional exchange only makes sense if there is a shared foundation. It is Balthasar's desire to demonstrate that such a foundation exists.[22]

What gives Balthasar hope that Catholic theology concurred in principle with Barth's theology is the 1940 *Church Dogmatics* II/1 on the doctrine of God, from which he quotes extensively in both articles. Balthasar considers this work important as Barth develops his account of the *analogia fidei* and thus partially adopts a concept he previously subjected to polemic. The truly exciting question for Balthasar is the extent to which Barth has come closer to the Catholic position, especially in light of the ecumenical significance of this issue.[23]

To discover the shared foundation which emerges in view of the principle of analogy, Balthasar deals with those sections of the *Church Dogmatics*

---

is to speak at all – as if we were both some theologians of union. And if one thinks about it we are still standing only before the terrible situation which has not become in the least more tolerable or satisfactory during its 400-year duration. Perhaps you have come to terms with this, resigned after long struggling and wrestling. I would rather batter my head on it than come to terms with it for a moment.'

[21] Cf. Balthasar (1944), p. 171.
[22] Cf. Balthasar (1944), p. 173, quoting KD II/1 (1940), p. 254.
[23] Cf. Balthasar (1944), p. 172.

which treat the limits of the knowledge of God.[24] Here, Barth first emphasizes that God can be known only through his revelation in order then to explain that the person is truly able to know God in his revelation if God has allowed himself to be known.[25] In this connexion, Barth introduces the concept of analogy.[26] Even though this section is interpreted in different ways, there is a general agreement that it depends upon how analogy is treated in the *Church Dogmatics*, and thus it is a matter of theological epistemology.[27] But Balthasar does not take this context into consideration when he assumes that analogy deals with the relationship of God and humanity.[28] This analogical relationship entails neither identity nor complete difference, but is instead a relationship which includes both proximity and distance. Furthermore, this relationship does not mean that God and humanity are located on the same plane, for the more a person seems to be like God, the more clearly is the dissimilarity between them revealed. Distance increases as proximity grows since it is a matter of the relationship between the absolute to the relative. The relationship between God and a human person is always an analogous relationship, for the ever greater dissimilarity between them is always present. We should note that Balthasar considered analogy to be something like a universal principle, and thus cannot be confined solely to the field of theological epistemology. Furthermore, analogy for Balthasar is not simply a philosophical or a purely theological concept. The relationship between God and humanity as expressed by this concept eludes any such categorizing.[29]

The current state of research seems to suggest that Balthasar's interpretation is highly unconventional, if not in fact an imaginative construct which cannot withstand a closer historical examination. Such a judgement, however, would not be doing Balthasar justice. After Barth had described the *analogia entis* as *the* invention of the Antichrist and the final reason for not becoming

---

[24] For what follows see KD II/1 (1940), pp. 200–87 (§ 27. Die Grenzen der Erkenntnis Gottes) [English translation: CD II/1, pp. 179–254 (§ 27. The Limits of the Knowledge of God)].

[25] Cf. KD II/1 (1940), pp. 200–29 (§ 27.1 Die Verborgenheit Gottes) [English translation: CD II/1, pp. 179–204] or KD II/1 (1940), pp. 229–87 (§ 27.2 Die Wahrhaftigkeit menschlicher Gotteserkenntnis) [English translation: CD II/1, pp. 204–54].

[26] Cf. KD II/1 (1940), pp. 252–75 [English translation: CD II/1, pp. 224–43].

[27] See Bruce McCormack, '§ 27 "The Limits of the Knowledge of God". Theses on the Theological Epistemology of Karl Barth', ZDT 15 (1999), pp. 75–86; Dirk-Martin Grube, 'Analogia fidei. Zum "Analogiegeschehen" bei Karl Barth', in *Wie läßt sich über Gott sprechen? Von der negativen Theologie Plotins bis zum religiösen Sprachspiel Wittgensteins*, ed. Werner Schüßler (Darmstadt: Wissenschaftliche Buchgesellschaft, 2008), pp. 117–31.

[28] For what follows see Balthasar (1944), pp. 174–7, with reference to KD II/1 (1940), pp. 253–5, 264–5, 269, 273.

[29] Cf. Balthasar (1944), p. 177.

Catholic, Catholic theologians almost unanimously classified his theology as Protestantism carried to the extreme and thus worthy of rejection. One of Balthasar's central concerns was to counteract this impression and reopen the possibility of a productive dialogue with Barth. While Balthasar was still working with the *Stimmen der Zeit* he published an article in which he emphatically supported the thesis that Barth's theology had undergone development.[30] He concedes that Barth's theology once followed the principle of dialectics, which explains his rejection of the *analogia entis*. Yet Barth's more recent publications have moved beyond such dialectics. While, for instance, in the *Epistle to the Romans* creation and sin were identified with each other, the two are conceptually disentangled and the finite can receive its own identity and independence.[31] Balthasar sees in Barth's theological development a difference between an earlier phase characterized by dialectics and a later phase associated with the *Church Dogmatics*. This interpretation raises the question of how the two phases are actually connected, for Barth's development appears to be neither totally discontinuous nor seamlessly continuity.

This question returns us to Balthasar's article in *Divus Thomas*. There he describes Barth's theological development, although without explicitly saying so, according to the Hegelian pattern of thesis, antithesis and synthesis.[32] His recourse to this pattern is quite ingenious for several reasons: Balthasar can explain to Catholic theologians that their disapproval of Barth was understandable as regards his dialectical phase, but is unjustified in the light of his new phase in the *Church Dogmatics*. He can also show Barth why it was (or maybe even still is) absolutely necessary to make analogy, not dialectics, the principle of theology. We could describe Balthasar's use of the Hegelian in this way: the first edition of the *Epistle to the Romans* is the *thesis*, its second edition and all of Barth's writings up to and including the Prolegomena to the *Church Dogmatics* are the *antithesis*, and the *synthesis* begins with the doctrine of God in *Church Dogmatics* II/1.

If dialectics simply described a way of speaking, Barth's recourse to it would be completely unproblematic.[33] As theology talks about a God who is unavailable even in his revelation, then dialectics can indeed be a necessary warning and corrective: every statement about God should at the same time be relativized by its counterstatement. Yet Balthasar thinks that dialectics

---

[30] Hans Urs von Balthasar, 'Karl Barth und der Katholizismus', in *Der Seelsorger – Beiheft* 3 (1938; F. 2, 1939), pp. 126–32.

[31] Cf. Balthasar (1939c), p. 131.

[32] Cf. Balthasar (1944), pp. 173–4, 186–201. The concepts used here already enable us to see that he is borrowing from Hegel. Balthasar speaks (p. 173) for example of a 'three step' which proceeds with an inner necessity in which all theological reflection takes place, and also of the 'law of a progressive self-finding of theology'.

[33] Cf. Balthasar (1944), pp. 177–86.

initially represented, for Barth, something more than a mere method. At least in the earlier phase of Barth's development, the one connected with the second edition of the *Epistle to the Romans*, he viewed God and humanity into in such a way that God and humanity were completely different from each other and that humanity, as such, stood as an ontic contradiction to God. In Balthasar's opinion this position was inconsistent, for differences are only possible on the basis of some common ground. If one assumes there to be an 'infinite qualitative difference' between God and humanity, as Barth does in the *Epistle to the Romans*, then no such common ground is possible. God and humanity were no longer simply different from each other: they were completed separated. For this reason Barth *had to* give up dialectics, understood as ontic contradiction, as a principle within his theology.

Balthasar understands the inner necessity of Barth's theological development in Hegel's sense.[34] In the first edition of the *Epistle to the Romans*, Barth understood God and humanity as identical to each other. This identity remained the unspoken premise of his thinking, which is why Barth insisted so vehemently on the absolute difference of the two in the second edition in 1922; the antithesis depends upon and follows the thesis. If God and humanity are so strictly separated from each other, a problematic situation arises for theology. Theology neither can explain how something like the incarnation is at all possible, nor can it understand sin to be humanity's opposition to God, which was Barth's real concern at that time. To be able to say what he had initially wanted to say, Barth *had to* move away from using identity and dialectics as principles of his theology and replace them with analogy. It is with analogy that the common ground between God and humanity could be presupposed for the first time; the antitheses were taken up in the synthesis.

As Balthasar sees it, the common ground necessary for being able to make and see differences is best formulated within and by a doctrine of creation. As a creature, the human being both is completely from God and for God and a free subject.[35] Creatureliness therefore signifies both humanity's dependence upon God and its independence from him; otherwise stated, independence only exists on the basis of dependence. The phenomenon of sin can only be thought of within this context. For if the human person had no real independence, as Barth presumed in both editions of the *Epistle to the Romans*, then sin could never be a real possibility.[36] At the moment when a human being opposes God upon whom he or she is completely dependent, he or she becomes nothing and simply disappears, as would the problem itself. Sin, as real opposition to God, is only possible on the basis of that independence which the concept of the subject entails. If sin actually is a

---

[34] For what follows see Balthasar (1944), pp. 186–201.
[35] Cf. Balthasar (1944), pp. 196–201.
[36] Cf. Balthasar (1944), pp. 201–16.

moral act, then it can neither abolish nor corrupt the subject's independence, as Barth had assumed in the second edition of the *Epistle to the Romans*.[37]

The relationship between God and humanity is neither one of identity nor of opposition; it is rather a relationship of dissimilar similarity, or similarity within dissimilarity. This relationship between Creator and creature is unbreakable, even if it becomes negative through sin, understood here as the creature's absurd attempt to challenge its dependence on its Creator.[38] Just as the human being is God's *creature* and, as such, is independent, he or she is still *God's* creature and thus dependent on God. For this reason the person can in no way stand on the same level as God. As Przywara and Barth agree, the human person is strictly subordinate to God.[39] This is how Balthasar understands the analogy which exists between God and the person.[40] Thus the differences between Przywara's *analogia entis* and Barth's *analogia fidei* are not as great as they may prima facie appear. For if a person recognizes, no matter whether through faith or reason, that he or she is a created being, then he or she will, at the same time, set his or her eyes upon his or her Creator. This recognition is, however, only possible at all because God has already revealed himself.[41] This is proof for Balthasar that Barth's accusations against Przywara and Catholicism in general are unfounded. Catholic theology also seeks to preserve the sovereignty of God, and check humanity's own attempts to grasp God.[42] If Barth charges Neo-Protestantism of levelling out any distance between God and humanity, he is, according to Balthasar, materially giving prominence to an objectively given revelation and formally relying on the principle of analogy. Both serve to preserve difference.[43] Barth thus shares with Catholic theology not only the aim of maintaining this difference, but also the method one should use to do so. Thus Barth's polemics completely miss the true Catholic understanding of analogy; at most they are directed at distortions of it. Attempting to grasp God always remains a possibility that is open to humanity. So too is it possible to misuse analogy, but even this misuse does not discredit or condemn the principle of analogy as such, but the various ways it can be put to use. Dogmatics needs to be occasionally reminded that God remains unavailable in his revelation, and in this way it needs dialectics. Dogmatics cannot, however, restrict itself merely to bemoaning the inadequacy of human concepts in relation to the reality of God. Dogmatics must use analogy in

---

[37] Cf. Balthasar (1944), pp. 204–8.
[38] Cf. Balthasar (1944), pp. 205, 208.
[39] Cf. Balthasar (1944), pp. 209–11, with reference to Erich Przywara, *Analogia Entis. Metaphysik*, vol. 1 (Munich: Kösel and Pustet, 1932) and RB (1922) et al.
[40] Cf. Balthasar (1944), pp. 211–3.
[41] Cf. Balthasar (1944), pp. 212–3.
[42] Cf. Balthasar (1944), pp. 213–4.
[43] Cf. Balthasar (1944), p. 214.

order to be able to make positive statements about God. In the doctrine of God in *Church Dogmatics* II/1, Barth has even treated the concept of being in this way.[44] Hence Balthasar raises the question whether in so doing Barth has not, at least tacitly, revised his original position expounded in the prolegomena which appeared a few years earlier: 'So still *Analogia entis* as "*the* invention of the Antichrist"?'[45]

In the course of his development, Barth had reached the stage of recognizing analogy as a theological principle and should be asked to what extent he could still reject a properly understood analogy of existence. Yet Balthasar admits that the decisive objection which Barth raises against such an analogy of being has, as yet, not been mentioned: for Barth, the *analogia entis* is the codeword for a natural theology which relativizes revelation by assuming the possibility of a relationship to God established by reason.[46] What is possible only through faith also appears to be possible through reason. Balthasar agrees with Barth, but only on this point: if the *analogia entis* were to serve to establish a relationship to God independently of revelation, he would be right in seeing it as a human grasping after God and condemning it as *the* invention of the Antichrist.[47] Balthasar needs to refute this objection as well, for if it were true it would abolish the shared ground just gained and show the confessional split to be insurmountable. He thus needs to prove that, understood in Przywara's sense, the *analogia entis* is not an expression of the natural theology against which Barth is feuding, a kind of theology which blends philosophy and theology, reason and faith together. Refuting this objection thus leads Balthasar to the question of the relationship between nature and grace.

7.3 *Analogie und Natur (1945)*

Balthasar turned resolutely against the 'two-storey thinking' typical of Neo-Scholasticism. Nature and grace cannot be defined independently of each other. While it is clear that grace is always grace for something which is described as 'nature,' one might be tempted to speak of nature in dissociation from the grace.[48] However, as nature and grace actually only appear together, then they must be defined in relationship to each other.[49] There is still an

---

[44] Cf. Balthasar (1944), p. 215, with reference to KD II/1 (1940), pp. 291–2 [English translation: CD II/1, p. 260].
[45] Balthasar (1944), p. 215, quoting KD I/1 (1932), p. VIII: 'Also immer noch *Analogia entis* als "*die* Erfindung des Antichrist"?'
[46] Cf. Balthasar (1944), p. 215.
[47] Cf. Balthasar (1944), pp. 215–6 related to pp. 171–2.
[48] Cf. Balthasar (1945), p. 16.
[49] Cf. Balthasar (1945), pp. 11, 23.

important differentiation to be made here, as an independent nature may serve to guarantee the effectiveness of grace.[50] In this respect, the First Vatican Council's teaching regarding the *duplex ordo* is completely appropriate.[51] In Balthasar's estimation the then current scholastic insufficiently observes the analogy between the concepts of nature as developed in theology and as alternatively developed in philosophy. In determining the relationship of nature and grace the textbooks usually start from the concept of nature borrowed from Aristotelian philosophy, according to which nature is the dynamic pattern existence, including the final end, of something which is coming into being.[52] To avoid the unavoidable conclusion that grace is necessary for the person to the extent in which his final end consists in the beatific vision (or *visio Dei*), grace is defined as supernatural. Grace, then, is that which is not nature. As one can only be defined in relation to the other, Balthasar thinks this merely formal distinction is highly inadequate. The result of this way of thinking is a concept of nature which hardly seems theologically relevant.[53] Moreover, it is not made clear that grace, as the grace of *God*, is not something which the human being has at his or her disposal, even if it is a question of definition.[54] Offering a purely formal definition of the relationship of nature and grace which disregards the relationship's material aspects is characteristic of Baroque and Neo-Scholasticism. Yet this method leads to a massive contraction when grace is primarily considered from the standpoint of its gratuitous nature rather than from the viewpoint of the God who actually gives grace.[55]

Balthasar's own account of the relationship between nature and grace should be understood against this background. Instead of beginning with the philosophical concept of nature usually presented in the textbooks, and inferring from it the concept of grace understood as the supernatural, Balthasar starts from the theological concept according to which nature is that which is not grace.[56] How nature should be understood theologically can only be determined *a posteriori*, from the perspective of salvation, and not *a priori*.[57] Indeed, one can only infer the condition of its possibility because of the reality of God's gracious self-communication. Nature, which, as such, is not in itself grace, stands out as the antechamber of revelation only because revelation is given.[58] This definition of nature is still purely formal, and so

---

[50] Cf. Balthasar (1945), pp. 3–8.
[51] Cf. Balthasar (1945), pp. 5–6, with reference to Denzinger 1795–6.
[52] Cf. Balthasar (1945), pp. 8–9, 10.
[53] Cf. Balthasar (1945), p. 11.
[54] Cf. Balthasar (1945), p. 14.
[55] Cf. Balthasar (1945), pp. 12–7.
[56] Cf. Balthasar (1945), p. 17.
[57] Cf. Balthasar (1945), p. 15.
[58] Cf. Balthasar (1945), p. 18: '*Indem* Offenbarung ergeht, hebt sich Natur von ihr als der Vorraum ab, der als solcher nicht selbst Gnade ist.'

one might ask whether a material definition of nature in itself, considered independently of grace, is possible. At this point Balthasar expressly protests against the concept of the *natura pura*. Although it is possible to envisage a hypothetical nature which remains entirely untouched by grace as grace is and remains free, it should also be made clear that in reality such a grace-less nature never exists. It appears that the scholastic tradition was not always aware of this fact.[59]

Here Balthasar is referring to the complex development of the Catholic doctrine of grace at the end of the sixteenth century. To ensure the absolute gratuity of grace, the concept of the *natura pura* was thought to be helpful. For Balthasar, however, such a strategy is highly problematic. In light of the factual unity of the orders of nature and grace, one can scarcely be differentiated from the other. As grace is not some sort of quantity at hand, it eludes a precise definition and, at most, might be described by an approximation which nevertheless always remains inadequate.[60] Since nature in itself cannot be defined independently of grace, its formal definition must finally coincide with its material definition. If the human being is truly to be able to understand revelation and receive grace, she or her must first be what philosophy calls a 'subject'.[61] Even Barth could not avoid this conclusion. If, in the *Epistle to the Romans* and the first volumes of the *Church Dogmatics*, there was a tendency to recognize only the graced and sanctified person as a true subject, then Barth outgrew such a tendency by *Church Dogmatics* II/1.[62]

In Balthasar's opinion, an analogy exists not only between philosophical and theological concepts of nature. Nature and grace are not two entirely different 'things', but two *modi* of the relationship between Creator and creature, just as expressed by the *analogia entis*.[63] Grace cannot be deduced

---

[59] Cf. Balthasar (1945), pp. 25–6.
[60] Cf. Balthasar (1945), pp. 26–7.
[61] Cf. Balthasar (1945), p. 29.
[62] Cf. Balthasar (1945), pp. 29–33, especially p. 33, with reference to KD II/1 (1940), pp. 729–30, 756.
[63] According to Balthasar, the analogy in the concept of nature as is developed above is itself already a reflection and expression of the analogy between nature and grace. This 'between' can always only appear in that 'in'. For nature and grace are not two comparable quantities comprehensible from a higher standpoint but are two forms of conditions, shapings, forms of existence of the one and the same *analogia entis*. Thus Balthasar (1945), p. 33: 'Die Analogie im Naturbegriff, wie sie oben entwickelt wurde, ist nun selber schon Spiegelung und Ausdruck der Analogie zwischen Natur und Gnade. Dieses Zwischen kann ja stets nur in jenem "In" erscheinen. Denn es handelt sich bei Natur und Gnade nicht um zwei von einem höheren Standpunkt aus überschaubare, vergleichbare Größen, sondern um zwei Zustandsformen, Ausprägungen, Seinsweisen der einen und selben Analogia entis.'
[64] For what follows see Balthasar (1945), pp. 34–8. It is unclear whether Balthasar is here

from nature as current Catholic theology obviously thinks, but neither can nature be deduced from grace, which is always a danger in Barth's theology.

When Balthasar emphasized that nature and grace are not two completely different realities, he is decidedly arguing against Neo-Scholasticism's theology of grace. This line of thought gives the impression that there is a tidy and well-defined 'natural' area to which grace is added. The formula traced back to Thomas Aquinas – *gratia supponit, extollit, non destruit, perficit naturam* – was interpreted in this way. The *potentia oboedientialis* then has the task of mediating between nature and grace. Balthasar certainly takes up these two formulae, but he interprets them differently.[64] As for the first formula, even if nature and grace must be both materially and logically distinguished, the two form, factually speaking, a strict unity, particularly in the person of Jesus Christ.[65] Although the human being can only experience through Christ what grace is, and thus what nature is as well, we should immediately add that through and in Christ we see what had been initially established in creation: the *abstractissimum* can be seen in the *concretissimum* without the two being identical to each other.[66] The *analogia entis* has a Christological form insofar as Creator and creature are normatively mediated together in the hypostatic union.[67] Balthasar thinks that these Christological points demonstrate that grace does not just superficially join nature. Likewise, he argues that we should interpret the second scholastic formula regarding the *potentia oboedientialis* in a similar way.[68] The decisive systematic question Balthasar poses in this regard is the reciprocal relationship between reality and possibility. As the creature's being forgiven is real, it must also be possible. Yet being forgiven cannot be either a possibility inherent within the person or solely a divine possibility, and thus a human impossibility.[69] In the first case it would not be the grace

---

following Erich Przywara's article 'Der Grundsatz "Gratia non destruit, sed supponit et perficit naturam"', *Scholastik* 17 (1942), pp. 178–86.

[65] Cf. Balthasar (1945), p. 34.
[66] Cf. Balthasar (1945), p. 35.
[67] Cf. Balthasar (1945), p. 38.
[68] For what follows see Balthasar (1945), pp. 38–49. It is not only on the basis of *Kontroverstheologie* that Balthasar pays attention to the *potentia oboedientialis* (p. 39): he thinks that the *potentia oboedientialis* is, for Karl Barth, the source of all Catholic errors. For if an 'ability' for grace is here being attributing to the human being, no matter how it is disguised – that is, that there is a possibility *within nature itself* that grace is at its disposal, is open for it, takes it up, or that nature can recognize grace as possible or even desired, maybe even prepared for it – then through this small opening would rush a deluge of 'naturalisms', which indeed seem to constitute the distinguishing essence of Catholicism.
[69] Cf. Balthasar (1945), pp. 38–9. Balthasar had already referred to this aspect of the paradoxical relationship of nature and grace (p. 33): while grace is, on the one hand,

of *God*, and in the second it would not be the *grace* of God. For Balthasar, however, the problem is solved if one asks about the subject of the *potentia oboedientialis*. Its subject is primarily God and only secondarily humanity, even if the latter is no less its subject. What matters most is paying attention to this sequence.[70] It is not simply that there is always a point of contact within humanity to which God must connect in order to communicate himself in grace and revelation. As Przywara also stressed, there is no precondition for the possibility of revelation; rather it becomes real in that revelation itself creates the conditions for its possibility.[71] These remarks show why Balthasar criticizes the 'philosophy of religion' approach of his fellow Jesuit Karl Rahner, who seems to posit a natural willingness on the part of humanity to receive God's revelation.[72] Scholasticism harboured uncertainties in this regard. On the one hand, Thomas Aquinas started out from a natural human desire, provable by philosophical means, for the *visio Dei*, and, on the other hand, thought he must accept for theological reasons that the beatific vision was beyond human understanding and yearning.[73] Balthasar, however, thought that the *potentia obedientialis* primarily signifies obedience, availability, service and is not an 'anticipation' of grace.[74]

Thus Balthasar criticized scholasticism's tendency to understand nature as a prerequisite for grace, for this overlooks the fact that both are always mediated together in Jesus Christ. Nevertheless, the other extreme of deducing nature from grace was also unacceptable. Certainly, grace is always and only the grace of Christ, just as all things are created through Christ and exist in him.[75] Yet Christ is one person in two natures, wholly God and wholly human. We can see in him the relationship between nature and grace, how they both differ from each other and also how they are related.[76] Although Barth is in danger of deducing nature from grace, he is at least well aware of the danger he is skirting.[77] This brings Balthasar back to his initial question.

---

the fulfilment and perfection of nature, without thereby presupposing an already present possibility, on the other hand, grace is not an extrinsic accessory but the innermost perfection of nature.

[70] Cf. Balthasar (1945), p. 44.
[71] Cf. Balthasar (1945), p. 45, with reference to Przywara (1932), pp. 86–91.
[72] Cf. Balthasar (1945), pp. 42–4 fn 1, with reference to Karl Rahner, *Hörer des Wortes* (Munich: Kösel-Pustet, 1941). Balthasar had already criticized Rahner's transcendental theological approach in a review article in *ZKT* 63 (1939), pp. 371–9, especially pp. 375–9.
[73] Cf. Balthasar (1945), p. 47, with reference to *Summa contra Gentiles* 3, 50 and *Summa theologiae* I–II q.114 a.3.
[74] Cf. Balthasar (1945), p. 48.
[75] Cf. Balthasar (1945), p. 49, quoting Colossians 1,15–7 (Vulgate).
[76] Cf. Balthasar (1945), p. 52.
[77] Cf. Balthasar (1945), pp. 53–5, with particular reference to *KD* II/1 (1940).

If sin, as human opposition to God, is possible, then there must be a relationship between the two. In Balthasar's opinion the concept of Creator and creature is suitable in a special way because it permits us to express equally both closeness and distance between God and humanity. This relationship is normed through Jesus Christ, who by virtue of his human nature stands totally on the side of the creature and through his divine nature stands totally on the side of the Creator. In the person of Jesus Christ, nature and grace form a real unity, although factually and logically they can be differentiated from each other. Thus it is not a matter of realities which differ from each other, build on each other, or can be derived from each other. Hence it is impossible to state the relationship between God and humanity without using the concept of analogy.[78]

Although Balthasar clearly has reservations towards the scholastic tradition, by no means does he completely reject it. In his articles he certainly criticizes some of the best known and most widely circulated authors of dogmatic textbooks of his time, namely Joseph Pohle (1852–1922), Bernhard Bartmann (1860–1938) and Ludwig Lercher (1864–1937).[79] However, when he defines nature as that which is not grace and thus names subtraction as the process which allows one to develop a theologically relevant conception of nature, he falls back on representatives of scholasticism. In particular, he uses the Spanish Jesuit Juan Martinez de Ripalda (1594–1648) and Johann Baptist Heinrich (1816–1891), professor at the Seminary in Mainz.[80] It seems as though Balthasar's preoccupation with Barth sensitized him to the weak points in the traditional doctrines regarding nature and grace. Nevertheless, he initially desired to overcome these deficiencies within the context of scholasticism. A few years later he would reach the conclusion that the real problem is scholastic theology itself, committed as it is to Aristotelianism and thus heavily influenced by philosophy.

At this point, a quick detour through Karl Rahner's thought might prove instructive. Rahner, although he was equally dissatisfied with the then contemporary textbook theology as his Swiss brother Jesuit, remained

---

[78] Cf. Balthasar (1945), p. 56.

[79] Cf. Balthasar (1945), p. 12, quoting Joseph Pohle, 'Natur und Übernatur', in *Religion, Christentum, Kirche. Eine Apologetik für wissenschaftlich Gebildete*, ed. Gerhard Esser and Joseph Mausbach, vol. 1 (Kempten: Kösel, 1911), pp. 315–476, 318; p. 12, quoting Bernhard Bartmann, *Lehrbuch der Dogmatik*, vol. 2 (Freiburg i.Br.: Herder, $^{4/5}$1921), p. 3; pp. 10–11, quoting Ludwig Lercher, *Institutiones Theologiae dogmaticae in usum scholarum*, vol. 2 (Innsbruck: Rauch, ^{3}1940), p. 344.

[80] Cf. Balthasar (1945), p. 15, with reference to Juan Martínez de Ripalda, *De ente supernaturali. Disputationes in universam theologiam*, vol. 1 (Bordeaux: Guillermus Millangius, 1634) or Balthasar (1945), pp. 11–12 fn 1 and p. 15, with reference to Johann Baptist Heinrich, *Dogmatische Theologie*, vol. 5 (Mainz: Kirchheim, ^{2}1888), pp. 368ff.

deliberately within the framework that Neo-Scholasticism offered him. While Rahner knew he was at home in scholastic theology, Balthasar clearly felt that not only was he not at home there, he was a complete stranger.[81] What Balthasar half-heartedly adopted for lack of a better alternative, Rahner chose deliberately. Exemplary in this regard are Rahner's theological reflections on grace.[82] Of particular importance here is an article published in 1939 which was given much consideration at the time.[83] In this piece Rahner expressly ignores the question of whether the fact that revelation and grace are what unite God and humanity could be equally or even better expressed using the concepts of personalistic philosophy. Instead, he attempts to deal with the problem using the classic terminology, and so he examines what 'uncreated grace' means. Rahner proceeded in a very similar way when, set off by the *Nouvelle Théologie* a few years later, he once again tackled, in an even more determined way, the relationship of nature and grace. In order to relate the two quantities without making them dependent upon each other, he introduced the concept of a 'supernatural existential' ('übernatürliches Existential') which combines both modern and scholastic aspects.[84]

---

[81] Cf. Bernard Sesboüé, 'La genese d'une œuvre ou comment sortir de la «néoscolastique»?', in *Balthasar, Rahner – Deux pensées en contraste*, ed. Henri Jérôme Gagey and Vincent Holzer (Paris: Bayard, 2005), pp. 47–67; Fergus Kerr, *Twentieth-Century Catholic Theologians. From Neoscholasticism to Nuptial Mysticism* (Malden, MA et al.: Blackwell, 2007), pp. 87–104, 121–44. Extremly helpful are the following of Sesboüé's (p. 48) remarks: 'L'un et l'autre sont sortis de la néoscolastique mais selon des itinéraires complètement différents. Rahner a cherché à dominer la scolastique pour pouvoir ensuite s'en libérer, tandis que Balthasar n'y est pratiquement jamais entré. Rahner s'est fait lui-même à partir d'une formation classique, tandis que Balthasar s'est laissé fasciner par une série de maîtres.'

[82] On the background to this see Paul Rulands, 'Selbstmitteilung Gottes in Jesus Christus: Gnadentheologie', in Andreas R. Batlogg et al., *Der Denkweg Karl Rahners. Quellen – Entwicklungen – Perspektiven* (Mainz: Grünewald, 2003), pp. 161–96, and Stephen J. Duffy, 'Experience of grace', in *The Cambridge Companion to Karl Rahner*, ed. Declan Marmion and Mary E. Hines (Cambridge et al.: Cambridge University Press, 2005), pp. 43-62. Rahner's thoughts on the doctrine of grace are collected in his *Theological Investigations* – that is, Rahner (1954) [English translation: Rahner (1961)].

[83] For what follows see Karl Rahner, 'Zur scholastischen Begrifflichkeit der ungeschaffenen Gnade', *ZKT* 63 (1939), pp. 137–57. Reprinted in ibid (1954), pp. 347–75.

[84] Cf. Karl Rahner, 'Über das Verhältnis von Natur und Gnade', ibid (1954), pp. 323–45. A first version of this article appeared as a reply to the article by an author who remained anonymous, namely D., 'Ein Weg zur Bestimmung des Verhältnisses von Natur und Gnade', *Orientierung* 14 (1950), pp. 138–41. Rahner's article appeared pp. 141–5. What exactly Rahner meant by the term is succinctly explained in his article 'Existential, übernatürliches', in *LTK*² 3 (1959), p. 1301.

Looking back at these different approaches today, it was in fact Rahner's tactic of extending Neo-Scholasticism even further from within which would prove to be more successful. Rahner became *the* Catholic theologian, even far beyond the bounds of German-speaking areas. His renown is connected not least with the fact that he used the scholastic concepts understood by all students, lecturers and priests, although he admittedly made some small, but still considerable, alterations and extensions to their meaning. Balthasar, by contrast, manoeuvred himself from the very beginning into the position of an outsider when he openly expressed his detachment from the theology then taught and came closer to Karl Barth, a thinker who was unacceptable to many Catholics at the time, not only because of his Protestantism. Balthasar also considered the central problem of the Neo-Scholastic theology of grace, or what one could call 'two-storey-thinking'. Yet Balthasar did not provide a solution to the problem which could be clearly formulated and consequently adopted. His two articles in *Divus Thomas*, for example, are rather wayward and roundabout. Thus it is not surprising that they were given little to no consideration within Catholic theology, and were not even mentioned in the *Church Dogmatics*. Clearly there was the need for a new approach.

8

BALTHASAR'S APPROPRIATION OF BARTH'S LINE OF THOUGHT (1948–1951)

8.1 A Dialogue on a Circuitous Route: Barth and the Nouvelle Théologie

'Soyez gai' ('be happy') – with these words Balthasar ended a letter to Henri de Lubac in July 1950.[1] Ever since his time as a student at the Jesuit seminary of Fourvière in Lyons, a close friendship connected Balthasar to the French scholar. Now, however, some members of this seminary had run into difficulties: several lecturers were relieved of their duties, subjected to strict censorship and encouraged to change their place of residence. The leadership of the Society of Jesus desired, by means of these rather heavy-handed measures, to prevent something far worse from happening, such as being put on the Index or even ecclesial prosecution. It was known that an encyclical which was to rule against the theological trend of the *Nouvelle Théologie*, supported by several Jesuits associated with Fourvière, was being prepared. Since Lubac counted as their spokesman, he was affected in particular by the repressive measures. Informed of this situation by Lubac, Balthasar's reaction was one of shock. In a letter he wrote to Lubac before the encyclical *Humani Generis* appeared in August, Balthasar relates that he could scarcely believe what he hears and that such a thing could happen is alarming and incomprehensible. Yet, in the end, as Balthasar attempted to encourage his former mentor, one would have to recognize the results of his research as true; it was only a matter of time. Balthasar then goes on to say that he has completed a book which essentially enacts a discussion between

---

[1] Elio Guerriero, *Hans Urs von Balthasar. Eine Monographie* (Freiburg i.Br.: Johannes, 1993), pp. 409–10 (Hans Urs von Balthasar to Henri de Lubac, letter dated July 1950).

him (Lubac) and Barth, and that he would like to dedicate this book to him since he owes him practically everything. In the meantime, Balthasar encourages Lubac not lose courage but go on working as if nothing had happened. As Balthasar assures Lubac, he will do all he can to make Lubac's research known in German-speaking countries.

The letter is remarkable insofar as Balthasar himself establishes a connexion between his monograph *Karl Barth. Darstellung und Deutung seiner Theologie* (published in October 1951) and Lubac's research. Astonishingly, however, this connexion has not been explored in subsequent literature. Taking this letter into consideration means that *Karl Barth* fits into the post-World War II discussions surrounding the relationship between nature and grace: Balthasar was attempting to find a solution for the problem mentioned by Lubac through recourse to Barth. This was why Balthasar wrote to his former mentor that he is basically conducting a discussion between him and Barth in his recently completed book.

Lubac encountered the topic which was to occupy him for the rest of his life fairly early on: the concept of the supernatural.[2] The fruit of many years of research, Lubac published his epoch-making monograph *Surnaturel* in 1946.[3] In this work he meticulously reconstructs how Catholic theology came to view the relationship of nature and grace as the relationship between the natural and the supernatural. This shift took place in the sixteenth century when grace threatened to become naturalized by theologians such as Bajus. To protect its gratuitous character, the doctrine of humanity's twofold goal and with it the doctrine of *natura pura* were introduced. The price of this protection, however, was that grace was uncoupled from a person's inner fulfilment.

Lubac's explosive theses met with lively interest far beyond the bounds of France. They brought attention to changes within the doctrine of grace made since the early modern period and in turn prompted numerous further studies. What had always appeared simply to be the Catholic position turned out, on closer inspection, to be greatly conditioned by time and circumstance.[4] Lubac's theses certainly did not meet unqualified agreement.[5]

---

[2] Cf. Georges Chantraine, 'La théologie du Surnaturel selon Henri de Lubac', NRT 119 (1997), pp. 218–35.

[3] Henri de Lubac, *Surnaturel. Études historiques* (Paris: Aubier, 1946). On the historical context cf. Étienne Fouilloux, 'Henri de Lubac au moment de la publication de *Surnaturel*', RevThom 101 (2001), pp. 13–30. Lubac presented his theses later, in a condensed form, in the article 'Le mystère du surnaturel', RSR 36 (1949), pp. 80–121.

[4] Cf. Henri Rondet, 'Le problème de la nature pure et la théologie au XVIe siècle', RSR 35 (1948), pp. 481–521; Pieter Smulders, 'De oorsprong van de theorie der zuivere natuur. Vergeten meesters der Leuvense school', Bijdragen 10 (1949), pp. 105–27; Juan Alfaro, *Lo natural y lo sobrenatural. Estudio histórico desde santo Tomás hasta Cayetano (1274–1534)* (Madrid: Consejo Superior de Investigaciones Cientificas, 1952).

[5] Generally speaking, the textbooks that appeared at the beginning of the 1950s did not pay any attention to Lubac (1946) and simply continued to use the traditional defini-

BALTHASAR'S APPROPRIATION OF BARTH'S LINE OF THOUGHT

What was controversial was less Lubac's historical analyses than his suggested definition of the relationship between nature and grace.[6] Instead of giving prominence to the freedom of grace and nature, Lubac wanted to emphasize the subordination of nature to grace: insofar as a human cannot exist without a connexion to God, there cannot be a *status naturae purae*.[7] His critics, however, fastened on this point. It appeared to them to be highly doubtful whether the gratuity of grace could be maintained if a human being, as such, could not be thought of without being connected to grace and the beatific vision.[8] Without mentioning Lubac by name, this was the very point of criticism offered by *Humani Generis*. In the encyclical, Pope Pius XII warns against certain views which endangered Catholic doctrine, among which he included relativizing the gratuity of the supernatural order.[9]

Lubac had named a pressing problem, but, as the ensuing debate demonstrated, he had not reached a satisfactory solution. Balthasar was also aware of this problem, regardless of the fundamental agreement he noted in the encouraging letter to his onetime mentor. In his book on Barth, in fact, Balthasar quite openly criticizes Lubac's concept, for while its intention was certainly genuinely Catholic, it could scarcely remain so if it were consistently developed.[10] This worry is in no way simply a reproof cribbed from *Humani Generis*. Balthasar was perfectly aware of the weaknesses in Lubac's attempt to overcome the dualism of nature and grace. He thought he could find the solution for this problem elsewhere: Barth's *Church Dogmatics*. What Balthasar thought was promising in Barth was what he himself was later to call 'Christocentrism' ('Christozentrik').

The year 1936 represents a clean break in Barth's theological development. After this year the centre of Barth's thought would no longer be theological

---

tion of grace as supernature. This is true, for instance, of Matthias Premm, *Katholische Glaubenskunde. Ein Lehrbuch der Dogmatik*, vol. 4 (Vienna: Herder, 1953), pp. 3–6 and Joseph Pohle, *Lehrbuch der Dogmatik*, ed. Josef Gummersbach, vol. 1 (Paderborn: Schöningh, [10]1952), pp. 565–9.

[6] There is, however, a growing number those who also question Lubac's historical analyses. Here we must mention Ralph McInerny, *Praeambula fidei. Thomism and the God of the philosophers* (Washington, D.C.: The Catholic University of America Press, 2006), pp. 69–90; Karim Schelkens and Marcel Gielis, 'From Driedo to Bellarmine. The Concept of Pure Nature in the 16th Century', *Augustiana* 57 (2007), pp. 425–48; Rupert Johannes Mayer, 'Zum *desiderium naturale visionis Dei* [. . .]', *Ang* 85 (2008), pp. 737–63.

[7] See the nuanced explanations by Michael Figura, *Der Anruf der Gnade. Über die Beziehung des Menschen zu Gott nach Henri de Lubac* (Einsiedeln: Johannes, 1979), pp. 199–211.

[8] A survey of the debate can be found in Figura (1979), pp. 328–53.

[9] Cf. DH 3891.

[10] Cf. Balthasar (1951), p. 308 [English translation: Balthasar (1992), p. 297]. Thus Balthasar (pp. 306–10, 412 fn 54 [English translation: Balthasar (1992), pp. 295–9]) agrees with Lubac's historical analyses but not with his systematic conclusions.

epistemology – that is, the spiritually effected knowledge of God – but Christology.[11] The background to this shift is Barth's interaction with traditional Reformed doctrine,[12] and in particular with the venerable doctrine of *double* predestination, which assumed that the individual was predestined either for heaven or hell. Stimulated by an international symposium held in Geneva in 1936 to celebrate the 400th anniversary of the city's Reformation, Barth reformulated this doctrine in the light of the insight that God's will can only be known by his work in Jesus Christ and thus we can only start from God's *one* will for salvation. The corollary of this claim is that since God turns to the human in Jesus Christ, theology is essentially Christology. Starting from this premise, Barth sets about subjecting his own theology to a comprehensive revision. This process, which extended over a long period, culminated in 1942 and Barth's doctrine of election in *Church Dogmatics* II/2. There we read:

> The election of grace is the eternal beginning of all the ways and works of God in Jesus Christ. In Jesus Christ God in His free grace determines Himself for sinful man and sinful man for Himself. He therefore takes upon Himself the rejection of man with all its consequences, and elects man to participation in His own glory.[13]

One is tempted to say that the volume entitled 'God's Election of Grace' represents the systematic heart of Barth's oeuvre. Everything that follows in the *Church Dogmatics* can be understood as a development of the earthshaking insight that theology is essentially Christology.[14]

---

[11] See Bruce McCormack, *Karl Barth's Critically Realistic Dialectical Theology. Its Genesis and Development 1909–1936* (Oxford: Clarendon Press, 1995), pp. 453–63.

[12] For what follows see Matthias Gockel, *Barth and Schleiermacher on the Doctrine of Election. A Systematic-Theological Comparison* (Oxford et al.: Oxford University Press, 2006), pp. 158–97.

[13] CD II/2, p. 94 (leading proposition of § 33. The Election of Jesus Christ), the translation of KD II/2 (1942), p. 101 (Leitsatz von § 33. Die Erwählung Jesu Christi). Also see p. 1 (Leitsatz von § 32. Die Aufgabe rechter Lehre von Gottes Gnadenwahl) [English translation: CD II/2, p. 3 (leading proposition of § 32. The Problem of a Correct Doctrine of the Election of Grace): 'The doctrine of election is the sum of the Gospel because of all words that can be said or heard it is the best: that God elects man; that God is for man too the One who loves in freedom. It is grounded in the knowledge of Jesus Christ because He is both the electing God and elected man in One. It is part of the doctrine of God because originally God's election of man is a predestination not merely of man but of Himself. Its function is to bear basic testimony to eternal, free and unchanging grace as the beginning of all the ways and works of God.'].

[14] Most important, in the respect, is Karl Barth's lecture *Die Menschlichkeit Gottes* (Zollikon and Zürich: Evangelischer Verlag, 1956).

BALTHASAR'S APPROPRIATION OF BARTH'S LINE OF THOUGHT

Incredibly enough, it is only at the end of the 1940s that Balthasar appears to have first noticed Barth's increasingly intense concentration on Jesus Christ. In fact, in his earlier articles on Barth the doctrine of election is not mentioned at all.[15] Only in the course of preparing a total of ten lectures which he had to hold in Basle on the topic of 'Karl Barth and Catholicism' between October 1948 and January 1949 does Balthasar appear to have examined it more closely.[16] This is indicated in a letter in which he reports on the hectic preparations for the lectures: he has, in fact, since 1942 no longer followed Barth's steadily increasing work.[17] When one considers all the things on which he had previously worked, one only has to think of his time-consuming work as translator, publisher and editor,[18] it is plausible that Balthasar found very little time to study Barth extensively. His debating partner in Basle had, however, not remained inactive; he had, moreover, produced his voluminous doctrine of creation which takes up more than 1,200 pages of the *Church Dogmatics*.[19] All this makes it very probable that Balthasar only took note of Barth's doctrine of election, which had appeared six years earlier, in the winter of 1948/1949, or at least it was only at this time that Balthasar studied it seriously. The incentive to do so may have been a report published at almost the same time in which Barth looks back at thought in the 1930s and refers to the 'Christological concentration' ('christologische Konzentration') which he increasingly carried out at that time.[20] Balthasar would later use the term 'Christocentrism' ('Christozentrik')

---

[15] Cf. Balthasar (1944); ibid (1945).

[16] On the series of lectures see Lochbrunner (2007), pp. 647–50. In the monograph entitled '*Karl Barth*' which followed in the wake of the lectures Balthasar goes into KD II/2 (1942) in more detail. As Balthasar (1951), p. 187, [English translation: Balthasar (1992), p. 174] declares, the doctrine of election is without doubt the most uniform and most carefully crafted part of the whole work. It is written with the greatest love, the heart of Barthian theology, a kind of dithyramb of almost 600 pages which one must read for oneself boldly and with careful rationality because any dry summary would necessarily distort it. Barth's universalistic doctrine of predestination confirmed what he had thought for a long time – so Balthasar confesses, looking back in his *Rechenschaft 1965* (Einsiedeln: Johannes, 1965), p. 6.

[17] Cf. Lochbrunner (2007), p. 649 (Hans Urs von Balthasar to Karl Thüer, letter dated 6 November 1948).

[18] Cf. Manfred Lochbrunner, *Hans Urs von Balthasar als Autor, Herausgeber und Verleger. Fünf Studien zu seinen Sammlungen (1942–1967)* (Würzburg: Echter, 2002).

[19] Cf. KD III/1 (1945); KD III/2 (1948).

[20] Cf. Karl Barth, '"Parergon"', *EvT* 8 (1948/1949), pp. 268–82, 272: '[Ich] hatte in diesen Jahren zu lernen, daß die christliche Lehre ausschließlich und folgerichtig und in allen ihren Aussagen direkt oder in direkt Lehre von Jesus Christus als dem uns gesagten lebendigen Wort Gottes sein muß, um ihren Namen zu verdienen und um die christliche Kirche in der Welt zu erbauen, wie sie als christliche Kirche erbaut sein will. [...] Meine neue Aufgabe war, alles vorher Gesagte noch einmal ganz anders, nämlich jetzt als eine Theologie der Gnade Gottes in Jesus Christus durchzudenken

to describe this aspect of Barth's theology.[21] In so doing, Balthasar wanted to capture the idea that Jesus Christ, the definitive, universal and unique revelation of God, is the basis of all theological knowledge.[22]

Since Balthasar only became aware of Barth's doctrine of election fairly late, Barth's Christological concentration was not yet clearly expressed in that series of lectures. Nevertheless, Balthasar appears to have quickly realized what had happened here. It is, at any rate, the concept of Christocentrism which would enable him to determine the relationship of nature and grace in a way he thought superior to that of Neo-Scholasticism. Balthasar had finally found a way of solving the problem which, as his articles from the beginning of the 1940s show, he had thought pressing for a long time. This also explains why he did all he could to publish his monograph on Karl Barth as quickly as possible. From the beginning of 1950 he hurried along the printing very eagerly, even though he saw himself confronted with quite different problems at that time. Given the choice by his superiors of leaving the Society of Jesus or giving up the leadership of the Community of John ('Johannesgemeinschaft'), of which he was a co-founder, Balthasar decided with a heavy heart to withdraw from the Jesuits.[23] Turning down a position in the chic health resort of St Moritz offered to him by the Diocese of Chur, Balthasar retreated to Zürich in order to be able to work intensively and concentratedly on the manuscript. At the same time he made arrangements with the publishing house so that the book could appear as soon as possible, preferably in the autumn of the same year. He also named possible adjudicators to church authorities in Chur who were responsible for granting ecclesiastical permission to print. While Karl Rahner was to draw up an unofficial report, he had in mind the official report of Johannes Feiner (1909–1985), a very moderate and ecumenically open-minded professor in the diocesan seminary.[24] The energy which Balthasar devoted to

---

und auszusprechen.' Barth described this task, and it is the formulation which matters here, as a 'christologische Konzentration'. In translation: 'In those years I had to learn that Christian doctrine, exclusively and consistently in all that it says, directly or indirectly is teaching about Jesus Christ as the living Word of God spoken to us in order to deserve its name and to edify the Christian Church in the world as it will be edified as a Christian Church. [...] My new task was to think through and express all that has already been said once again in a quite different way, namely as a theology of the Grace of God in Jesus Christ.'

[21] Cf. Balthasar (1951), pp. 40, 46–7 and *passim* [English translation: Balthasar (1992), pp. 30, 37]. On the term see Marc Cortez, 'What does it mean to call Karl Barth a "christocentric" theologian?', *SJT* 60 (2007), pp. 127–43.

[22] Cf. Hans Urs von Balthasar, 'Drei Merkmale des Christlichen', *Wort und Wahrheit* 4 (1949), pp. 401–15, 407–8.

[23] On what follows see Lochbrunner (2007), pp. 650–1.

[24] On their relationship see Manfred Lochbrunner, 'Johannes Feiner und Hans Urs von Balthasar', in *Hans Urs von Balthasar und seine Theologenkollegen. Sechs Beziehungsgeschichten* (Würzburg: Echter, 2009), pp. 481–513.

his project can be seen particularly in that he was already able to complete the manuscript in July. As he wrote in his letter to Henri de Lubac at that time: 'Soyez gai' – that is, 'be happy'.

If Balthasar had hoped to have the work already printed by the autumn, more than a year was to elapse before *Karl Barth* would actually appear. The reason for this delay was not only because Rahner declined on the grounds of overwork wherefore a new referee, Robert Grosche[25], had to be appointed. More crucial was the publication of the encyclical *Humani Generis* in August, as it caused Balthasar to look at the work with greater circumspection. He recalled the typescript already in the hands of the publisher, Hegner in Cologne, in order to check through it once again, and thus *Karl Barth* is virtually peppered with – naturally approving – quotations from the encyclical. In this way he clearly desired to circumvent possible difficulties. He was, however, only partly successful. The Jesuit Engelbert Gutwenger (1905–1985) in Innsbruck accused him of making the same mistake as Henri de Lubac: making nature subordinate to grace and thereby questioning its gratuity.[26] Balthasar, who was already well aware of the difficulties the representatives of the *Nouvelle Théologie* now faced, hastily endeavoured to dispel this accusation. He promptly wrote a rejoinder which appeared, together with a riposte from Gutwenger, in the same year.[27] Balthasar's reply is remarkable in that he now presented his reflections with reference to Karl Rahner's 'supernatural existential', thereby protecting an open flank – unless Gutwenger did not want to come out openly against his colleague in Innsbruck and question his orthodoxy, he had to keep silent.[28] Thus there was nothing that Gutwenger could do except grit his teeth and give way.[29] Although everything ended without serious consequences for Balthasar, this episode reveals how carefully he had to proceed, even more so as *Karl Barth* genuinely contained dogmatic dynamite.

---

[25] On Grosche's relationship to Barth cf. Chapter 3.
[26] See Engelbert Gutwenger, 'Natur und Übernatur. Gedanken zu Balthasars Werk über die Barthsche Theologie', *ZKT* 75 (1953), pp. 82–97, 86–92. At that time other theologians classified '*Karl Barth*' as part of the discussion which had been initiated by the *Nouvelle Théologie*, e.g. Léopold Malevez, 'La gratuité du surnaturel', *NRT* 75 (1953), pp. 561–86, 673–89, and Richard Bruch, 'Das Verhältnis von Natur und Übernatur nach der Auffassung der neueren Theologie', *TGl* 46 (1956), pp. 81–102.
[27] Cf. 'Der Begriff der Natur in der Theologie. Eine Diskussion zwischen Hans Urs von Balthasar, Zürich, und Engelbert Gutwenger S.J., Innsbruck', *ZKT* 75 (1953), pp. 452–64. Balthasar's statement can be found on pp. 452–61, Gutwenger's riposte on pp. 461–4.
[28] Cf. Balthasar and Gutwenger (1953), p. 453.
[29] Cf. Balthasar and Gutwenger (1953), p. 461.

8.2 Karl Barth (1951)

8.2.1 A Contribution on Theological Methodology

The title Hans Urs von Balthasar gave to his 1951 monograph is simple and unpretentious: *Karl Barth. Darstellung und Deutung seiner Theologie.* What he set forth in almost 400 pages, however, baulks an immediate attempt at interpretation, so diverse are the themes mentioned. He treats at least two considerably problematic areas – the *analogia entis* and the relationship of nature and grace – and, as if that were not enough, Balthasar also attaches an ecumenical significance to the whole. Up until now research has concentrated on this latter aspect, so that *Karl Barth* is read almost exclusively as a contribution to ecumenical dialogue.[30]

Although this perspective surely has a high heuristic value, it cannot explain everything. Thus an alternative interpretation will be suggested in what follows. This reading is based on the assumption that Balthasar is less concerned with a confrontation with the contents of Barth's work and far more interested in offering a new form of Catholic theology. Not without reason does he refer both explicitly and implicitly to Hegel. Indeed, one might argue that Hegel's philosophy, particularly the idea of the independent movement of thought expounded therein, is the subject of *Karl Barth*.[31] In contrast to Hegel, however, Balthasar does not want to describe how the Spirit in the form of absolute knowledge becomes the idea of itself. Much more prosaically, but no less boldly, he aims to reach a new form through confronting traditional Catholic theology with Barth's way of thinking. Thus the emphasis in what follows falls less upon the theological contents of *Karl Barth* and more upon theological methodology or teaching on principles.

In this respect, *Karl Barth* hardly stands alone in twentieth-century Catholic theology. In the 1960s and 1970s similar theological efforts were undertaken in the realization of the ever more evident end of the Neo-Scholastic system which equally gripped theology and philosophy and had been dominant in Catholicism for a long time. These efforts were, in particular, focused on transcendental philosophy.[32] Balthasar, by contrast,

---

[30] Cf. Thompson (1994); John Webster, 'Balthasar and Karl Barth', in *The Cambridge Companion to Hans Urs von Balthasar*, ed. David Moss and Edward T. Oakes (Cambridge et al.: Cambridge University Press, 2004), pp. 241–55; Howsare (2005), pp. 77–99; Werner Löser, 'Von Balthasars Karl-Barth-Buch – eine theologische Würdigung', in *Karl Barth – Hans Urs von Balthasar. Eine theologische Zwiesprache*, ed. Wolfgang W. Müller (Zürich: Theologischer Verlag Zürich, 2006), pp. 71–96; Wigley (2007), pp. 11–48.

[31] Cf. Balthasar (1951), p. 419 (Register) [English translation: Balthasar (1992), p. 420 (Index)].

[32] Cf. Henri Bouillard, *Logique de la foi* [...] (Paris: Aubier, 1964); Bernard Lonergan, *Method in Theology* (London: Darton Longman & Todd, 1972); Karl Rahner,

argued from a historical perspective. This approach is fitting given the influence the *Nouvelle Théologie* had on him, for its main characteristic was the emphasis on the historicity of revelation and the development of dogmas along with an increasing recourse to the Bible.[33] At least as regards methodology, Balthasar's break with Neo-Scholasticism is far more drastic than in any other theologian, as he clearly privileges the historically concrete over the speculatively abstract. Conversely, the theology committed to transcendental philosophy remains tied to Neo-Scholasticism. The key to understanding Balthasar's reflections is his insight into the complex correlation between human thinking and divine revelation. It is clear that there must be a fundamental difference between the two, which means that revelation can never be obtained speculatively. What is understood in this way is *per definitionem* not God. Revelation can, however, only be grasped by thought, as otherwise it would not be an unveiling of something previously veiled. Yet modern theology's 'turn to the subject' renders this claim problematic. If knowledge is always and only perspectival, and thus dependent on the context of what is to be known, then there is neither a super-reason nor a super-language which allows what has been known to be formulated clearly and in a way that is valid for all time. Even if what is thought is unconditioned, thought itself remains conditioned in many ways. The relationship which exists between human thought and divine revelation is, as such, variable.

How one deals with this insight represents a considerable challenge. One must, for example, carefully consider whether the same thing can really be thought in different ways. This question becomes even more acute if theology is considered a function of the Church insofar as Church unity, at least to a certain extent, requires unity in thought. Thus, in late nineteenth and early twentieth-century Catholicism only *one* form of thought – the Neo-Scholastic incarnation of Thomism – was claimed to be true to revelation. The magisterium played a considerable part in giving the impression that Catholic theology was fixed on a particular metaphysical position. There was a potential danger, however, of overlooking not only the fundamental difference between thought and revelation, but also the fact that all thought is essentially inadequate because it is perspectival and contextual. These remarks lead us directly to Balthasar's *Karl Barth*.

In Balthasar's estimation, hardly anyone shows so clearly how little modern Thomism was free of shortcomings – particularly as regards the relationship between nature and grace – than Henri de Lubac and his

---

Grundkurs des Glaubens. Einführung in den Begriff des Christentums (Freiburg i.Br. et al.: Herder, 1976).

[33] Cf. Rudolf Voderholzer, 'Die Bedeutung der so genannten "Nouvelle Théologie" (insbesondere Henri de Lubacs) für die Theologie Hans Urs von Balthasars', in Kasper (2006), pp. 204–28, especially pp. 205–12.

Surnaturel.[34] Lubac's embedding of Thomas Aquinas in his historical intellectual context made a lasting impression on Balthasar. Just as his former mentor, Balthasar sees Thomas on the threshold between the patristic period, which was predominantly interested in theology, and the modern age, which primarily thinks philosophically; that is, Thomas comes from the old and strides towards the new. Balthasar calls this position 'transitionality'.[35] This transitionality can be seen all too clearly when one looks at the Thomist concept of nature which oscillates between philosophy and theology.[36] Its weak points became evident in the late sixteenth century when the Louvain theologian Michael Baius maintained that grace was essential for nature. For if the human being, as Thomas expressly taught, was basically designed to contemplate God, then God cannot refuse him grace. Provided each final goal requires the possibility of its achievement, nothing speaks against this conclusion, at least purely in a philosophical sense. For theological reasons, however, one cannot move from the dynamic aspect of the human nature to its final end in the *visio Dei*. It is precisely here that Balthasar sees the problem, for modern Thomism's preference for philosophy means that the emphasis is placed on the gratuity of grace and thus grace is defined as super-nature, as that which once again transcends the nature in which it stands. It is, then, no surprise that the definitions of grace found in the Neo-Scholastic textbooks are absurd.[37] There is a double contravention of elementary formal logic in that the terminus of what is to be defined is already used in the definition itself. To determine 'the natural' on which the concept of 'the supernatural' depends, the concept of nature is presupposed as the static and dynamic plan for the essence of what is coming into being.[38]

Although Balthasar shrinks back from stating this in plain language, Thomism as such is the problem. While such a sentiment might be faintly glimpsed in *Karl Barth*, Balthasar lets it shine through in an article entitled 'Thomas von Aquin im kirchlichen Denken heute'.[39] In this piece, published

---

[34] Cf. Balthasar (1951), p. 306 with p. 404 fn 1, both relating to Lubac (1946), especially pp. 431–80 [English translation: Balthasar (1992), p. 295]. Balthasar was to argue in a very similar way in *Herrlichkeit. Eine theologische Ästhetik*, vol. 3/1,1 (Einsiedeln: Johannes, 1965), pp. 354–70.

[35] Cf. Lubac (1946), pp. 187–321 or Balthasar (1951), pp. 278–82 with p. 404 [English translation: Balthasar (1992), pp. 267–70].

[36] For what follows see Balthasar (1951), pp. 284–7 [English translation: Balthasar (1992), pp. 272–5].

[37] Cf. Balthasar (1951), p. 287 with p. 405 fn 9 [English translation: Balthasar (1992), pp. 275–6].

[38] Cf. Balthasar (1951), p. 287 [English translation: Balthasar (1992), pp. 275–6].

[39] Hans Urs von Balthasar, 'Thomas von Aquin im kirchlichen Denken heute', *Gloria Dei* 8 (1953), pp. 65–76. Similar considerations can be found in Balthasar's article 'Was soll Theologie? Ihr Ort und ihre Gestalt im Leben der Kirche', *Wort und Wahrheit*

in 1953, he speaks of a renewed dephilosophizing of theology.[40] This line is unmistakably directed towards Thomism, the tendency of which, according to Balthasar, is to measure revelation philosophically and reappraise it rationally.[41] Theology, however, should devote itself to God's saving acts in history.[42] Thus Balthasar is concerned with a *theological change in theology*, meaning that he desires to place God's address to humanity in Jesus Christ at the centre of theology, an address which philosophically is underivable because it is free.

If one looks back at the monograph on Karl Barth which appeared two years earlier, one can see that Balthasar is already assuming as much and looking for ways to formulate what is Catholic in a way different to that of Neo-Scholasticism. He creates space for such a possibility through establishing that there is a fundamental difference between thought and revelation.[43] In this way we can see thought in all its limitedness, and it becomes clear that there cannot be only *one* model by which we can unfold revelation in our thinking.[44] Particularly important to Balthasar is

---

8 (1953), pp. 325–32. Reprinted under the title 'Der Ort der Theologie', in *Verbum Caro. Skizzen zur Theologie I* (Einsiedeln: Johannes, 1960), pp. 159–71.

[40] Balthasar (1953), p. 69: '"Entphilosophisierung der Theologie"'.

[41] Cf. Balthasar (1953), p. 68.

[42] Cf. Balthasar (1953), pp. 75–6. How Balthasar interpreted Thomas has only been appraised with regards to his theological trilogy; see James J. Buckley, 'Balthasar's use of the Theology of Aquinas', *The Thomist* 59 (1995), pp. 517–45.

[43] For one thing, Balthasar draws attention to the limitedness of thought without wishing to contest the unconditionality of what is thought; see Balthasar (1992), p. 12, a translation of ibid (1951), p. 22: 'Historical and cultural epochs can often be characterized by distinctive styles and modes of thought, some of which are sharply, and other often faintly, different from each other. Now these styles of thought can for the most part be neutral respecting the content of the thoughts being expressed, so that the same content of basic truths (let us call these basic truths *philosophia perennis*) can be couched in these various "languages". Yet at the same time, these forms, like language itself, can have their own rules – but on the other hand, as languages are wont to do, they have their own laws and can give a slight nuance in a perceptible way to contents expressed. Worldly truth is created and, in spite of all its participation in the immutability of the Eternal, has its historical dimension which displays its fullness in a wealth of forms and languages.' Balthasar expresses himself in a very similar way at another point, namely Balthasar (1992), p. 218, a translation of ibid (1951), p. 229: 'Revelation has never revealed that it has been predestined to be expressed in one, single human thought *form* (this is not to say anything against the content of a "perennial philosophy").' On the other hand, he points out (p. 263 [English translation: Balthasar (1992), p. 251]) that the revelation upon which theology has to reflect is greater than that which can be understood, for, as *God's* revelation, it is as infinite and mysterious as God himself.

[44] Cf. Balthasar (1951), p. 265 [English translation: Balthasar (1992), p. 253].

how reflection on content is organized, and here he uses the term 'mode of thought' ('Denkform').[45] His interest is not necessarily revelation itself but how revelation is understood in diversely conditioned modes of thought. To this end, Balthasar first presents Barth's thinking and the mode of thought he uses and then does the same for Catholicism.[46] However, these two parts, which form the core of the monograph, do not simply stand alongside each other, but are inwardly connected. As Balthasar stresses, Barth's thought questions Catholic theology and requires a response. Since Barth genuinely has something to say, he must be listened to attentively and understood; it is not a matter here of simply replying or brusquely retorting. The answer to a concrete question should be a new self-understanding of the one questioned.[47] Balthasar does not explicate this, but (once again) Hegelian dialectics are in the background: in the movement of thought which he develops surrounding the *Church Dogmatics*, Balthasar attributes the role of the 'thesis' to the Thomism of Neo-Scholasticism and that of the 'antithesis' to the *Church Dogmatics*. He explains how they fundamentally differ by considering the various pairs of concepts such as metaphysics and history, possibility and reality, general and particular, existence and act. The basic question is: in what relationship does the one stand to the other? While Thomas – and with him Neo-Scholasticism – draws conclusions from the abstract to the concrete, Barth deduces the abstract from the concrete. In Balthasar's assessment these two modes of thought are diametrically opposed.[48]

---

[45] Cf. Balthasar (1951), pp. 201–3 [English translation: Balthasar (1992), pp. 189–90] defines what is meant by this term as follows: A mode of thought is a conscious or unconscious philosophy, a world-view, a thought pattern. For the history of the term cf. Helmut G. Meier, 'Denkform', in *Historisches Wörterbuch der Philosophie* 2 (1972), pp. 104–7.

[46] Cf. Balthasar (1951), pp. 65–259 or pp. 261–386 [English translation: Balthasar (1992), pp. 57–247 or pp. 249–378].

[47] Cf. Balthasar (1951), p. 27 [English translation: Balthasar (1992), p. 17].

[48] According to Balthasar (1951), p. 187 [English translation: Balthasar (1992), p. 174], it is Barth's central thesis that one may only understand the mystery of God through his self-revelation in Jesus Christ; that every return to an 'abstract' God, as philosophy represents him, leads to disastrous consequences for theology everywhere, and here more than ever. At another point – Balthasar (1992), p. 265, a translation of ibid (1951), pp. 276–7 – he explains: 'Now Thomas' style of thinking with its decided predilection for induction (working from below, drawing examples from here for the realm above and finally explaining theology in philosophical terms) obviously stands in sharp contrast to Barth's exclusively theological way of thinking, far more so than with any other thinker's method. However much Barth might have felt at home with the *theological* rationality of Anselm, he could not feel at ease with St. Thomas' *philosophical* rationality.' Balthasar speaks of induction, pp. 276, 293 [English translation: Balthasar (1992), pp. 265]; of deduction pp. 254, 313 [English translation: Balthasar (1992), pp. 242, 302].

BALTHASAR'S APPROPRIATION OF BARTH'S LINE OF THOUGHT

Corresponding to the Aristotelian way of thinking, Thomist thought is definitely 'from below'. Philosophy, consequently, is given decisive significance before and within theology.[49] The general concepts and principles contained therein are inferred on the way of abstraction, beginning with experience and sensory nature. But, as Balthasar objects, this represents a predominantly philosophical method which can only find a limited application within theology. For even in his historically contingent revelation, God is *the* absolute concrete in whom there is nothing abstract. Since Thomism does not begin with God's free acts in history but from those necessary truths of reason which are basically accessible to the human person, there is a danger that the person achieves definitional dominion over God and thereby restricts God's sovereignty.

Barth, by contrast, attempts to begin directly with God's revelation in Jesus Christ; that is, with the concrete in order to reach the abstract. Balthasar finds an easily remembered simile to illustrate this:

> We could describe this thought as a kind of hourglass, where the two contiguous vessels (God and creature) meet only at the narrow passage through the center: where they both encounter each other in Jesus Christ. The purpose of the image is to show that there is no other point of contact between the two chambers of the glass. And just as the sand flows only from top to bottom, so too God's revelation is one-sided, flowing from his gracious decision alone. But of course the sand flows down into the other chamber so that the sand there can really *increase*. In other words, there *is* a countermovement in the other chamber, but only because of the first movement, the initiative of the first chamber. Everything, however, depends in the final analysis on the funnel at the center. This narrowest of passageways is verily the decisive one. It is the *actus*, the point of contact, the event, from which everything we call nature and condition derives its being.[50]

Jesus Christ, for Barth, is more than simply the Revealer, and is the only ground of human knowledge of God. At work in the background is the strong influence of German Idealism, particularly Schleiermacher, on Barth's thought.[51] In the manner of idealism, Barth takes a transcendental point which unites the differences within itself to be the origin of thought. Balthasar is basically asking us to reflect upon the fact that while a philosophical schema

---

[49] For what follows see Balthasar (1951), pp. 273–8, especially pp. 276–7 [English translation: Balthasar (1992), pp. 261–6, especially pp. 263–6].
[50] Balthasar (1992), pp. 197–8, a translation of Balthasar (1951), p. 210.
[51] For what follows see Balthasar (1951), pp. 210–59 [English translation: Balthasar (1992), pp. 199–247].

is being used here, it is filled with theological content and thus is immediately broken apart. For Barth does not regard human consciousness as the point which moves and stirs thought, as do typical accounts of consciousness. Instead, he places at this point an encounter between completely opposed realities: of the gracious God and sinful humanity, of the revelation understood as the Word of God and human faith. In the end, the point of unity is Jesus Christ, wholly God and wholly man.[52]

Balthasar certainly protests against dismissing Barth's theology simply as veiled philosophy, as a kind of crypto-idealistic speculation.[53] Yet he also thinks that he must show how the theological content in the philosophical form is actually being forced into an all too rigid schema. At the very least, Barth tends to succumb, against his own intentions, to the constraints of the idealistic system.[54] This becomes particularly clear when Barth attempts to deduce anthropology from Christology. If the unity of God and humanity is given most perfectly in Jesus Christ, then he is not merely the Revealer and thereby the ground of human knowledge of God, but he is also the ground of human existence. Thus Balthasar speaks, quite ambiguously in fact, of the 'Christological narrowing' ('christologische Engführung') which characterizes Barth's thinking.[55] With this theological neologism he is saying that Barth wants to affirm that the relationship between God and humanity is opened up only by the incarnate God. At the same time he points critically to the contraction at work when humanity is seen only in connexion to Jesus Christ. Instead of choosing an open and flexible mode of thinking as would be appropriate to revelation, Barth tends to fit theological data into a closed metaphysical frame. From this 'Christological narrowing' also comes the more far-reaching problematic nature of his ecclesiology. If the relationship between God and humanity has already been established in Jesus Christ, then disbelief simply represents an impossible possibility. To the extent in which the human being, as such, has always already been elected in Jesus Christ by God, then only that which has always existed, albeit hidden, is brought to light in the Church: God's sovereignty in relation to everything which he himself is not.[56] Thus there cannot be a particular community which could

---

[52] Cf. Balthasar (1951), p. 214 [English translation: Balthasar (1992), p. 203].
[53] Cf. Balthasar (1951), pp. 228–9 [English translation: Balthasar (1992), pp. 218–9].
[54] Cf. Balthasar (1951), pp. 251–9 [English translation: Balthasar (1992), p. 240–7].
[55] Cf. Balthasar (1951), pp. 253–5 [English translation: Balthasar (1992), pp. 241–3]. 'Narrowing' is a means of intensification, frequently used in music, particularly in fugues. The entries of the themes no longer simply supersede one another but follow one another in such brief intervals that they are pushed together like a telescope. Balthasar refers to this background in *Karl Barth. Darstellung und Deutung seiner Theologie* (Cologne: Hegner, ²1962), p. II fn 1 [English translation: Balthasar (1992), p. 393 fn 2].
[56] Cf. Balthasar (1951), pp. 257–8 [English translation: Balthasar (1992), pp. 245–6].

be distinguished from an unbelieving world, but only a community which witnesses the triumph of faith.

This would fundamentally relativize the significance of the Church – it would be in danger of being dispersed into the world. Here we also find an explanation for the ever-present, sharply anti-institutional strain in Barth.[57]

Thus far Balthasar's critical exposition, which aims, among other things, to prove that Barth's supposedly exclusively theological way of thinking is, after all, latently philosophical to the extent in which the 'Christological narrowing' is basically a metaphysical concentration.[58] Balthasar thinks that the same structural problem reoccurs in the Thomism of Neo-Scholasticism, for in both cases the thought form (in one case Aristotelian, in the other idealist) crowds out revelation, crams it into a corset and so limits its freedom. Thus, both the thesis and antithesis are inadequate, and so Balthasar finally arrives at the synthesis. In this synthesis the modes of thought of Thomism and Barth are 'resolved'. Instead of moving from the abstract to the concrete or from the concrete to the abstract, thought should begin where both are given in full effect: Jesus Christ.[59] What for today's reader might sound fairly unspectacular turns out, on closer reflection, to be revolutionary, for Balthasar is aiming for nothing less than a novel instantiation of Catholic theology which reflects on its own principles and genuine methods, and in so doing begins with the ineductible fact of revelation.[60] In concrete terms this means a turn to God's concrete self-revelation which includes a renunciation of a Thomism so heavily determined by metaphysics. Hence Balthasar is attempting to offer a theology oriented by salvation history ('Heilsgeschichte') and thus Christocentric in nature. It should, then, be fairly clear why Balthasar thinks that Barth's theology could provide crucial help in the production of a new style of Catholic theology.[61]

In the preceding chapter we saw how Balthasar had already picked up on some of Barth's insights through his consideration of the *Church Dogmatics*.[62]

---

[57] Cf. Balthasar (1951), p. 258 [English translation: Balthasar (1992), p. 246].
[58] Cf. Balthasar (1951), p. 258 [English translation: Balthasar (1992), p. 246–7].
[59] Cf. Balthasar (1951), p. 278 [English translation: Balthasar (1992), p. 266].
[60] Cf. Balthasar (1951), pp. 274–8 [English translation: Balthasar (1992), pp. 262–6]: Taking up a formulation of Vatican I (DH 3019), Balthasar pleads several times for a theology which is aware of its own principles and methods. Such a theology could be nothing other than a *scientia de singularibus*. In so doing he turns explicitly against Thomas Aquinas (*Summa theologiae* I q. 1 a. 2 arg. 2), who desires to consider God's saving acts in history merely as examples of his eternal wisdom. This approach explains why Balthasar, at least with regards to his intention, stands closer to nominalism.
[61] Cf. Balthasar (1951), p. 278 [English translation: Balthasar (1992), p. 266].
[62] For what follows see Balthasar (1951), pp. 124–81 [English translation: Balthasar (1992), pp. 114–67].

Here the central point of reference was the 1945 *Church Dogmatics* III/1 on the doctrine of creation. Here Barth argues that creation is the external basis of the covenant and that the covenant is the internal basis of creation.[63] To translate these remarks into the conceptuality of the Catholic theology taught at that time, one could say that the orders of creation and salvation certainly differ but are still related to each other.[64] Balthasar expounds the precise way in which the two are connected through the concepts of 'setting' ('Setzen') and 'presupposing' ('Voraussetzen').[65] The order of creation/nature is thus 'presupposed' in the order of salvation/grace so that the latter is placed after the former.[66] This arrangement, however, only becomes clear in the light of the 'setting', the revelation in Jesus Christ.[67] This is the central insight which Balthasar draws from the *Church Dogmatics*: the orders of creation and salvation certainly differ, but they are mediated together in Jesus Christ, in whom they first become visible. Balthasar then undertakes a re-reading of the nature-grace problem with this kind of Christocentrism in hand.[68] What he says about the nature-grace problem is more like a sketch than a polished systematics. Yet the cursory nature of his remarks is hardly surprising since he is primarily concerned with achieving a new mode of thought for Catholicism beyond Neo-Scholasticism. It is also not too important how he defines the relationship of nature and grace; far more significant is the fact that he does it differently than Neo-Scholasticism. In *Karl Barth*, the search for a new methodology is more pressing than finding the immediate solution to a dogmatic problem.

---

[63] Cf. Balthasar (1951), pp. 131–6, with reference to KD III/1 (1945), pp. 103–377 [English translation: Balthasar (1992), pp. 121–5]. What Barth develops here is in the context of KD III/1 (1945), pp. 44–377 (§ 41. Schöpfung und Bund). Instead of following this insight Barth tends to reduce the order of creation to that of salvation in the following volumes of the *Church Dogmatics*, or at least according to Balthasar (1951), pp. 139–48 with reference to KD III/2 (1948) and KD III/3 (1950) [English translation: Balthasar (1992), p. 128–36].

[64] Cf. Balthasar (1951), p. 131 [English translation: Balthasar (1992), p. 121]: What Barth names 'creation' and 'covenant' Balthasar calls 'the order of nature' and 'the order of the incarnation and salvation'. In an even more scholastic way, he writes (p. 313 [English translation: Balthasar (1992), p. 302]) that there is an absolute priority of the order of grace before that of nature (*in ordine intentionis*) and the relative priority of the order of creation before that of grace (*in ordine executionis*).

[65] Cf. Balthasar (1951), pp. 129–31 [English translation: Balthasar (1992), pp. 118–20]. Certainly in KD III/I (1945) Barth uses concepts from the semantic field of 'setting' (pp. 252, 254), but not in the sense of idealist philosophy. For the historical background to these concepts see Thomas Leinkauf and Tobias Trappe, 'Setzen/Setzung', in *Historisches Wörterbuch der Philosophie* 9 (1995), pp. 697–721.

[66] Cf. Balthasar (1951), pp. 134–6 [English translation: Balthasar (1992), pp. 123–5].

[67] Cf. Balthasar (1951), p. 137 [English translation: Balthasar (1992), p. 126].

[68] Cf. Balthasar (1951), pp. 278–386, especially pp. 335–86 [English translation: Balthasar (1992), pp. 267–378, especially pp. 326–78].

8.2.2 Barth's Theological Development

Balthasar was firmly convinced that the *Church Dogmatics* could help point the way towards an alternative formulation of what was 'Catholic' than the one found in Neo-Scholasticism. In this hope, however, he stood largely alone. In the 1940s and early 1950s, Catholic theologians only sporadically considered Barth while still publishing a great deal on Emil Brunner (from whom Barth had become estranged), particularly as regards the question of natural theology.[69] Balthasar was therefore lead to the opinion that there was an almost total lack of interest in the *Church Dogmatics*.[70] The popular prejudice was that Barth is the absolute embodiment of Protestant obstinacy.[71] This sentiment was not least due to Barth's remark that the *analogia entis* is *the* invention of the Antichrist.[72] Barth was understood in the light of the strict differentiation between God and humanity presupposed in this invective. Hence Balthasar points to a study by Jérôme Hamer (1916–1996) published in 1949.[73] The Belgian Dominican bases his writing primarily on the prolegomena of the *Church Dogmatics* and comes to the conclusion that Barth's whole style of theology is characterized by this idea: revelation is never something given but is always an unattainable event.[74] As was typical in Catholic theology at that time, Hamer paid no attention to the steadily increasing emphasis upon Christology over pneumatology clearly noticeable in Barth's thinking from the 1930s. Balthasar does not mention the other publications which show that the *Epistle to the Romans* led to the

---

[69] Cf. Dahlke (2010), p. 202 fn 70.

[70] Cf. Balthasar (1951), p. 21 [English translation: Balthasar (1992), p. 11]: 'There is certainly no doubting the general intellectual apathy and sloth prevailing in wide circles of Catholicism today – perhaps in unconscious imitation of Hegel's famous master-slave dialectic! Nor can it be disputed how many Catholics feel it is better to know as little as possible of Protestant theology. I venture to say that one could count on two hands – perhaps even one – the Catholic theologians who regard Barth's *Dogmatics* as required reading.'

[71] Cf. Balthasar (1951), p. 33 [English translation: Balthasar (1992), p. 23–4].

[72] Cf. Balthasar (1951), pp. 56–7, with reference to KD I/1 (1932), pp. VIII–IX [English translation: Balthasar (1992), p. 49]. How persistent and widespread this assessment was can be seen in the fact that it can be found in the authoritative Neo-Scholastic textbooks produced at that time, e.g. in Pohle (1952), p. 138 and Johannes Brinktrine, *Die Lehre von Gott*, vol. 1 (Paderborn: Schöningh, 1953), pp. 43–4, both with reference to KD I/1 (1932). We must also refer to Johannes Cornelis Groot, *Karl Barth en het theologische Kenprobleem* (Heiloo: Kinheim, 1946), pp. 147–58.

[73] Cf. Balthasar (1951), p. 69, with reference to Jérôme Hamer, *Karl Barth. L'occasionalisme théologique de Karl Barth. Étude sur sa methode dogmatique* (Paris: Desclée, 1949) [English translation: Balthasar (1992), p. 61].

[74] Cf. Hamer (1949), pp. 167–72.

perception that Barth still considered the relationship of God and humanity exclusively in the sense of the 'infinite qualitative difference'.[75]

The stigma of being a 'dialectical theologian' stuck to Barth. To make him acceptable to Catholic theologians at all, Balthasar first had to offer proof that such was not the case, or at least no longer the case, for it could hardly be denied that dialectics had played a central part in the *Epistle to the Romans*. This shift meant that both the continuity and discontinuity in Barth's theological development up to the *Church Dogmatics* had to be determined. As Balthasar sees it there are two options, both of which, however, have their difficulties. To think that there is no development in Barth's theology neither corresponds to the actual facts nor does it take seriously his numerous retractions.[76] Likewise, it is also unconvincing merely to presume that the style of theology expressed in the *Epistle to the Romans* has been overcome by the *Church Dogmatics* and is thus obsolete.[77] To avoid these problems and to enable one to think of continuity and discontinuity Balthasar falls back upon, although he admittedly does not explain it in this way, what Hegel called 'resolution' ('Aufhebung'): the positive of preservation through the negative of cancellation. In considering Barth's theological development Balthasar asks 'how much "analogy" overcame "dialectic" or how much, on the contrary, "analogy" managed to preserve and carry along the latter.'[78]

Although he considers the *Church Dogmatics* to be the mature form of Barth's theology, Balthasar certainly does not think that everything written before it is rendered obsolete and only interesting as historical artefacts. For it appears to him that what is later developed in the *Church Dogmatics* is already laid out in the *Epistle to the Romans*. Only in the *Church Dogmatics* does it become completely clear what Barth was aiming for from the start.[79]

The Hegelian concept of resolution describes a process which includes both termination and preservation. When the figurative is proved to be such and is ruled out, the real continues to exist; indeed, it comes into the foreground even more clearly than previously. Balthasar desires to understand Barth's theological development in this sense.[80] Barth's development takes place in

---

[75] See Johannes Hessen, *Die Geistesströmungen der Gegenwart* (Freiburg i.Br.: Herder, 1937), pp. 155–9; Friedrich Maria Rintelen, '"Der Römerbrief" und "Das Evangelium"', *TGl* 34 (1942), pp. 330–3, with reference to RB (1922/⁶1933); Yves Congar, 'Barth', in *Catholicisme* 1 (1948), pp. 1267–8; Michael Schmaus, *Katholische Dogmatik*, vol. 3,2 (Munich: Hueber, ³/⁴1951), p. 95.

[76] Cf. Balthasar (1951), p. 68, with reference to RB (1922/⁴1926), KD I/2 (1938), pp. 55–6; KD II/1 (1940), p. 715 [English translation: Balthasar (1992), p. 60].

[77] Cf. Balthasar (1951), pp. 69–71 [English translation: Balthasar (1992), pp. 62–3].

[78] Balthasar (1992), p. 63, a translation of Balthasar (1951), p. 71.

[79] Cf. Balthasar (1951), pp. 69–70 [English translation: Balthasar (1992), p. 62].

[80] For what follows see Balthasar (1951), pp. 67–181 (Darstellung) [English translation: Balthasar (1992), pp. 59–167 (Exposition)].

three stages: in the first Barth was still under the influence of liberal theology, in the second stage his thinking was completely stamped by dialectics.[81] In his early writings up to and including the revision of the *Epistle to the Romans* contradiction was not merely a rhetorical device, but was in fact a basic ontological assumption. Yet this is precisely where the problem lies. If everything about the relationship between God and humanity is to be said with the 'infinite qualitative difference', it would be impossible even to approach the mystery of the incarnation speculatively; how God could really become human in Jesus Christ finally remains inexplicable.[82] For this reason Barth gradually shifts to analogy, the third stage in his thinking.[83] This change does not take place abruptly but is a process extending over many years and which is only concluded in the *Church Dogmatics* II/1 of 1940.[84] Within this development, Barth's study on Anselm plays a special role, as it reveals for the first time that Barth no longer sees God and humanity as completely opposed to each other but connected in Jesus Christ.[85] Barth's thinking only attains its true and complete form when he places a Christology oriented by Chalcedon at its very centre.[86] On the basis of the insight that Jesus Christ is at one and the same time wholly God and wholly human can the finite, which previously seemed insignificant in the face of the infinite, be positively characterized.[87]

One could, of course, object that Balthasar is forcing the course of Barth's theological development into a pattern borrowed from philosophy; what is far more complicated and complex is schematized too strongly. As obvious as the objection may be, it remains unconvincing: when Balthasar relies on the Hegelian concept of resolution he is able to do Barth a high degree of justice. Of particular significance in this regard is an article, first available in German at the end of the 1940s, in which Barth looked back at his own

---

[81] Cf. Balthasar (1951), pp. 71–93 (Die Periode der Dialektik) [English translation: Balthasar (1992), pp. 64–85 (The Dialectical Period)].

[82] Cf. Balthasar (1951), p. 79 [English translation: Balthasar (1992), p. 72].

[83] Cf. Balthasar (1951), pp. 93–123 (Die Wendung zur Analogie) [English translation: Balthasar (1992), pp. 86–113 (The Conversion to Analogy)].

[84] Cf. Balthasar (1951), pp. 116–7 [English translation: Balthasar (1992), p. 107]. Balthasar argues in a similar fashion elsewhere, namely pp. 124–5, with reference to KD I/2 (1938), pp. 134–221 (§ 15. Das Geheimnis der Offenbarung) and KD II/1 (1940) [English translation: Balthasar (1992), p. 115].

[85] Cf. Balthasar (1951), pp. 101–2, with reference to Karl Barth, *Fides quaerens intellectum. Anselms Beweis der Existenz Gottes im Zusammenhang seines theologischen Programms* (Munich: Kaiser, 1931) [English translation: Balthasar (1992), p. 93].

[86] Cf. Balthasar (1951), pp. 124–81 (Die Vollgestalt der Analogie) [English translation: Balthasar (1992), pp. 114–67 (The Centrality of Analogy)].

[87] Cf. Balthasar (1951), p. 124 [English translation: Balthasar (1992), p. 114–5].

theological development from 1928 to 1938.[88] He expressly desires that his own theological development should be interpreted as a 'consolidation' or, alternatively, a 'deepening'.[89] Barth notes that he has made himself increasingly free of philosophical premises and has reflected ever more deeply upon Jesus Christ. In this process of 'Christological concentration', decisive significance should not be given to the document *Nein!*, which he wrote against Emil Brunner, but to the earlier study *Fides quaerens intellectum*.[90]

Balthasar leans on this article on several different occasions.[91] He follows Barth's own self-assessment even as he arranges Barth's development by the Hegelian concept of resolution. He understands what Barth names 'consolidation' as an increasing emancipation from philosophical premises in favour of a stronger consideration of Christology; that is, there is a fundamental continuity in the apparent discontinuity of Barth's thinking. Insofar as resolution signifies a movement in which real breaks do not occur, Balthasar can also conclude from Barth's autobiographical article that the study on Anselm played a *special* role but not a *decisive* one in the transition from the *Epistle to the Romans* to the *Church Dogmatics*.[92] Balthasar's recourse to Hegel means that it is not necessary for him to maintain that there are breaks in Barth's theological development in order to show that Barth's thinking only sorted itself out after a lengthy process.

With the concept of resolution, however, Balthasar is not only reacting to Barth's own self-assessment. We must bear in mind that the primary addressees of this study are Catholic theologians. As Balthasar firmly stresses he does not want to offer an introduction to Barth's work, which can best be achieved simply by reading it for oneself.[93] Rather, his concern is to tackle a theological problem felt to be of the utmost importance at the time: the relationship between the order of nature and that of grace. What Barth

---

[88] Cf. Barth (1948/1949), pp. 268–75. This text is the original of an autobiographical outline by Barth himself which previously was only available in an American translation published in 1938.

[89] Cf. Barth (1948/1949), p. 272: 'Vertiefung'.

[90] Cf. Barth (1948/1949), p. 272, with reference to ibid (1931) and *Nein! Antwort an Emil Brunner* (Munich: Kaiser, 1934).

[91] Cf. Balthasar (1951), pp. 69, 101–2, 417, with reference to Barth (1948/1949), pp. 268–75 [English translation: Balthasar (1992), pp. 62, 93, XV].

[92] Cf. Balthasar (1951), pp. 101–2, with reference to Barth (1931) [English translation: Balthasar (1992), p. 93]. Hence it is not the case that Balthasar identifies *Fides quaerens intellectum* as a break in Barth's theological development. Rather he considers the study on Anselm as the first clear expression of Barth's final position (p. 155 [English translation: Balthasar (1992), p. 143]). He vaguely locates the 'turning-point' itself to be around 1930 (p. 101 [English translation: Balthasar (1992), p. 93]). At another point Balthasar speaks of the turn around 1930 to be towards a positive concept of the creature (p. 145 [English translation: Balthasar (1992), p. 133]).

[93] Cf. Balthasar (1951), p. 10 [English translation: Balthasar (1992), p. XVIII].

himself describes as 'Christological concentration' appears to Balthasar to be a promising avenue. For in the person of Jesus Christ there are two natures which are neither completely separate nor fully identical with each other. Balthasar's earth-shaking realization was that this Christological truth could be applied to the problem of nature and grace. Yet as Barth had anything but a good standing in the Catholic theology of that time – his name still tainted with the radicalism of his early writings – it had to be shown why his more recent thinking stood out significantly from his earlier theology. Balthasar resorted to Hegel to direct the attention of Catholic theologians from the *Epistle to the Romans* to the *Church Dogmatics*.

8.2.3 On Bruce McCormack's Criticism of Balthasar

Hence Balthasar saw the solution to the problem of the relationship between the natural and the supernatural in what he called Barth's 'Christocentrism', or what Barth himself called his 'Christological concentration'. With this mind we should explore the debates regarding Balthasar's reconstruction of Barth's theological development which flare up occasionally. This debate was begun by Bruce McCormack (b.1952), professor at Princeton Theological Seminary, who explicitly understands his 1995 *Karl Barth's Critically Realistic Dialectical Theology* to be a critical debate with Balthasar.[94] As McCormack puts it, while in *Karl Barth* Balthasar emphasizes the discontinuity in Barth's theological development, he wishes to strengthen the continuity. Hence McCormack argues that Barth was always a dialectical theologian, not only in the phase connected with the *Epistle to the Romans*.[95]

McCormack's argument has both met with agreement[96] and provoked opposition, bringing advocates of Balthasar on to the scene in the process.[97] Most recently, however, the debate seems to have run stale and entered a holding period as both camps produce reasons for their opinions. Instead of reviewing and assessing both sides of the debates in what follows, a change in perspective will be suggested. If until now the *historical truth* of Balthasar's

---

[94] Cf. McCormack (1995), pp. 1–28.
[95] Cf. McCormack (1995), p. 18.
[96] Cf. John Webster, *Karl Barth* (London and New York: Continuum, 2000), pp. 22–4 with p. 45 fn 3; Gary Dorrien, *The Barthian revolt in modern theology. Theology without weapons* (Louisville, KY: Westminster John Knox Press, 2000), pp. 144–5, 163–5; Christophe Chalamet, *Dialectical Theologians. Wilhelm Herrmann, Karl Barth and Rudolf Bultmann* (Zürich: Theologischer Verlag Zürich, 2005), pp. 225–49.
[97] Cf. Reinhard Hütter, 'Barth between McCormack and von Balthasar. A dialectic', *Pro Ecclesia* 8 (1999), pp. 105–9; Stephen D. Wigley, 'The von Balthasar thesis. A re-examination of von Balthasar's study of Barth in the light of Bruce McCormack', in *SJT* 56 (2003), pp. 345–59; ibid (2007), pp. 39–44; Timothy Stanley, 'Returning Barth to Anselm', *Modern Theology* 24 (2008), pp. 413–37.

or McCormack's interpretation has been in question, we should now look at the *theological-political interest* that drives each of them. It is entirely clear that Balthasar's study of Barth was impelled by his concern to move and invigorate Catholic theology beyond the boundaries of Neo-Scholasticism. What has not been taken into account in the debate so far is that McCormack also has a goal in mind when he criticizes Balthasar and advances an alternative model for understanding Barth's theological development; he too is not simply interested in a purely historical reconstruction. McCormack wants to break up a classification of Barth's theology frequently offered in Anglo-Saxon circles and which McCormack blames Balthasar for having encouraged. For instance, it was while relying on Balthasar's work that Thomas F. Torrance (1913–2007) and Hans W. Frei (1922–1988) created the 'myth' of Barth as a neo-orthodox theologian.[98] With his criticism of Balthasar, McCormack is actually aiming at the interpretation of Barth which, at least in Anglo-American theology, has been dominant for decades. Thus we should first look at the connexion he establishes between Balthasar's thesis and what he calls the 'neo-orthodox' version of Barth.

Hans W. Frei counts as one of the most distinguished American systematic theologians of the twentieth century.[99] During his years of teaching at Yale he made numerous students, many of whom are now professors themselves, conversant with Barth's thinking. Frei had already dealt with Barth's theological development in his 1956 dissertation, which is replete with references to Balthasar's study.[100] He attempted to understand Barth's development itself as dialectic: heavily influenced by liberal theology, Barth was initially convinced that God is immanent to the individual believer; after his break with the theology of his teachers Barth emphasized the transcendence of God; finally, however, Barth came to see the relationship between God and humanity analogically, by thinking in terms of *similarity within dissimilarity*.[101] Frei explicitly relies here on Balthasar's arguments.[102]

---

[98] Cf. McCormack (1995), pp. 23–5.
[99] Cf. John F. Woolverton, 'Hans W. Frei in Context. A Theological and Historical Memoir', *ATR* 79 (1997), pp. 369–93.
[100] Hans W. Frei, *The Doctrine of Revelation in the Thought of Karl Barth, 1909 to 1932. The Nature of Barth's Break with Liberalism* (PhD diss., Yale University, 1956): in the first of three parts of the dissertation Barth's theological development between 1909 and 1932 is described (pp. 1–202), in the second the historical context explained (pp. 203–428) and in the third an interpretation of Barth's understanding of revelation during his break with liberal theology presented (pp. 429–549). A summary then follows (pp. 550–77).
[101] Cf. Frei (1956), pp. 1–6.
[102] Cf. Frei (1956), p. 4 fn 2, with reference to Balthasar (1951), pp. 93–123 (Die Wendung zur Analogie).

BALTHASAR'S APPROPRIATION OF BARTH'S LINE OF THOUGHT

But he goes beyond these when he describes the study on Anselm not simply as a 'turning-point' but even as a 'revolution'.[103]

Torrance, who had studied in Basle in the 1930s and later became a professor in Edinburgh, also lent his emphatic support to Barth's theology. He drove forward the translation of the *Kirchliche Dogmatik* into English and helped Barth's thought become an extensive influence, particularly in Scotland, which is still perceptible in both academic theology and in the life of the Church.[104] The extent to which his interpretation of Barth was indebted to Balthasar, whose book he had immediately reviewed after it appeared, is most readily apparent in his 1962 introduction to Barth's early theology.[105] Here Torrance differentiates between three phases within Barth's development. While Barth was initially heavily indebted to liberal theology, he then became a dialectical theologian after his break with the theology of his teachers. Nevertheless, it is the *Church Dogmatics* which, according to Torrance, represents the fully developed form of Barth's thought.[106]

Why Frei and Torrance were more interested in the *Church Dogmatics* than, for example, in the *Epistle to the Romans*, can be explained against the background of a theological project common to both. All their lives they strove for a doctrinal orthodoxy under conditions of modernity, which is why they were greatly interested in Barth's more developed and explicitly dogmatic theology. For both Frei and Torrance, Barth was a model for

---

[103] Frei (1956), p. 6: 'The turning point in this development away from dialectical theology toward a theology of analogy is Barth's book on Anselm of Canterbury's *Proslogium*, which he wrote between the two editions of *The Doctrine of the Word of God*.' With these 'two editions' he means CD (1927) and KD I/1 (1932). Cf. also pp. 193–200, with reference to Barth (1931), especially pp. 193–4: 'Barth's book on Anselm is absolutely indispensable for a knowledge of the revolution in his thought between the two editions of *The Doctrine of the Word of God*.'

[104] See D. Densil Morgan, *Barth Reception in Britain* (London and New York: T & T Clark, 2010).

[105] Thomas F. Torrance, *Karl Barth. An Introduction to his Early Theology, 1910–1931* (London: SCM Press, 1962). In the first part of the study the person and work of Karl Barth are presented (pp. 13–25), his theological development is handled in the second section (pp. 27–198), and in the third Barth's position in modern theology forms the central theme (pp. 199–217). How much Torrance was influenced by Balthasar can be particularly seen in this last section, which he concludes with a quotation from Balthasar's study on Barth that is almost two pages long; cf. pp. 216–7, quoating from Balthasar (1951), pp. 35–6. The following lines introduce the Balthasar quotation (p. 216): 'None of Barth's contemporaries discerns or appreciates more the positive relation of his theology to historic culture than Hans Urs von Balthasar. It is therefore fitting to end this study with a fine tribute from him to Barth.' – Torrance's review of Balthasar (1951) appeared in the daily newspaper, *The Scotsman* (14 April 1952).

[106] Cf. Torrance (1962), pp. 33–47, especially p. 34 fn 2, with reference to Balthasar (1951), pp. 220–9 or pp. 48–132 or pp. 133–98, especially p. 140 fn 1, with reference to Balthasar (1951), pp. 92–123 (Die Wendung zur Analogie).

navigating a *via media* between the arbitrariness of liberalism and the rigidity of fundamentalism.[107] They saw in him a kind of 'Church Father of the Modern Age'. McCormack sees in this line of interpretation the production of a neo-orthodox Barth created under the influence of Balthasar's book. Why does he oppose such a reading of Barth and insist that Barth was always a dialectical theologian? Addressing this question might advance the debate surrounding Barth's development, which has, admittedly, recently become a bit stale.

An answer is found when one considers that those church communities which appeal to the confessions of the Reformers have had to accept massive losses in membership in the USA. Both the Lutherans and Reformed are increasingly in danger of being wiped out between the Catholic and Orthodox Churches on the one side, and the Free Churches and Pentecostal groups on the other.[108] In a productive appropriation of Barth's thought McCormack, himself a part of the Presbyterian tradition, hopes for material for a clear-cut, theologically justified, Reformed Protestantism which he wants to place in between a hierarchical Christianity attached to tradition and one which is pragmatic and without traditions.[109] In order to be free from the Church's doctrinal tradition without losing all connexion to it, he wants to understand Barth as a dialectical theologian.[110] In this way Barth's thought can also be taken up by various denominations and trends, particularly the steadily growing evangelical movement.[111] This last group has traditionally had a rather reserved attitude to Barth, as it considered him to be a neo-orthodox theologian. In McCormack's view, if there is to be a

---

[107] Cf. Hans W. Frei, 'Five Types of Theology', in *Types of Christian Theology* (New Haven, CT and London: Yale University Press, 1992), pp. 28–55, 38–46 or Thomas F. Torrance, *Karl Barth. Biblical and Evangelical Theologian* (Edinburgh: T&T Clark, 1990).

[108] Such a scenario, verifiable by statistics, is drawn by Bruce McCormack, 'Karl Barth's Christology as a Resource for a Reformed Version of Kenoticism', *International Journal of Systematic Theology* 8 (2006), pp. 243–51, 251.

[109] See Bruce McCormack, 'The Barth Renaissance in America. An Opinion', *Princeton Seminary Bulletin* 23 (2002), pp. 337–40. McCormack makes similar reflections in two further articles, namely in 'The End of Reformed Theology? The Voice of Karl Barth in the Doctrinal Chaos of the Present', in *Reformed Theology. Identity and Ecumenicity*, ed. Wallece M. Alston and Michael Welker (Grand Rapids, MI: Eerdmans, 2003), pp. 46–65 and 'Is there a Future for "Church Dogmatics"?', *TZ* 66 (2010), pp. 306–17.

[110] This can be clearly seen in Bruce McCormack, 'The Actuality of God. Karl Barth in Conversation with Open Theism', in *Engaging the Doctrine of God. Contemporary Protestant Perspectives*, ed. ibid (Grand Rapids, MI: Baker and Edinburgh: Rutherford House, 2008), pp. 185–242.

[111] Cf. Bruce McCormack, 'The Being of Holy Scripture is in Becoming. Karl Barth in Conversation with American Evangelical Criticism', *The Princeton Theological Review* 9 (2004), pp. 4–15.

return to a genuinely Protestant theology in the USA it will most likely come about through recourse to the works of Karl Barth.

Thus if one asks about the *theological-political interest* connected to each reconstruction of Barth's theological development and not about its *historical truth*, the recent debate appears in a completely new light. Both Balthasar and McCormack have a vested interest in their interpretations of Barth's development: in the former it is to overcome the dualism of two orders, while in the latter it is to achieve a genuinely Protestant way of thinking. They also have different impressions of Barth to overcome: while Balthasar has to counteract the sense that Barth is still a dialectical theologian, McCormack wants to dispel the view of Barth as presenting an all too rigid neo-orthodoxy.

What does this historicizing and contextualizing of Balthasar's and McCormack's position contribute to the debate surrounding Barth's theological development? First, we must stress that the historical question is in no way superfluous, for each characterization of Barth's development has systematic implications which could prove significant. Recognizing the fundamental perspectivity of knowledge, however, should protect us from reaching rash conclusions and internecine reproaches. Additionally, we could even ask whether Balthasar's and McCormack's interpretations of Barth are complementary. In any case, that Balthasar's *Karl Barth* can stir such emotions should be taken as an indication of the quality and status of the work. In fact, this work already had an astonishing attraction in the 1950s, as will be shown in the following section.

8.2.4 On the Immediate History of its Effect and Reception

A reappraisal of the effect and reception of *Karl Barth* would surely need a study of its own. Balthasar's monograph was not only acknowledged, beyond the bounds of language and denomination, in almost all the relevant theological periodicals of the time, but even daily newspapers reported on it at length.[112] This fact is all the more astonishing because interest in Barth was waning at the beginning of the 1950s.[113] One cause of this decline might

---

[112] Cf. Hans Markus Wildi (revisor), *Bibliographie Karl Barth*, vol. 2 (Zürich: Theologischer Verlag Zürich, 1992), p. 67. For reference to other publications not noted there I thank Ms. Cornelia Capol (Basle).

[113] Cf. Balthasar (1951), p. 31. In the English translation [Balthasar (1992), p. 21], the passage reads as follows: 'We will not be conversing with Barth because he is the head of a strong current in contemporary Protestantism. Schools of thought are transient phenomena that ebb and flow with the times. And not few are the voices that claim, perhaps rightly and not without a certain satisfaction, that Barth's influence is already waning. But then there are also times when it is not a bad sign for a person to be losing influence.'

be found in the heated controversy about Rudolf Bultmann's programme of demythologization which also attracted the attention of Catholic theologians at that time.[114] Nevertheless, in the course of the 1950s there appeared numerous contributions on questions of fundamental theology and dogmatics prompted by *Karl Barth*.[115] In this connexion special mention must be made of the dissertations of Henri Bouillard (1908–1981) and Hans Küng (b.1928), both benevolently attended by Balthasar.[116]

In the 1920s there had certainly been a lively consideration of Barth in francophone Catholic theology, but no study ever achieved the influence of Bouillard's.[117] Interestingly, this work had an auspicious origin in a somewhat awkward situation. As a result of the encyclical *Humani Generis*, the Jesuit had to give up his teaching-post at the seminary of Fourvière and move to Paris, where he began to study Barth's work.[118] The fruit of his studies was an expansive three-volume work with which he earned the state doctorate at the Sorbonne in June 1956.[119] Barth journeyed with Balthasar from Basle to the oral defence of the thesis, and Hans Küng was also present.[120]

Küng owed even more than Bouillard to Balthasar. In February 1957, Küng, who previously had undertaken studies at Rome, received a doctorate in Balthasar's presence at the Parisian Institut Catholique with a work on the doctrine of justification in Barth and in Catholic theology.[121]

---

[114] On this see Klaus Hollmann, *Existenz und Glaube. Entwicklung und Ergebnisse der Bultmann-Diskussion in der katholischen Theologie* (Paderborn: Bonifacius-Druckerei, 1972), pp. 80–110.

[115] Cf. Dahlke (2010), p. 212 fn 118.

[116] Cf. KBA 9353.359 (Hans Urs von Balthasar to Karl Barth, undated letter [presumably summer 1953], translated): 'Bouillard sends greetings and would like to present you with two chapters as a foretaste of his visit. May I send them to you? Do you have the time and inclination for this? He has an observant, critical intellect. – A young theologian from Rome (Küng, Sursee), alert, also wants to write a dissertation thesis on you; I pointed him for a change to ethics ([. . .] possibly to "Word of God" and "Jesus Christ").'

[117] On the significance of Bouillard's study for the francophone area see Benoît Bourgine, 'Die Rezeption der Hermeneutik Barths in der katholischen Theologie Frankreichs und Belgiens', in *Karl Barths Theologie als europäisches Ereignis*, ed. Martin Leiner and Michael Trowitzsch (Göttingen: Vandenhoeck und Ruprecht, 2008), pp. 30–47, 33–4.

[118] Cf. Michel Castro, 'La rencontre de Henri Bouillard avec Karl Barth et la relation de l'homme à Dieu', *Greg* 88 (2007), pp. 512–32.

[119] Cf. Henri Bouillard, *Karl Barth*, 3 vols (Paris: Aubier, 1957). As Bouillard makes clear (vol. 1, p. 272), he owes a great deal to Balthasar (1951). They had both studied in Lyons in the 1930s.

[120] Cf. the accounts by Lubac (1989), p. 72 and Hans Küng, *Erkämpfte Freiheit. Erinnerungen* (Munich and Zürich: Piper, 2002), pp. 178–9.

[121] Cf. Hans Küng, Rechtfertigung. Die Lehre Karl Barths und eine katholische Besinnung (Einsiedeln: Johannes, 1957).

BALTHASAR'S APPROPRIATION OF BARTH'S LINE OF THOUGHT

Balthasar fostered his young Swiss compatriot energetically by publishing his dissertation and by sending out numerous review copies to ensure that *Rechtfertigung* was widely received. The study was, at any rate, a calculated success. Küng requested a cover letter from Barth, and published an article in the periodical *Una Sancta*, which was widely read in ecumenical circles.[122] Even more decisive was Küng's remarkable and trenchantly formulated conclusion arguing that the doctrine of justification, properly understood, should no longer be seen as a doctrine that divides the Church.[123] Such a conclusion had to cause a sensation, as it was arguing that the Church schism existing since the Reformation had been overcome. With this drum-roll, Küng became one of the best-known younger theologians worldwide, and soon became a professor at the highly reputed university of Tübingen.

Whether Küng was really correct in his thesis is, however, quite a different matter. Even if his representation of Barth's doctrine of justification and his interpretation of the Council of Trent are correct – of which, incidentally, there should be no serious doubt – there is the question of whether he does not downplay the differences between Barth and Martin Luther.[124] While the German Reformer sees humanity as always facing temptation, which is why the person who has been baptized always has to ensure his or her justification anew, in Barth's view, humanity is already reconciled with God through Jesus Christ.[125] Küng, however, raises the impression that Barth represents Protestantism as a whole,[126] an assumption that has been vehemently contested on the Protestant side.[127] Thus, Küng may have reached

---

[122] Cf. Karl Barth, 'Ein Brief an den Verfasser', in Küng (1957), pp. 11–4 or Hans Küng, 'Ist in der Rechtfertigungslehre eine Einigung möglich?', *Una Sancta* 12 (1957), pp. 116–21.

[123] Cf. Küng (1957), p. 274.

[124] In the first part of his study, Küng describes Barth's doctrine of justification and in the second part formulates an answer to it from the perspective of Catholic theology. Cf. Küng (1957), pp. 19–101 or pp. 103–276.

[125] Cf. Carl E. Braaten, *Justification. The Article by Which the Church Stands or Falls* (Minneapolis, MN: Augsburg Fortress, 1990), pp. 63–79; Gerhard Sauter, 'Rechtfertigung VI. Das 19. und 20. Jahrhundert', in *TRE* 28 (1997), pp. 336–52, 341; Alister E. McGrath, *Iustitia Dei. A History of the Christian Doctrine of Justification* (Cambridge et al.: Cambridge University Press, ³2005), pp. 392–406.

[126] Cf. Küng (1957), pp. 274–6; ibid, 'Katholische Besinnung auf Luthers Rechtfertigungslehre heute', in *Theologie im Wandel*, ed. Joseph Möller et al. (Munich et al.: Wewel, 1967), pp. 449–68.

[127] Cf. Peter Brunner, 'Trennt die Rechtfertigungslehre die Konfessionen? Neue Wege in der Kontroverstheologie', *Die neue Furche* 30 (1959), pp. 524–36; ibid, 'Rechtfertigung und Kircheneinheit. Katholisches Dogma, lutherisches Bekenntnis und Karl Barth', *Die neue Furche* 30 (1959), pp. 594–608; Alister E. McGrath, 'Justification: Barth, Trent and Küng', *SJT* 34 (1981), pp. 517-29; Eberhard Jüngel, *Das Evangelium von der Rechtfertigung des Gottlosen als Zentrum des christlichen Glaubens. Eine theologische Studie in ökumenischer Absicht* (Tübingen: Mohr Siebeck, ⁵2006), pp. 15–26.

an agreement with Barth, but not with Lutheran theology. *Rechtfertigung* is a masterly achievement of theological politics, but it certainly is not the milestone on the way to ecumenical agreement that Küng and his associates tend to portray it as being.[128] The dissertation was by all means an important work, but we can mention many other efforts which have led to similar rapprochements on the doctrine of justification.[129]

It is clear that Küng saw in Barth resources for the renewal of Catholic theology.[130] Moreover, a close friendship developed between the two such that in 1968, Küng even gave an address at Barth's funeral.[131] While Barth clearly got on splendidly with Küng, he and Balthasar became increasingly estranged, a situation which will be covered in the next chapter.

---

[128] Cf. Dahlke (2010), p. 214 fn 131.

[129] Cf. Birgitta Kleinschwärzer-Meister, *In allem auf Christus hin. Zur theologischen Funktion der Rechtfertigungslehre* (Freiburg i.Br. et al.: Herder, 2007), pp. 27–8; Karl Lehmann, '"Einig im Verständnis der Rechtfertigungsbotschaft? – Erfahrungen und Lehren im Blick auf die gegenwärtige ökumenische Situation"' [1998], in *Die Gemeinsame Erklärung zur Rechtfertigungslehre. Dokumentation des Entstehungs- und Rezeptionsprozesses*, ed. Friedrich Hauschildt et al. (Göttingen: Vandenhoeck und Ruprecht, 2009), pp. 849–72, 851–7.

[130] Cf. 'Karl Barths Lehre vom Wort Gottes als Frage an die katholische Theologie', in *Einsicht und Glaube*, Festschrift Gottlieb Söhngen, ed. Heinrich Fries and Joseph Ratzinger (Freiburg i.Br. et al.: Herder, 1962), pp. 75–97.

[131] Cf. Hans Küng, 'Ansprache', in *Karl Barth 1886–1968. Gedenkfeier im Basler Münster* (Zürich: EVZ-Verlag, 1969), pp. 43–6. Küng writes of this in *Umstrittene Wahrheit. Erinnerungen* (Munich and Zürich: Piper, 2007), pp. 138–40.

9

BALTHASAR'S LATER WRITINGS ON BARTH'S THOUGHT (AFTER 1951)

9.1 The Relationship between Christology and Pneumatology

In 1953, Karl Barth noticed, with considerable pleasure, a 'Christological renaissance' taking place within Catholic theology.[1] What he primarily, but not exclusively, had in mind was Balthasar's *Darstellung und Deutung*. Barth finds that he is far better understood in this monograph than in the vast majority of the books in the small library which had accumulated around him, especially as regards his focus on Jesus Christ and the Christian concept of reality implied in him which he had striven for in the *Church Dogmatics*. Yet immediately following this praise there comes a serious reservation. Looking at several religious biographies which Balthasar had previously published, Barth remained sceptical as to whether, in the light of the 'saints' portrayed, Jesus Christ was still the object and origin of the Christian faith.[2]

Barth's quite frank accusation that Balthasar relativizes the person and work of Jesus Christ is highly informative, for it allows us to see clearly the different systematic points which still exist in spite of all the common ground. The two differ significantly as regards their Pneumatology and Christology. When the accent is placed on God's ever-new self-revelation in

---

[1] On what follows see KD IV/1 (1953), p. 858 [English translation: CD IV/1, p. 768].
[2] Cf. KD IV/1 (1953), pp. 858–9, with reference to Hans Urs von Balthasar, *Therese von Lisieux. Geschichte einer Sendung* (Olten: Hegner and Summa, 1950); ibid, *Elisabeth von Dijon und ihre geistliche Sendung* (Cologne and Olten: Hegner, 1952); ibid, *Reinhold Schneider. Sein Weg und sein Werk* (Cologne and Olten: Hegner, 1953) [English translation: CD IV/1, pp. 768–9].

the Holy Spirit, God's unparalleled presence in the man, Jesus of Nazareth, is diminished. If, on the contrary, this temporally and spatially describable presence is emphasized, the question arises as to how one should move from Christ to Christians.

Barth's theology was heavily characterized by Christology ever since Barth had made the doctrine of election central to his thought. As the relationship between God and humanity was definitively established in Jesus Christ – that is, God has determined himself to be the God of humanity and thus made humanity the people of this God – the essential event has taken place once and for all. Thus, the Christian is a person who accepts the divine lordship of God already established in Jesus Christ and *in this way* allows it to become real.[3] Balthasar, by contrast, places more emphasis on Pneumatology. Just as Christ fulfilled the will of the Father, the Christian must look for the task God has assigned to him or her and accept it freely. This happens in and through the Holy Spirit who is the same now as then. Thus the Christian life is a constant *imitatio Christi*; such a life is to be analogous to the life of Christ.[4] This difference helps explain why Balthasar argues in *Karl Barth* that ecclesiology is a persistently problematic area for Barth[5], for if Christology takes precedence over pneumatology, it is difficult to see the Church as the Body of Christ progressing through time. As much as Balthasar may have come closer to Barth's way of thinking, even adopting some important insights from him, considerable differences between the two are still readily apparent. These differences became clearer the more Balthasar started to develop his own theology, an argument which will hopefully be proven in the conclusion.

9.2 God in His Revelation

As is typically stressed in current Catholic theology, revelation does not mediate something about God but God *himself*, and since God includes

---

[3] Cf. KD III/3 (1950), pp. 67–326 (§ 49. Gott der Vater als Herr seines Geschöpfes) [English translation: CD III/3, pp. 58–288 (§ 49. God the Father as Lord of His Creature)]. For an interpretation of this section, see Paul T. Nimmo, *Being in Action. The Theological Shape of Barth's Ethical Vision* (London and New York: T&T Clark, 2007), pp. 118–25. That Barth's Christology does not simply overwhelm pneumatology can be seen in KD III/3 (1950), pp. 275–9 [English translation: CD III/3, pp. 242–6]. Nevertheless, the extent to which Christology dominated his thinking is particularly clear in his lecture *Die Menschlichkeit Gottes* (Zollikon and Zürich: Evangelischer Verlag, 1956).

[4] Cf. Balthasar (1951), p. 386 [English translation: Balthasar (1992), p. 377–8]. This also explains why Balthasar attaches such importance to the saints in his work.

[5] Cf. Balthasar (1951), pp. 393–7 (Die Kirche) [English translation: Balthasar (1992), pp. 386–9 (The Church)].

humanity in his infinity, this revelation can only be partially perceived and understood through infinite approximation. Self-revelation and self-communication have become central theological concepts in the twentieth century, and not least because they forced open the constrictions of Neo-Scholasticism's didactic-theoretical understanding of revelation.[6] A quick look at the thought of the Dominican Réginald Garrigou-Lagrange (1877–1964), one of the most important Neo-Scholastic thinkers,[7] will allow a clearer view of these constraints. Garrigou-Lagrange maintains that in his revelation to humanity, God reveals previously hidden, or at least unclear, truths. Through the teaching of the Old Testament prophets, and finally through Jesus Christ, the person is made aware of the end for which he or she was created: eternal contemplation of the divine being. Revelation ultimately is, for Garrigou-Lagrange, a propositional instruction whose truth is guaranteed by an external authority.[8] How revelation occurs plays a subordinate role to revelation's content: the *what* is far more decisive than the *how*. Yet revelation cannot possibly amount only to teaching about propositional content, and so Vatican II established in its Constitution *Dei Verbum* that God has revealed himself in word *and* deed.[9] One should remember, however, that similar attempts had been undertaken in Catholic theology even before the magisterium tried to offer a more comprehensive account of revelation than that of Neo-Scholasticism. Balthasar's voluminous work *Glory of the Lord*, in particular, should be mentioned in this regard. In *Glory of the Lord*, Balthasar lays the epistemological foundation upon which his whole trilogy was to rest. The 1961 introductory volume, *Seeing the Form*, is of primary significance here.[10] Its title is already programmatic, for Balthasar is not concerned with simple analytical knowledge of a propositional content, but rather with the synthetic awareness of a multidimensional complex of meaning which he describes as 'figure' ('Gestalt'). The figure presenting itself and giving itself to be known is God's self-proclamation, which is anything but abstract: it should be studied in all its reality insofar as God's splendour

---

[6] Cf. Max Seckler, 'Der Begriff der Offenbarung', in *Handbuch der Fundamentaltheologie*, ed. Walter Kern et al., vol. 2 (Tübingen: Francke, ²2000), pp. 41–61, 42–8.

[7] For what follows see Reginaldus Garrigou-Lagrange, *De revelatione per Ecclesiam catholicam proposita*, vol. 1 (Rom: Ferrari, ³1925), pp. 56–72 (Definitio et divisio Revelationis). The extent to which Garrigou-Lagrange represented the doctrine then current can be seen Pope Benedict XV's explicit recommended of his tract in 1919 (p. 6). According to Kerr (2007), p. 10, he was the 'model Thomist – not only in Dominican mythology'.

[8] Cf. Garrigou-Lagrange (1925), pp. 64–8.

[9] Cf. DH 4202.

[10] Hans Urs von Balthasar, *Herrlichkeit. Eine theologische Ästhetik*, vol. 1 (Einsiedeln: Johannes, 1961).

shines out in the apparently insignificant Jesus Christ.[11] With this approach, Balthasar is unmistakeably turning against Neo-Scholasticism's didactic-theoretical understanding of revelation.[12]

Even if the theological aesthetics developed in *Seeing the Form* may be unique in the history of Catholic theology, they by no means simply dropped from the sky. The borrowings are unmistakeable, and one can clearly see representatives of philosophical aesthetics who, unlike Kant, did not place all the emphasis on the subject's setting up of the object in the act of knowledge, but on the object's allowing itself to be known. Johann Georg Hamann (1730–1788) and Johann Wolfgang Goethe (1749–1832) are, for instance, quoted extensively. Yet for a Catholic theologian it is far more astonishing how often Balthasar makes reference to Barth.[13] Balthasar attributes to him, for example, the historical service of having overcome the deeply rooted devaluation of aesthetics within Protestant theology. Here he is referring to the section of *Church Dogmatics* II/1 where God's eternity and glory are also treated in the context of God's revelation.[14] In spite of all the praise which Balthasar gives to this theological move, he qualifies his approval when noting that Barth attempts to reach this beauty by purely theological means and does not want to countenance any connexion between the splendour of God and the beauty of the world.[15] Yet such a connexion must exist, for God reveals himself not only in the history attested to in the Old and New Testaments, but also in creation.[16] If God unveils himself in being as well as in act, then there is neither an ontology free of theology nor a theology apart from ontology. Both, however, do not stand unconnected to each other, for even though God's revelation in creation and in Christ are different, they are not separated from each other. Balthasar explains how the two are connected by recourse to a figure of thought borrowed from the *Church Dogmatics*: that creation is the external basis of the covenant and the covenant the internal basis of creation.[17] As already in his earlier writings, this idea also plays a prominent part in *Seeing the Form*, without, however, this dependence being explicitly noted. According to Balthasar, the revelation of the triune God in Christ is not the mere extension or intensification of God's revelation in creation. Equally, however, the two are intimately

---

[11] Cf. Balthasar (1961), pp. 445–505.
[12] Cf. Benjamin Dahlke, '"Wahr-nehmung göttlichen Erscheinens"? Rückfragen an Hans Urs von Balthasars theologische Ästhetik', *TTZ* 120 (2011), pp. 269–82.
[13] Cf. Balthasar (1961), p. 659. The high esteem in which Barth is held in *Glory of the Lord* in general, and particularly in *Seeing the Form*, has already been covered in the secondary literature and most recently explored by Wigley (2007), pp. 49–87.
[14] Cf. Balthasar (1961), 49–53, with reference to KD II/1 (1940), pp. 685–764 (§ 31.3 Gottes Ewigkeit und Herrlichkeit).
[15] Cf. Balthasar (1961), p. 53.
[16] Cf. Balthasar (1961), pp. 413–44.
[17] Cf. KD III/1 (1945).

related in such a way that, seen from God's final plan, God's revelation in creation took place for the sake of the revelation in Christ and served as its preparation. God's revelation in Christ, however, was intended to synthesize, over and above every hope and expectation on the part of the creature, all that is heavenly and earthly in one divine-human Head, and thereby bestow upon him a gracious culmination, the majesty of which, belonging to the *kyrios* of the world, should radiate over the whole of creation. Then the form of the world itself, which as such was already a revelation of the divine 'doxa', becomes in Christ and through the Holy Spirit poured out through him a temple which, like the tabernacle and Solomon's temple, holds within itself the *kabôd* of God.[18]

Clearly, Barth would hardly have formulated what Balthasar is saying about the function of the revelation in Christ in a different way. For Barth, creation certainly is the external basis of the covenant, but no special splendour falls back on creation from this relation. In the section of the *Church Dogmatics* mentioned above, Barth typically abstains from ontological considerations and instead devotes himself to interpreting statements in the Old Testament dealing with the theology of creation as referring to Jesus Christ.[19]

For Balthasar, however, a kind of theological contraction occurs when Barth places the focus entirely on God's revelation in Jesus Christ. Balthasar's aim, then, is to extend our theological ken. Having initially gone over in *Seeing the Form* how the history of theology shows a de-aestheticizing of revelation on both the Protestant and Catholic sides, he raises the question of which way should now be pursued. Should theology follow Karl Barth, who himself rediscovers the inner beauty of theology and revelation, or should theology maintain that there is no real relationship between this theological beauty and the beauty of the world (a sentiment perhaps also included in Barth's position) and thereby deny, despite the danger this enterprise holds, that a true meeting with antiquity is possible, necessary or even forced upon us.[20]

Such thoughts are typical of Balthasar's treatment of Barth up until the early 1960s. In his attempt to formulate what was Catholic differently than it has been done by Neo-Scholasticism, Balthasar appeals to and follows Barth's reflections but still modifies them at certain crucial points. The methodological procedure which he uses in so doing is highly reminiscent of Hegelian dialectics. He places the philosophy-laden Neo-Scholasticism (the thesis) over against a putatively purely theological *Church Dogmatics* (the antithesis) and so reaches a way of thought in which being and action, the worldliness of the world and the divinity of God, are compatible with each other (the synthesis). The more clearly the contours of his 'Reformed

---

[18] Cf. Balthasar (1961), p. 415.
[19] Cf. KD III/1 (1945), pp. 258–377 (§ 41.3 Der Bund als innerer Grund der Schöpfung), with reference above all to Gen. 1-2.
[20] Cf. Balthasar (1961), pp. 75–6.

Catholicism' (as one might put it) become apparent, the further he moves away from Barth. While Barth increasingly focused on the *history* of the covenant between God and humanity perfected in Jesus Christ, Balthasar grounds this history in *metaphysics* and thus a theological ontology forms the basis of his theology.[21] This subtle yet crucial difference explains why we can detect a constantly increasing estrangement between the two. Barth himself spoke of this in a letter that he wrote to Balthasar in October 1962.[22] In retrospect, their relationship to each other was like that of two ships which meet at sea, greet each other in friendly fashion and then sail past again. As Barth himself emphasizes, he only wants to pursue and do theology, a position which is clearly not comprehensible for Balthasar. Barth is, then, unable to follow Balthasar into a hereafter of philosophy and theology, and so he ended with the wish that all might be better in heaven.

Although the contact between them did not completely break off in the 1960s, it did decrease to a very modest measure. How far the two ships, to stay with the simile, had moved away from each other can be seen from two lectures delivered at a meeting of the Ecumenical Dialogue-Commission of Switzerland at the end of February 1968. While Barth was highly delighted with the ecclesial renewal taking place everywhere – he was thinking of Vatican II – Balthasar expressed himself far more cautiously. In a letter which he had written to Barth in May 1940 he still remarked that the tremendous element of truth that Protestantism offered to Christianity had not yet been truly and fully assimilated in Catholic theology because the Counter-Reformation had turned too much against Protestantism.[23] Now, however, Balthasar warns against relinquishing basic Catholic convictions in ecumenical dialogue:

> Today's ecumenical conversations are frequently admittedly understood as a common search for the Christian truth looking up to our mutual Lord, but also as a radical reduction of what is the supposed 'essential', with the elimination of all additions which are dispensable and which disturb the understanding. It is clear that under such requirements the Catholic partner will necessarily come off worse, for the Reformation 450 years ago already lightened the ship of all its alleged 'ballast' and speaks today, not without satisfaction in view of the inner Catholic developments, of 'a lot to catch up on'. Since in the course of its history Protestantism has taken on the most varying and inconsistent forms: strict orthodoxy, pietism in the old and more recent

---

[21] See Nicholas J. Healy, *The Eschatology of Hans Urs von Balthasar. Being as Communion* (New York: Oxford University Press, 2005).

[22] For what follows see KBA 9262.177 (Karl Barth to Hans Urs von Balthasar, letter dated 30 October 1962, copy).

[23] Cf. KBA 9340.234 (Hans Urs von Balthasar to Karl Barth, letter dated 4 May 1940).

style of Schleiermacher, and finally liberalism even to the extreme of a 'theology after the death of God', the ecumenical agreement on the basis of such throwing off of ballast can likewise proceed on the most diverse levels, and the surrender of Catholic (above all allegedly 'Counter-Reformation') goods can then be summarily pushed ahead to a greater or less extent.[24]

Remarkably, Balthasar does not mention that from the beginning of the 1940s he himself had actively endeavoured to achieve a form of Catholic theology far beyond baroque and Neo-Scholasticism, and that he undertook such a project in a productive confrontation with Barth's theology. Balthasar creatively adopted the Christological concentration which can be seen in the *Church Dogmatics* and made Christocentrism the cornerstone of his own thought.[25] Barth's thought certainly plays a part in the trilogy of *Glory of the Lord*, *Theo-Drama* and *Theo-Logic*, but in comparison with Balthasar's earlier publications, Barth's contributions have become less prominent. Balthasar had certainly been aware of the *Church Dogmatics* and appropriated aspects of it, but had then set about moving beyond it.

As has been explained in the previous chapters, the fact that Balthasar worked on the *Church Dogmatics* at all fits together with his engagement with Neo-Scholasticism, the hallmark of which is the differentiation of the natural and the supernatural orders. If, on the one hand, the natural knowledge of God is emphasized as a reaction to modern rationalism, there emerges on the other hand, for the sake of the gratuity of grace, an independent sphere free of grace. Neo-Scholasticism was in turn heavily indebted to and oriented by philosophy. Against this movement Balthasar pleaded for a *theological turn in theology*. In his view the orders of grace and of nature are certainly different from each other, but they cannot be treated as completely separate. Rather they must be determined from Jesus Christ who unites both in his own person. This insight has strong and deep roots in Karl Barth's thinking. After Balthasar moved to Basle in 1940 he devoted himself to studying the *Church Dogmatics*. He pulled insights from Barth's work which he then used as an outline of Catholic theology far removed from Neo-Scholasticism. The more he developed this outline, the further he distanced himself from Barth. Indeed, eventually his conversation partner in Basle became only one influence among many, even if he remained an important one.

---

[24] Hans Urs von Balthasar, 'Einigung in Christus [...]', ibid and Karl Barth, *Einheit und Erneuerung der Kirche* (Freiburg/Schweiz: Paulusverlag, 1968), pp. 19–37, 36 (translated). On Balthasar's attitude towards Vatican II cf. Peter Henrici, 'Hans Urs von Balthasar und das Zweite Vatikanische Konzil', *Schweizerische Zeitschrift für Religions- und Kulturgeschichte* 104 (2010), pp. 239–50.

[25] This already becomes apparent in Hans Urs von Balthasar, *Glaubhaft ist nur Liebe* (Einsiedeln: Johannes, 1963), especially pp. 33–9.

SUMMARY

In this study the Catholic reception of Karl Barth's work in German-speaking theology from 1922 to 1958 has been sketched. Since the results were presented at the end of the respective chapters, we can do without presenting them again. Rather, in what follows I will attempt to relate the conclusions of these forays into Barth and Catholicism to the epistemological interests which have guided the study so far.

Karl Barth and Catholic Theology

When a mature Barth looked back over his life in 1960 it was clear that what had taken place between himself and Catholic theology was a particular source of joy for him. Perhaps no Protestant theologian since the Reformation had experienced so much criticism but also approval from its ranks than he. Apart from a small number of exceptions, Catholics seemed to provide the most comprehensive presentations, the most brilliant analyses and the most interesting judgements of his work.[1]

In fact, almost all of his major publications met with a lively interest among Catholics, including the *Epistle to the Romans* (Chapter 1), the study on Anselm, *Fides quaerens intellectum* (Chapter 4) or the *Church Dogmatics* (Chapters 5–9). Whether criticism or agreement was the dominant tone substantially depended on how strongly dialectics was thought to play a part in his theology. In the 1920s and early 1930s two positions regarding Barth's work clashed. On the one side the 'infinite qualitative difference of time and eternity', which Barth called the central idea in the *Epistle to the Romans*, was considered a problem. If God always makes himself visible in the Holy Spirit, one can say nothing meaningful about God and any type of mediation of revelation in the Church becomes superfluous (Chapter 2). On the other side, Catholic interpreters rejoiced that, with Barth, Protestantism was sorting itself out to the extent that real theology was once again being pursued in the tradition of the Reformers. This was of great interest for inter-denominational conversations because no real points of contact had been possible with liberal Protestant theology (Chapter 3). But when Barth, in the preface to the first volume of the *Church Dogmatics*, described the *analogia entis* as *the* invention

---

[1] Cf. Karl Barth, 'How my mind has changed', *EvT* 20 (1960), pp. 97–106, 104–5.

SUMMARY

of the Antichrist and the only real reason why one could not become Catholic, the first line of interpretation won the upper hand (Chapter 5).

Barth himself was responsible for this reaction, for in the *Church Dogmatics* he initially developed a theology that corresponds to revelation by dissociating it from Neo-Protestantism on the one side, and Catholicism on the other. In his view, a characteristic feature of the Roman 'heresy' is the *analogia entis*, which he regards as the embodiment of natural theology and thus humanity's inexcusable grasping after God. When, however, he had found a starting-point for his theology in the doctrine of election, the polemical and functional need to differentiate his theology from Catholicism became unnecessary. From the 1940s, at the very latest, Barth was developing his theology in the light of the fact that in Jesus Christ God has determined himself to be the *God of humanity* and at the same time has determined humanity to be *God's people*. Yet these additional developments were no longer recognized on the Catholic side, for Barth was still thought to be a dialectic theologian. This is why Hans Urs von Balthasar had to explain laboriously why his debating partner in Basle was not the very embodiment of Protestant recalcitrance when he was trying to offer a new form of theology beyond Neo-Scholasticism with the help of the the 'Christological concentration' he found in the *Church Dogmatics* (Chapters 6–9).

Although Barth constantly engaged in an intensive academic and personal exchange with Catholic theologians, he never gave up his distance to Catholicism. His fundamental disagreement with Catholicism rested on theological grounds: Barth's concern was for the truth of faith in the God who had shown himself, in Jesus Christ, to be the God of humanity. As the various Churches testify in their own way, God's merciful acts as related in Scripture are of the utmost importance. Thus no Church can claim that it is the true Church, for it must first become a true Church.[2] In the course of Vatican II, which Barth described as a 'Council of Reform' and greeted with satisfaction, his reservations against Catholicism softened somewhat.[3] In September 1966 he journeyed to Rome to inform himself about the new orientation being encouraged in Catholicism.[4] The Constitution on Revelation, *Dei Verbum*, appeared particularly important to him because

---

[2] Cf. Benjamin Dahlke, 'Karl Barth und der Katholizismus. Zu einer komplexen Beziehung', *Brixner Theologisches Forum* 120,2 (2009), pp. 22–37; Angelo Maffeis, 'Karl Barth, un teologo tra le confessioni cristiane', *Hermeneutica. Annuario di filosofia e teologia* (2009), pp. 27–66; Georg Plasger, 'Kirche als ökumenisches Ereignis. Die Einheit der Kirchen in der einen Kirche Jesu Christi', in *Karl Barth im europäischen Zeitgeschehen (1935–1950)* [...], ed. Michael Beintker et al. (Zürich: Theologischer Verlag Zürich, 2010), pp. 471–83.

[3] Cf. Karl Barth, *Ad Limina Apostolorum* (Zürich: EVZ-Verlag, 1967), pp. 23, 59; ibid, 'Kirche in Erneuerung', ibid and Hans Urs von Balthasar, *Einheit und Erneuerung der Kirche* (Freiburg/Schweiz: Paulusverlag, 1968), pp. 9–18, 13.

[4] Cf. Santiago Madrigal, 'K. Barth, A las puertas de San Pedro', in *Memoria del Concilio*.

of the increased importance it clearly allotted to Holy Scripture.[5] While the First Vatican Council emphasized the place and importance of natural theology, the historical revelation of God as witnessed to in Scripture was not given a central position. In this way, the Council was only expressing in words what was already thought in Catholic theology, a claim which should now be developed more fully.

Catholic Theology and Karl Barth

A timeless metaphysics lies behind the Neo-Scholasticism which came to be, for all intents and purposes, the dominant form of Catholic theology in the nineteenth century (and not least because of the assistance offered to it by the Church's magisterium). A *philosophia perennis* was encouraged in the face of the modern awareness of history, for modern historical understanding ties truth claims to their original context and thus qualifies their absoluteness, a strategy which seems to endanger faith.[6] Yet the more the historical boundedness of Neo-Scholasticism itself came into view, the less it was able to hold on to its monopoly. If Neo-Scholasticism had already fragmented in the decades prior to Vatican II, it simply disappeared in the wake of the Council.[7] The ascending historical focus plunged Catholic theology into a crisis with which it has been plagued ever since. The issue of historical understanding within theology is still under debate and its outcome seems to be completely open.[8]

Diez evocaciones del Vaticano II (Madrid: Desclée de Brouwer, 2005), pp. 277–96; Gilles Routhier, 'L'ombre de Karl Barth à Vatican II', *Etudes Théologiques et Religieuses* 86 (2011), pp. 1–24.
[5] Cf. Barth (1967), 58–9.
[6] Cf. Gerald McCool, *Catholic Theology in the Nineteenth Century. The Quest for a Unitary Method* (New York: Seabury, 1977); Georg Essen, '"es wackelt alles!" Modernes Geschichtsbewusstsein als Krisis katholischer Theologie im 19. und 20. Jahrhundert', *Cristianesimo nella Storia* 22 (2001), pp. 565–604.
[7] Michel Fourcade, 'Thomisme et antithomisme à l'heure de Vatican II', *RevThom* 108 (2008), pp. 301–25 clarifies the internal and external factors which played a part in the replacing of Neo-Scholasticism.
[8] Cf. Gianfranco Coffele, 'Storia della teologia', in *La Teologia del XX secolo. Un bilancio*, ed. Giacomo Canobbio and Piero Coda, vol. 1 (Rom: Città Nuova, 2003), pp. 249–325; John M. McDermott, 'The Path and Progress of Twentieth-Century Catholic Theology', *Josephinum Journal of Theology* 15 (2008), pp. 11–42. We should also take into account the conclusion of Bernard Lonergan, *Method in Theology* (London: Darton, Longman & Todd, 1972), p. 281: 'The era dominated by Scholasticism has ended. Catholic theology is being reconstructed.' For an overview on the often divergent approaches in contemporary Catholic systematics cf. *Wozu Fundamentaltheologie? Zur Grundlegung der Theologie im Anspruch von Glaube und Vernunft*, ed. Josef Meyer zu Schlochtern and Roman A. Siebenrock (Paderborn et al.: Schöningh, 2010).

SUMMARY

The period considered in this study thus represents a phase of transition. If the majority of theologians were still influenced by Neo-Scholasticism – one reason why Barth's completely different way of thinking remained foreign to them – a few not only became aware of Barth's work, but made it their own as well. In this connexion, special mention must be made of Gottlieb Söhngen and Hans Urs von Balthasar who, from their study of the *Church Dogmatics*, gleaned insights for a theology not based on some timeless metaphysics.[9] The emphasis upon salvation history ('Heilsgeschichte') and, in turn, upon a theology centred on Christ, which they propagated, was to leave its mark on Catholic dogmatics in the second half of the twentieth century. Thus it is no exaggeration if we understand the Catholic reception of Barth as a stimulus for the renewal of Catholic theology in the time leading up to Vatican II. Indeed, one might examine whether and to what extent Barth's thinking actually influenced individual documents of the Council, particularly *Dei Verbum* and *Lumen Gentium*.[10] We should also note, however, that some theologians who eventually did cross the standard theological frontiers, such as the unique Anselm Stolz and Erich Przywara, do not fit into this narrative. Although they had also distanced themselves from Neo-Scholasticism, they could only engage with Barth's theology in a highly limited fashion.[11]

Barth's work was also studied intensively on the Catholic side after the period covered here, a situation which continues even up until the present. Yet the context of Catholic theology has, to state the obvious, changed considerably, as what is at stake is no longer the renewal of Catholic thought in the face of the fossilization of Neo-Scholasticism, but of its reconstruction in the light of the problems modernity presents and the apparent arbitrariness of post-modernism. Barth now offers his services as a debating partner for very different reasons, not least because of the fact that he recalls theology to its particular and genuine task:

> [I]s there not even in the field of scholarship a great deal of so-called work, e.g., the effort put into examinations for examinations' sake in one's best years, or the work done on the conveyor belt which brings

---

[9] Cf. Chapter 5.5 or Chapters 6–9.
[10] Helpful here are the remarks of John Yoccum, 'What's Interesting about Karl Barth? Barth as Polemical and Descriptive Theologian', *International Journal of Systematic Theology* 4 (2002), pp. 29–44, 38: 'It would be far too simplistic to ascribe these developments to Barth's impact, but some of the key figures in twentieth century Catholic theology – von Balthasar, Congar, Daniélou, Rahner, to mention some of the most important – acknowledge a large debt to Barth.'
[11] Cf. Chapter 4.3, Chapter 1.4 or Chapter 5.6.

up a constant stream of dissertations from the libraries only to return them, and sometimes finally, to the same shelves, or a proportion of literary labour, which is obviously designed and undertaken for the sake of some return, but which does not contribute quite so obviously to the true well-being of man.[12]

---

[12] CD III/4, p. 531, a translation of KD III/4 (1951), p. 609.

BIBLIOGRAPHY

Abbreviations

Cath(M): Catholica
CD (1927): Barth (1927)
DH: *Enchiridion symbolorum definitionum et declarationum de rebus fidei et morum*, ed. Heinrich Denzinger, revised by Peter Hünermann (Freiburg i.Br. et al.: Herder, [39]2001).
DT: Divus Thomas
KD I–IV (1932–1967): Barth (1932–1967)
NZSTh: Neue Zeitschrift für Systematische Theologie
RB (1922): Barth (1922)
StZ: Stimmen der Zeit
ZDT: Zeitschrift für dialektische Theologie

Unpublished Sources

With permission of the 'Nachlaßkommission', unpublished sources from the Karl Barth-Archiv (Basle) were used. The documents are quoted as KBA. Thanks are due to Dr. Hans-Anton Drewes, the archive's director.

Primary Literature

Adam, K. (1926a), 'Die Theologie der Krisis'. *Hochland*, 23, (2), 271–86.
—(1926b), 'Karl Heim und das Wesen des Katholizismus'. *Hochland*, 23, (2), 447–69, 586–608.
Allers, R. (1936), *Anselm von Canterbury. Leben, Lehre, Werke*. Vienna: Thomas-Verlag Jakob Hegner.
Balthasar, H. U. von, *Geschichte des eschatologischen Problems in der modernen deutschen Literatur. Abhandlung zur Erlangung der Doktorwürde der Philosophischen Fakultät I der Universität Zürich* (Zürich 1930). Reissued as *Geschichte des eschatologischen Problems in der modernen deutschen Literatur*. Freiburg i.Br.: Johannes, 1998.
—(1933), 'Die Metaphysik Erich Przywaras'. *Schweizerische Rundschau*, 33, 489–99.
—(1937–1939), *Apokalypse der deutschen Seele. Studien zu einer Lehre von letzten Haltungen*, 3 vols. Salzburg and Leipzig: Pustet.

BIBLIOGRAPHY

—(1938), 'Die Krisis der protestantischen Theologie'. *StZ*, 134, 200–1.
—(1938; F. 2, 1939), 'Karl Barth und der Katholizismus'. *Der Seelsorger – Beiheft*, 3, 126–32.
—(1939), Untitled review article. *ZKT*, 63, 371–9.
—(1944), 'Analogie und Dialektik. Zur Klärung der theologischen Prinzipienlehre Karl Barths' *DT*, 22, 171–216.
—(1945), 'Analogie und Natur. Zur Klärung der theologischen Prinzipienlehre Karl Barths', *DT*, 23, 3–56.
—(1990), 'Es stellt sich vor: Hans Urs von Balthasar' [1945], in *Mein Werk. Durchblicke*. Einsiedeln and Freiburg i.Br.: Johannes, pp. 9–14.
—(1949), 'Drei Merkmale des Christlichen', *Wort und Wahrheit*, 4, 401–15.
—(1951), *Karl Barth. Darstellung und Deutung seiner Theologie*. Cologne: Hegner. [English translation: *The Theology of Karl Barth. Exposition and Interpretation*, trans. Edward T. Oakes (San Francisco: Ignatius Press, 1992)].
—(1952), *Schleifung der Bastionen. Von der Kirche in dieser Zeit*. Einsiedeln: Johannes. [English translation: *Razing the Bastions. On the Church in this Age*, trans. Brian McNeil (San Francisco: Ignatius Press, 1993)].
—(1953), 'Thomas von Aquin im kirchlichen Denken heute'. *Gloria Dei*, 8, 65–76.
—(1953), 'Was soll Theologie? Ihr Ort und ihre Gestalt im Leben der Kirche'. *Wort und Wahrheit*, 8, 325–32.
—(1957), 'Eschatologie', in J. Feiner et al. (ed.), *Fragen der Theologie heute*. Einsiedeln et al.: Benziger, pp. 403–21.
—(1961), *Herrlichkeit. Eine theologische Ästhetik*, vol. 1. Einsiedeln: Johannes.
—(1962), *Karl Barth. Darstellung und Deutung seiner Theologie*. Cologne: Hegner.
—(1963), *Glaubhaft ist nur Liebe*. Einsiedeln: Johannes.
—(1965), *Herrlichkeit. Eine theologische Ästhetik*, vol. 3/1,1. Einsiedeln: Johannes.
—(1965), *Rechenschaft 1965*. Einsiedeln: Johannes.
—(1966), *Cordula oder der Ernstfall*. Einsiedeln: Johannes.
—(1968), 'Einigung in Christus [...]', ibid and K. Barth, *Einheit und Erneuerung der Kirche*. Freiburg/Schweiz: Paulusverlag, pp. 19–37.
—(1974), *Der antirömische Affekt*. Freiburg i.Br. et al.: Herder.
—(1981), 'The anti-Roman attitude'. *Communio: International Catholic Review*, 8, 307–21.
—(1984), *Unser Auftrag. Bericht und Entwurf*. Einsiedeln: Johannes.
—(1989), 'Versuch eines Durchblicks durch mein Denken'. *Internationale katholische Zeitschrift Communio*, 18, 289–93.
Balthasar, H. U. von and Barth, K. (1968), *Einheit und Erneuerung der Kirche*. Freiburg/Schweiz: Paulusverlag.
Balthasar, H. U. von and Gutwenger, E. (1953), 'Der Begriff der Natur in der Theologie. Eine Diskussion zwischen Hans Urs von Balthasar, Zürich, und Engelbert Gutwenger S.J., Innsbruck'. *ZKT*, 75, 452–64.
Barth, K. (1919), *Der Römerbrief*. Bern: Bäschlin.
—(1922), *Der Römerbrief*. Munich: Kaiser.
—(1927), *Die christliche Dogmatik im Entwurf*, vol. 1. Munich: Kaiser.
—(1927), 'Der Begriff der Kirche', *Zwischen den Zeiten*, 5, 365–78.
—(1931), *Fides quaerens intellectum. Anselms Beweis der Existenz Gottes im Zusammenhang seines theologischen Programms*. Munich: Kaiser.

BIBLIOGRAPHY

—(1932–1967), *Die Kirchliche Dogmatik*, 4 vols in 13. Munich et al.: Kaiser et al. [English translation: *Church Dogmatics*, trans. Thomas F. Torrance et al. (Edinburgh: T & T Clark)].

—(1934), *Nein! Antwort an Emil Brunner*. Munich: Kaiser.

—(1935), 'Das Evangelium in der Gegenwart', in *Das Evangelium in der Gegenwart*. Munich: Kaiser, pp. 18–36.

—(1935), *Die Kirche und die Kirchen*. Munich: Kaiser.

—(1935), *Credo* [...]. Munich: Kaiser.

—(1938), *Gotteserkenntnis und Gottesdienst nach reformatorischer Lehre* [...]. Zollikon: Verlag der Evangelischen Buchhandlung Zollikon [English translation: *The Knowledge of God and the Service of God according to the Teaching of the Reformation* (London: Hodder and Stoughton,[3]1955)].

—(1947), *Die protestantische Theologie im 19. Jahrhundert. Ihre Vorgeschichte und ihre Geschichte*. Zollikon and Zürich: Evangelischer Verlag.

—(1948/1949), 'Parergon', *EvT*, 8, 268–82.

—(1956), *Die Menschlichkeit Gottes*. Zollikon and Zürich: Evangelischer Verlag.

—(1957), 'Ein Brief an den Verfasser', in Küng, H., Rechtfertigung. Die Lehre Karl Barths und eine katholische Besinnung. Einsiedeln: Johannes, pp. 11–14.

—(1958), *Fides quaerens intellectum. Anselms Beweis der Existenz Gottes im Zusammenhang seines theologischen Programms*. Zollikon: Evangelischer Verlag.

—(1960), 'How my mind has changed'. *EvT*, 20, 97–106.

—(1967), *Ad Limina Apostolorum*. Zürich: EVZ-Verlag.

—(1968), 'Kirche in Erneuerung', ibid and H. U. von Balthasar, *Einheit und Erneuerung der Kirche*. Freiburg/Schweiz: Paulusverlag, pp. 9–18.

—(1974), 'Karl Barth – Eduard Thurneysen. Briefwechsel', vol. 2, ed. E. Thurneysen, *Gesamtausgabe V. Briefe*. Zürich: Theologischer Verlag Zürich.

—(1997), 'Karl Barth. Gespräche 1964–1968', ed. E. Busch, *Gesamtausgabe IV. Gespräche*. Zürich: Theologischer Verlag Zürich.

—(2000), 'Karl Barth – Eduard Thurneysen. Briefwechsel', vol. 3, in C. Algner (ed.), *Gesamtausgabe V. Briefe*. Zürich: Theologischer Verlag Zürich.

—(2004), 'Briefe des Jahres 1933', ed. E. Busch, Zürich: Theologischer Verlag Zürich.

—(2008), 'Karl Barth – Charlotte von Kirschbaum. Briefwechsel', vol. 1, ed. R.-J. Erler, *Gesamtausgabe V. Briefe*. Zürich: Theologischer Verlag Zürich.

—(2010), 'Der Römerbrief', ed. C. van der Kooi, *Gesamtausgabe II. Akademische Werke*. Zürich: Theologischer Verlag Zürich.

Bartmann, B. (1928), *Lehrbuch der Dogmatik*, 2 vols. Freiburg i.Br. et al.: Herder.

—(1932), *Lehrbuch der Dogmatik*, vol. 2. Freiburg i.Br.: Herder.

—(1934), 'Die Dogmatik von Karl Barth'. *TGl*, 26, 205–13.

Bauhofer, O. (1932/1933), 'Katholische Tendenzen im Protestantismus?', *Schweizerische Rundschau*, 32, 562–4.

—(1933), 'Dialektik oder Theologie'. *Cath(M)*, 2, 49–60.

Bouillard, H. (1957), *Karl Barth*, 3 vols. Paris: Aubier

Brinktrine, J. (1953), *Die Lehre von Gott*, vol. 1. Paderborn: Schöningh.

Brugger, W. (1959), *Theologia Naturalis*. Pullach: Berchmanskolleg Verlag.

Cappuyns, Maieul. (1934), 'L'argument de saint Anselme'. *Recherches de Théologie Ancienne et Médiévale*, 6, 313–30.

BIBLIOGRAPHY

Congar, Y. (1948), 'Barth', *Catholicisme*, 1, 1267–8.
Deneffe, A. (1932), 'Review of Barth (1931)'. *Scholastik*, 7, 608.
Diekamp, F. (1930), *Katholische Dogmatik nach den Grundsätzen des heiligen Thomas*, 3 vols. Münster: Aschendorff.
—(1938), *Katholische Dogmatik nach den Grundsätzen des heiligen Thomas*, vol. 1. Münster: Aschendorff.
Engert, J. (1923/1924), 'Metaphysik und Historismus im Christentum'. *Hochland*, 21, (1), 502–17, 638–51.
—(1926), *Studien zur theologischen Erkenntnislehre*. Regensburg: Manz.
Fehr, J. (1936a), 'Der Weg zur dialektischen Theologie'. *DT*, 14, 163–80.
—(1936b), 'Zweierlei Offenbarung? Gedanken zu einer protestantischen Kontroverse'. *DT*, 14, 399–420.
—(1937a), 'Die Offenbarung als ,Wort Gottes' bei Karl Barth und Thomas von Aquin'. *DT*, 15, 55–64.
—(1937b), 'Offenbarung und Analogie. Ihr Verhältnis in dialektischer und thomistischer Theologie'. *DT*, 15, 291–307.
—(1938a), 'Offenbarung und Glaube. Ihr Verhältnis in dialektischer und thomistischer Theologie'. in *DT*, 16, 15–32.
—(1938b), 'Offenbarung, Heilige Schrift und Kirche. Ihr Verhältnis in dialektischer und thomistischer Theologie'. *DT*, 16, 309–30.
—(1939b), "Offenbarungstheologie'. Eine Buchbesprechung', *DT*, 17, 99–107.
—(1939a), *Das Offenbarungsproblem in dialektischer und thomistischer Theologie*. Freiburg i.Ue. and Leipzig: Verlag der Universitätsbuchhandlung Freiburg.
—(1941), 'Karl Barths theologische und geistesgeschichtliche Bedeutung'. *Schweizerische Kirchenzeitung*, 109, 121–3, 133–6.
Feuerer, G. (1933), *Der Kirchenbegriff der dialektischen Theologie*. Freiburg i.Br.: Herder.
Feuling, D. (1934), 'Das Gotteswort der Offenbarung'. *Benediktinische Monatsschrift*, 16, 123–30.
—(1936), *Hauptfragen der Metaphysik. Einführung in das philosophische Leben*. Salzburg and Leipzig: Pustet.
Geiselmann, J. R. (1930), 'Dialektische Theologie'. *LTK* 3, 279–82.
Getzeny, H. (1931), 'Strömungen in der protestantischen Theologie der Gegenwart'. *Der katholische Gedanke*, 4, 43–57.
Gierens, M. (1930), 'Die "dialektische Theologie" in katholischer Sicht'. *StZ*, 118, 196–206.
Gilson, É. (1934), 'Sens et nature de l'argument de saint Anselme'. *Archives d'Histoire doctrinale et littéraire du Moyen Âge*, 9, 5–51.
Groot, J. C. (1946), *Karl Barth en het theologische Kenprobleem*. Heiloo: Kinheim.
Grosche, R. (1926), *Der Kolosserbrief in Homilien erklärt*. Paderborn: Schöningh.
—(1930), *Wenn du die Gabe Gottes kenntest*. Frankfurt a.M.: Verlag der Carolus-Druckerei.
—(1930), 'Augustin und die dialektische Theologie. Eine Auseinandersetzung mit Karl Barth'. *Akademische Bonifatius-Korrespondenz*, 45, 86–98.
—(1932), 'Die dialektische Theologie und der Katholizismus'. *Cath(M)*, 1, 1–18.
—(1932), 'Die katholisch-protestantische Auseinandersetzung'. *Cath(M)*, 1, 96.
—(1932), 'Evangelisches Denken und Katholizismus'. *Cath(M)*, 1, 191–3.
—(1933), 'Fünf Thesen zur Mariologie'. *Cath(M)*, 2, 24–42.

BIBLIOGRAPHY

—(1935), 'Simul peccator et iustus. Bemerkungen zu einer theologischen Formel'. *Cath(M)*, 4, 132–9.
—(1935), 'Karl Barth und die Analogia entis'. *Cath(M)*, 4, 185–6.
—(1938), *Pilgernde Kirche*. Freiburg i.Br.: Herder.
—(1939), 'Zum Gespräch zwischen den Konfessionen'. *Cath(M)*, 8, 85–6.
—(1952), 'Zum Wiedererscheinen der Catholica'. *Cath(M)*, 9, 1–3.
—(1958), *Et intra et extra. Theologische Aufsätze*. Düsseldorf: Patmos.
Haecker, T. (1934), 'Analogia trinitatis'. *Hochland*, 31, (2), 499–510.
—(1934), *Schöpfer und Schöpfung*. Leipzig: Hegner.
Hamer, J. (1949), *Karl Barth. L'occasionalisme théologique de Karl Barth. Étude sur sa methode dogmatique*. Paris: Desclée.
Heinrichs, M. (1954), *Theses Dogmaticae*, vol. 2. Hong Kong: Studium Biblicum O.F.M.
Hessen, J. (1937), *Die Geistesströmungen der Gegenwart*. Freiburg i.Br.: Herder.
Keller, H. (1932), 'Review of KD I/1 (1932)'. *Benediktinische Monatsschrift*, 14, 324–5.
Kolping, A. (1939), *Anselms Proslogion-Beweis der Existenz Gottes. Im Zusammenhang seines spekulativen Programms* Fides quaerens intellectum. Bonn: Hanstein.
Küng, H. (1957), *Rechtfertigung. Die Lehre Karl Barths und eine katholische Besinnung*. Einsiedeln: Johannes.
—(1957), 'Ist in der Rechtfertigungslehre eine Einigung möglich?'. *Una Sancta*, 12, 116–21.
—(1962), 'Karl Barths Lehre vom Wort Gottes als Frage an die katholische Theologie', in H. Fries and J. Ratzinger (ed.), *Einsicht und Glaube*, Festschrift Gottlieb Söhngen. Freiburg i.Br. et al.: Herder, pp. 75–97.
—(1967), 'Katholische Besinnung auf Luthers Rechtfertigungslehre heute', in Joseph Möller et al., *Theologie im Wandel*. Munich et al.: Wewel, pp. 449–68.
—(1969), 'Ansprache', in *Karl Barth 1886–1968. Gedenkfeier im Basler Münster*. Zürich: EVZ-Verlag, pp. 43–6.
—(2002), *Erkämpfte Freiheit. Erinnerungen*. Munich and Zürich: Piper.
—(2007), *Umstrittene Wahrheit. Erinnerungen*. Munich and Zürich: Piper.
Nigg, W. (1939), 'Review of Fehr (1939a)'. *Neue Zürcher Zeitung* (25 October, 1939).
Pohle, J. (1931–1933), *Lehrbuch der Dogmatik*, ed. M. Gierens, 3 vols. Paderborn: Schöningh.
—(1952), *Lehrbuch der Dogmatik*, ed. J. Gummersbach, vol. 1. Paderborn: Schöningh.
Pribilla, M. (1935), 'Nach vierhundert Jahren'. *StZ*, 129, 155–68.
Przywara, E. (1923), *Religionsbegründung. Max Scheler – J.H. Newman*. Freiburg i.Br.: Herder.
—(1923), 'Gott in uns oder Gott über uns? (Immanenz und Transzendenz im heutigen Geistesleben.)'. *StZ*, 105, 343–62.
—(1924), 'Ringen um Gott'. *StZ*, 107, 347–52.
—(1925), 'Neue Religiösität?'. *StZ*, 109, 18–35.
—(1926), 'Neue Theologie? Das Problem protestantischer Theologie'. *StZ*, 111, 348–60.
—(1927), *Religionsphilosophie katholischer Theologie*. Munich and Berlin: Oldenbourg.

BIBLIOGRAPHY

—(1929), 'Eschatologismus'. *StZ*, 117, 229–35.
—(1929), 'Das katholische Kirchenprinzip'. *Zwischen den Zeiten*, 7, 277–302.
—(1929), *Das Geheimnis Kierkegaards*. Munich and Berlin: Oldenbourg.
—(1930), 'Protestantismus II. Beurteilung vom Standpunkt des Katholizismus'. *RGG²*, 3, 1600–3.
—(1932), *Analogia Entis. Metaphysik*, vol. 1. Munich: Kösel and Pustet.
—(1932), 'Sein im Scheitern – Sein im Aufgang'. *StZ*, 123, 152–61.
—(1933/1934), 'Dynamismus'. *StZ*, 126, 155–68.
—(1935), 'Religiöser und weltlicher Mensch'. *StZ*, 129, 200–2.
—(1937), 'Luther konsequent'. *Scholastik*, 12, 386–92.
—(1938–1940), *Deus semper maior. Theologie der Exerzitien*, 3 vols. Freiburg i.Br.: Herder.
—(1940), 'Die Reichweite der Analogie als katholischer Grundform'. *Scholastik*, 25, 339–62, 508–32.
—(1940), 'Review of Volk (1938)'. *StZ*, 137, 132.
—(1940), 'Review of Ries (1939)'. *StZ*, 137, 132.
—(1942), 'Der Grundsatz "Gratia non destruit, sed supponit et perficit naturam"'. *Scholastik*, 17, 178–86.
—(1955), 'Um die analogia entis' [1952/1955], in *In und gegen. Stellungnahmen zur Zeit*. Nürnberg: Glock und Lutz, pp. 277–81.
Rahner, K. (1936), 'Die deutsche protestantische Christologie der Gegenwart'. *Der Seelsorger*, 1, 189–202.
—(1941), *Hörer des Wortes. Zur Grundlegung einer Religionsphilosophie*. Munich: Kösel-Pustet.
—(1960), 'Kleine Bemerkungen zum dogmatischen Traktat "De Trinitate"', in L. Lenhart (ed.), *Universitas. Dienst an Wahrheit und Leben*, Festschrift Albert Stohr, vol. 1. Mainz: Grünewald, pp. 130–50.
—(1997), *Sämtliche Werke*, vol. 4. Solothurn et al.: Benziger and Herder.
Ries, J. (1939), *Die natürliche Gotteserkenntnis in der Theologie der Krisis im Zusammenhang mit dem Imagobegriff bei Calvin*. Bonn: Hanstein.
Rintelen, F. M. (1934), *Wege zu Gott. Eine kritische Abhandlung über das Problem des Gotterfassens in der deutschen protestantischen Theologie der Nachkriegszeit*. Würzburg: Becker.
—(1935), 'Das Verhängnis der protestantischen Theologie'. *TGl*, 27, 453–65.
—(1942), 'Der Römerbrief" und "Das Evangelium'. *TGl*, 34, 330–3.
—(1983), *Erinnerungen ohne Tagebuch*. Paderborn: Bonifatius.
Rosenmöller, B. (1933), 'Katholische Kontroverstheologie'. *Cath(M)*, 2, 48.
Schmaus, M. (1951), *Katholische Dogmatik*, vol. 3, 2. Munich: Hueber.
—(1960), *Katholische Dogmatik*, vol. 1. Munich: Hueber.
Schmitt, F. S. (1933), 'Der ontologische Gottesbeweis Anselms'. *TRev*, 32, 217–23.
—(1957), 'Anselm v. Canterbury'. *LTK²*, 1, 592–4.
—(1972), 'Der ontologische Gottesbeweis und Anselm'. *Analecta Anselmiana*, 3, 81–94.
Söhngen, G. (1932), 'Die katholische Theologie als Wissenschaft und als Weisheit'. *Cath(M)*, 1, 49–69.
—(1934), 'Analogia entis: Gottähnlichkeit allein aus Glauben?'. *Cath(M)*, 3, 113–36.
—(1934), 'Analogia entis: Die Einheit in der Glaubenswissenschaft'. *Cath(M)*, 3, 176–208.
—(1935), 'Bonaventura als Klassiker der analogia fidei'. *Wissenschaft und Weisheit*, 2, 97–111.

—(1935), 'Natürliche Theologie und Heilsgeschichte. Antwort an Emil Brunner'. *Cath(M)*, 4, 97–114.
—(1935), 'Wunderzeichen und Glaube. Biblische Grundlegung der katholischen Apologetik'. *Cath(M)*, 4, 145–64.
—(1936), 'Philosophie'. *LTK*, 8, 244–7.
—(1942), 'Analogia entis oder analogia fidei?'. *Wissenschaft und Weisheit*, 9, 91–100.
—(1956), 'Analogia entis in analogia fidei', in Ernst Wolf et al., *Antwort*, Festschrift Karl Barth. Zollikon and Zürich: Evangelischer Verlag, pp. 266–71.
—(1962), 'Natürliche Theologie. I. Im katholischen Verständnis'. *LTK*², 7, 811–6.
—(1962), 'Neuscholastik'. *LTK*², 7, 923–6.
—(1965), 'Die Weisheit der Theologie durch den Weg der Wissenschaft', in J. Feiner and M. Löhrer (ed.), *Mysterium Salutis. Grundriss heilsgeschichtlicher Dogmatik*, vol. 1. Einsiedeln et al.: Benzinger, pp. 905–80.
Stolz, A. (1932), 'Review of Barth (1931)', *DT*, 10, 560–1.
—(1933), 'Zur Theologie Anselms im Proslogion'. *Cath(M)*, 2, 1–24.
—(1934), '"Vere esse" im Proslogion des hl. Anselm'. *Scholastik*, 9, 400–9.
—(1935), 'Das Proslogion des hl. Anselm'. *RBén*, 47, 331–47.
—(1936), *Theologie der Mystik*. Regensburg: Pustet.
—(1937), 'Einleitung', in *Anselm von Canterbury*. Munich: Kösel-Pustet. pp. 7–43.
—(1939–1943), *Manuale theologiae dogmaticae*, 6 vols. Freiburg i.Br.: Herder.
Tanner, W. (1940), 'Review of Fehr (1939a)', *Kirchenblatt für die reformierte Schweiz*, 96, 26–9.
Volk, H. (1938), *Die Kreaturauffassung bei Karl Barth. Eine philosophische Untersuchung*. Würzburg: Becker.
—(1939), *Emil Brunners Lehre von der ursprünglichen Gottebenbildlichkeit des Menschen*. Emsdetten: Lechte.
—(1940), Review of Ries (1939). *TRev*, 39, 215–17.
—(1950), *Emil Brunners Lehre von dem Sünder* [1943]. Münster: Regensberg.
Walkenbach, A. (1955) *Der Glaube bei Karl Barth. Dargestellt im Licht seiner kirchlichen Dogmatik* [1949]. Limburg: Lahn-Verlag.
Weisweiler, H. (1933), 'Review of KD I/1 (1932)', *Scholastik*, 8, 599–601.
—(1939), 'Natur und Übernatur in Glaube und Theologie'. *Scholastik*, 14, 346–72.
Wittig, J. (1922), 'Die Erlösten'. *Hochland*, 19, (2), 1–26.
—(1923/1924), 'Neue religiöse Bücher'. *Hochland*, 21, (1), 415–30.
Wyser, P. (1941), 'Review of Fehr (1939a)', *DT*, 19, 332–40.

Secondary Literature

Adam, K. (1924), *Das Wesen des Katholizismus*. Augsburg: Haas und Grabherr.
Alfaro, J. (1952), *Lo natural y lo sobrenatural. Estudio histórico desde santo Tomás hasta Cayetano (1274–1534)*. Madrid: Consejo Superior de Investigaciones Cientificas.
'Allers, Rudolf' (1995), in *Deutsche Biographische Enzyklopädie*, 1, 91.
Alston, W. P. (2005), 'Religious Language', in W. J. Wainwright (ed.), *The Oxford Handbook of Philosophy of Religion*. Oxford et al.: Oxford University Press, pp. 220–44.
Ameriks, K. (2006), *Kant and the Historical Turn. Philosophy as Critical Interpretation*. Oxford: Clarendon Press.

BIBLIOGRAPHY

Arnold, C. (2010), 'Internal church reform in catholic Germany', in J. van Eijnatten and P. Yates (ed.), *The Churches*. Leuven: Leuven University Press, pp. 159–84, 215–21.

Avon, D. (2005), 'Une école théologique à Fourvière?', in É. Fouilloux and B. Hours (ed.), *Les jésuites à Lyon. XVIe–XX^{e}siècle*. Lyons: ENS Editions, pp. 231–46.

Axt-Piscalar, C. (2006), 'Kontinuität oder Abbruch? Karl Barths Prolegomena zur Dogmatik im Lichte der Theologie des 19. Jahrhunderts – eine Skizze', TZ, 62, 433–51.

Batlogg, A. R. (2003), 'Vom Mut, Jesus um den Hals zu fallen. Christologie', ibid *Der Denkweg Karl Rahners. Quellen - Entwicklungen - Perspektiven*. Mainz: Grünewald. et al., pp. 277–99.

— (2005), 'Hans Urs von Balthasar und Karl Rahner: zwei Schüler des Ignatius', in M. Striet and J.-H. Tück (ed.), *Die Kunst Gottes verstehen. Hans Urs von Balthasars theologische Provokationen*. Freiburg i.Br. et al.: Herder, pp. 410–46.

Batlogg, A. R. et al. (2003), *Der Denkweg Karl Rahners. Quellen – Entwicklungen – Perspektiven*. Mainz: Grünewald.

Bauer, E. J. (1990), 'Bernhard Rosenmoeller (1883–1974)', in E. Coreth et al. (ed.), *Christliche Philosophie im katholischen Denken des 19. und 20. Jahrhunderts*, vol. 3. Graz et al.: Styria, pp. 159–71.

Bauhofer, O. (1938), 'Bemerkungen zu Emil Brunners Christlicher Anthropologie', StZ, 134, 327–31.

Beintker, M. et al. (ed.), (2005), *Karl Barth in Deutschland (1921–1935). Aufbruch – Klärung – Widerstand [...]*. Zürich: Theologischer Verlag Zürich.

Berkhof, L. (1932), *Reformed Dogmatics*, vol. 1. Grand Rapids, MI: Eerdmans.

Betz, J. R. (2005, 2006), 'Beyond the Sublime: The Aesthetics of the analogia entis', *Modern Theology*, 21, 367–411 and 22, 1–50.

Beutel, A. (2009), *Kirchengeschichte im Zeitalter der Aufklärung. Ein Kompendium*. Göttingen: Vandenhoeck und Ruprecht.

Bieler, M. (2006), 'Die kleine Drehung. Hans Urs von Balthasar und Karl Barth im Gespräch', in W. Kasper (ed.), *Logik der Liebe und Herrlichkeit Gottes. Hans Urs von Balthasar im Gespräch, Festschrift Karl Lehmann*, Mainz: Grünewald, pp. 318–38.

Bonhoeffer, D. (1931), *Akt und Sein. Transzendentalphilosophie und Ontologie in der systematischen Theologie*. Gütersloh: Bertelsmann.

Bouillard, H. (1964), *Logique de la foi [...]*. Paris: Aubier.

Bourgine, B. (2008), 'Die Rezeption der Hermeneutik Barths in der katholischen Theologie Frankreichs und Belgiens', in M. Leiner and M. Trowitzsch (ed.), *Karl Barths Theologie als europäisches Ereignis*. Göttingen: Vandenhoeck und Ruprecht, pp. 30–47.

Braaten, C. E. (1990), *Justification. The Article by Which the Church Stands or Falls*. Minneapolis, MN: Augsburg Fortress.

Brazier, P. (2005), 'Barth and Rome. A Critical engagement with Catholic thinkers'. *Downside Review*, 123, 137–52.

Bressan, F. (2001), 'Alla ricerca della figura spirituale della teologia e del teologo: l'Introductio in *Sacram Theologiam* di Anselm Stolz o.s.b. (1900–1942)'. *Benedictina*, 48, 61–96.

Brinktrine, J. (1938), *Offenbarung und Kirche. Fundamental-theologische Vorlesungen*, vol. 1. Paderborn: Schöningh.

BIBLIOGRAPHY

Brodkorb, C. (2002), 'Rintelen, Friedrich Maria', in E. Gatz (ed.), *Die Bischöfe der deutschsprachigen Länder 1945–2001*. Berlin: Duncker und Humblot, pp. 347–9.

Bromiley, G. (1988), 'The Influence of Barth after World War II', in N. Biggar (ed.), *Reckoning with Barth* [...]. Oxford: Mowbray, pp. 9–23.

Bruch, R. (1956), 'Das Verhältnis von Natur und Übernatur nach der Auffassung der neueren Theologie'. *TGl*, 46, 81–102.

Brunner, P. (1959), 'Trennt die Rechtfertigungslehre die Konfessionen? Neue Wege in der Kontroverstheologie'. *Die neue Furche*, 30, 524–36.

—(1959), 'Rechtfertigung und Kircheneinheit. Katholisches Dogma, lutherisches Bekenntnis und Karl Barth'. *Die neue Furche*, 30, 594–608.

Buckley, J. J. (1995), 'Balthasar's use of the Theology of Aquinas'. *The Thomist*, 59, 517–45.

Burkard, D., (2006), '... Unam Sanctam (Catholicam?). Zur theologiegeschichtlichen Verortung des Ökumenismusdekrets "Unitatis redintegratio" aus der Sicht des Kirchenhistorikers', in T. Franz and H. Sauer (ed.), *Glaube in der Welt von heute. Theologie und Kirche nach dem Zweiten Vatikanischen Konzil*, Festschrift Elmar Klinger vol. 1. Würzburg: Echter, pp. 57–109.

Busch, E. (1975), *Karl Barths Lebenslauf. Nach seinen Briefen und autobiographischen Texten*. Munich: Kaiser.

—(1986), 'God is God. The Meaning of a Controversial Formula and the Fundamental Problem of Speaking about God'. *Princeton Seminary Bulletin*, 7, 101–13.

—(1995), 'Weg und Werk Karl Barths in der neueren Forschung'. *TRu*, 60, 273–99, 430–70.

Busch, E. et al. (1966), *Parrhesia*, Festschrift Karl Barth. Zürich: EVZ-Verlag.

Castro, M. (2007), 'La rencontre de Henri Bouillard avec Karl Barth et la relation de l'homme à Dieu'. *Greg*, 88, 512–32.

Chalamet, C. (2005), *Dialectical Theologians. Wilhelm Herrmann, Karl Barth and Rudolf Bultmann*. Zürich: Theologischer Verlag Zürich.

—(2008), 'Est Deus in Nobis? Die frühen Jahre der Barth-Przywara-Debatte', in M. Leiner and M. Trowitzsch (ed.), *Karl Barths Theologie als europäisches Ereignis*. Göttingen: Vandenhoeck und Ruprecht, pp. 271–90.

Chantraine, G. (1997), 'La théologie du Surnaturel selon Henri de Lubac'. *NRT*, 119, 218–35.

Coffele, G. (2003), 'Storia della teologia', in G. Canobbio and P. Coda (ed.), *La Teologia del XX secolo. Un bilancio*, vol. 1. Rom: Città Nuova, pp. 249–325.

Congar, Y. (1937), *Chrétiens désunis. Principes d'un 'œcuménisme' catholique*. Paris: Cerf.

Cortez, M. (2007), 'What does it mean to call Karl Barth a "christocentric" theologian?'. *SJT*, 60, 127–43.

Dahlke, B. (2009), 'Karl Barth und der Katholizismus. Zu einer komplexen Beziehung'. *Brixner Theologisches Forum*, 120, (2), 22–37.

—(2010), *Die katholische Rezeption Karl Barths. Theologische Erneuerung im Vorfeld des Zweiten Vatikanischen Konzils*. Tübingen: Mohr Siebeck.

—(2010), 'Das Zerbrechen der Dialektischen Theologie in katholischer Sicht'. *Cath(M)*, 64, 67–78.

—(2011), 'Karl Barth und die Erneuerung der katholischen Theologie', in *Jahrbuch der Akademie der Wissenschaften zu Göttingen (2010)*. Berlin and New York: Walter de Gruyter, pp. 201–6.

BIBLIOGRAPHY

—(2011), '"Wahr-nehmung göttlichen Erscheinens"? Rückfragen an Hans Urs von Balthasars theologische Ästhetik'. *TTZ*, 120, 269–82.

Daniélou, J. (1946), 'Les orientations présentes de la pensée religieuse'. *Études*, 249, 5–21.

Delgado, M. (ed.) (2000), *Das Christentum der Theologen im 20. Jahrhundert. Vom 'Wesen des Christentums' zu den 'Kurzformeln des Glaubens'*. Stuttgart: Kohlhammer.

Desmazières, A. (2005), 'Le sens d'une soumission. La réception française de l'encyclique *Humani generis* (1950–1951)'. *RevThom*, 105, 273–306.

Diekamp, F. (1930), *Katholische Dogmatik nach den Grundsätzen des heiligen Thomas*, 3 vols. Münster: Aschendorff.

Dierken, J. (2005), 'Karl Barth (1886–1968)', in F. W. Graf (ed.), *Klassiker der Theologie*, vol. 2. Munich: Beck pp. 223–57.

Donneaud, H. (2003), 'Une école thomiste en sa tradition contemporaine. XIXe–XXe siècles', in S.-T. Bonino et al.: *Thomistes ou de l'actualité de saint Thomas d'Aquin*. Paris: Parole et Silence, pp. 255–64.

Dorrien, G. (2000), *The Barthian revolt in modern theology. Theology without weapons*. Louisville, KY: Westminster John Knox Press.

Drewes, H.-A. (2005), 'Karl Barth und Hans Urs von Balthasar – ein Basler Zwiegespräch', in M. Striet and J.-H. Tück (ed.), *Die Kunst Gottes verstehen. Hans Urs von Balthasars theologische Provokationen*. Freiburg i.Br. et al.: Herder, pp. 367–83.

Duffy, S. J. (2005), 'Experience of grace', in D. Marmion and M. E. Hines (ed.), *The Cambridge Companion to Karl Rahner*. Cambridge et al.: Cambridge University Press, pp. 43–62.

Dupré, L. (2000), 'Philosophy and the Natural Desire for God. An Historical Reflection'. *International Philosophical Quarterly*, 40, 141–8.

Engelbert, P. (1988), *Geschichte des Benediktinerkollegs St. Anselm in Rom* [...]. Rom: Pontificio Ateneo S. Anselmo.

Ernesti, J. (2007), *Ökumene im Dritten Reich*. Paderborn: Bonifatius.

Ernesti, J. and Thönissen, W. (ed.) (2008), *Die Entdeckung der Ökumene. Zur Beteiligung der katholischen Kirche an der Ökumene*. Paderborn: Bonifatius and Frankfurt: Lembeck.

Essen, G. (2001), '"es wackelt alles!" Modernes Geschichtsbewusstsein als Krisis katholischer Theologie im 19. und 20. Jahrhundert'. *Cristianesimo nella Storia*, 22, 565–604.

Faber, E.-M. (2005), 'Künder der lebendigen Nähe des unbegreiflichen Gottes. Hans Urs von Balthasar und Erich Przywara', in M. Striet and J.-H. Tück (ed.), *Die Kunst Gottes verstehen. Hans Urs von Balthasars theologische Provokationen*. Freiburg i.Br. et al.: Herder, pp. 384–409.

Feckes, K. (1938), 'Übernatürlich'. *LTK*, 10, 354–6.

Fergusson, D. (ed.) (2010), *The Blackwell Companion to Nineteenth-Century Theology*. Oxford et al.: Blackwell-Wiley.

Figura, M. (1979), *Der Anruf der Gnade. Über die Beziehung des Menschen zu Gott nach Henri de Lubac*. Einsiedeln: Johannes.

—(2005). 'Das Geheimnis des Übernatürlichen. Hans Urs von Balthasar und Henri de Lubac', in M. Striet and J.-H. Tück (ed.), *Die Kunst Gottes verstehen. Hans Urs von Balthasars theologische Provokationen*. Freiburg i.Br. et al.: Herder, pp. 349–66.

BIBLIOGRAPHY

Fischer, N. (ed.) (2005), *Kant und der Katholizismus. Stationen einer wechselhaften Geschichte.* Freiburg i.Br. et al.: Herder.

Fisichella, R. (ed.) (1996), *Storia della teologia*, vol. 3. Rom and Bologna: Edizioni Dehoniane.

Foley, G. (1961), 'The Catholic Critics of Karl Barth in Outline and Analysis'. *SJT*, 14, 136–55.

Forster, M. (1993), 'Hegel's dialectical method', in F. C. Beiser (ed.), *The Cambridge Companion to Hegel.* Cambridge et al.: Cambridge University Press, pp. 130–70.

Fouilloux, É. (2001), 'Henri de Lubac au moment de la publication de Surnaturel'. *RevThom*, 101, 13–30.

—(2003), 'I movimenti di riforma nel pensiero cattolico dal XIX al XX secolo'. *Cristianesimo nella Storia*, 24, 659–76.

Fouilloux, É. and Hours, B. (ed.) (2005), *Les jesuites à Lyon.* Lyons: ENS Editions.

Fourcade, M. (2008), 'Thomisme et antithomisme à l'heure de Vatican II'. *RevThom*, 108, 301–25.

Frei, H. W. (1956), *The Doctrine of Revelation in the Thought of Karl Barth, 1909 to 1932. The Nature of Barth's Break with Liberalism.* PhD diss., Yale University.

—(1992), 'Five Types of Theology', in *Types of Christian Theology.* New Haven, CT and London: Yale University Press, pp. 28–55.

Garrett, S. M. (2009), 'Glancing into the Cathedral of Hans Urs von Balthasar's Theology – A Review Essay'. *Christian Scholar's Review*, 39, 91–105.

Garrigou-Lagrange, R. (1925), *De revelatione per Ecclesiam catholicam proposita*, vol. 1. Rom: Ferrari.

Geiselmann, J. R. (1940), *Johann Adam Möhler. Die Einheit der Kirche und die Wiedervereinigung der Konfessionen. Ein Beitrag zum Gespräch zwischen den Konfessionen.* Vienna: Friedrich Beck.

Gockel, M. (2006), *Barth and Schleiermacher on the Doctrine of Election. A Systematic-Theological Comparison.* Oxford et al.: Oxford University Press.

Griffiths, P. J. and Hütter, R. (ed.) (2005), *Reason and the Reasons of Faith.* London and New York: T&T Clark.

Grube, D.-M. (2007), 'God or the Subject? Karl Barth's Critique of the "Turn to the Subject"'. *NZSTh*, 50, 308–24.

—(2008), 'Analogia fidei. Zum "Analogiegeschehen" bei Karl Barth', in W. Schüßler (ed.), *Wie läßt sich über Gott sprechen? Von der negativen Theologie Plotins bis zum religiösen Sprachspiel Wittgensteins.* Darmstadt: Wissenschaftliche Buchgesellschaft, pp. 117–31.

Guerriero, E. (1993), *Hans Urs von Balthasar. Eine Monographie.* Freiburg i.Br.: Johannes.

Gunton, C. (2002), *Act and Being.* London: SCM Press.

Gutwenger, E. (1953), 'Natur und Übernatur. Gedanken zu Balthasars Werk über die Barthsche Theologie'. *ZKT*, 75, 82–97.

Hart, D. B. (2003), *The Beauty of the Infinite. The Aesthetics of Christian Truth.* Grand Rapids, MI and Cambridge: Eerdmans.

Hasenkamp, G. (1983), 'Erinnerungen an Robert Grosche. Wie es zur Gründung der CATHOLICA und zu deren Weiterführung nach dem Kriege kam'. *Cath(M)*, 37, 163–71.

BIBLIOGRAPHY

Hausberger, K. (1998), 'Der "Fall" Joseph Wittig (1879–1949)', in H. Wolf (ed.), *Antimodernismus und Modernismus in der katholischen Kirche. Beiträge zum theologiegeschichtlichen Vorfeld des II. Vatikanums*. Paderborn et al.: Schöningh, pp. 299–322.

Healy, N. J. (2005), *The Eschatology of Hans Urs von Balthasar. Being as Communion*. New York: Oxford University Press.

Hege, B. A. R. (2008), 'Liberal Theology in the Weimar Era. Schleiermacher and the Question of Religious Subjectivity in the *Methodenstreit* between Georg Wobbermin and Karl Barth'. *TZ*, 64, 33–48.

Heim, K. (1925), *Das Wesen des evangelischen Christentums*. Leipzig: Quelle und Meyer.

Heinrich, J. B. (1888), *Dogmatische Theologie*, vol. 5. Mainz: Kirchheim.

Hemming, L. P. (2004), '*Analogia non Entis sed Entitatis*. The Ontological Consequences of the Doctrine of Analogy'. *International Journal of Systematic Theology*, 6, 118–29.

Henrici, P. (2010), 'Hans Urs von Balthasar und das Zweite Vatikanische Konzil'. *Schweizerische Zeitschrift für Religions- und Kulturgeschichte*, 104, 239–50.

Herms, E. (2009), '"Neuprotestantismus". Stärken, Unklarheiten und Schwächen einer Figur geschichtlicher Selbstorientierung des evangelischen Christentums im 20. Jahrhundert'. *NZSTh*, 51, 309–39.

Hollmann, K. (1972), *Existenz und Glaube. Entwicklung und Ergebnisse der Bultmann-Diskussion in der katholischen Theologie*. Paderborn: Bonifacius-Druckerei.

Holtmann, S. (2007), *Karl Barth als Theologe der Neuzeit. Studien zur kritischen Deutung seiner Theologie*. Göttingen: Vandenhoeck und Ruprecht.

—(2008), 'Karl Barth als Theologe der Neuzeit. Die Deutungen Trutz Rendtorffs, Falk Wagners und Friedrich Wilhelm Grafs', in M. Leiner and M. Trowitzsch (ed.), *Karl Barths Theologie als europäisches Ereignis*. Göttingen: Vandenhoeck und Ruprecht, pp. 331–47.

Howard, T. A. (2006), *Protestant Theology and the Making of the Modern German University*. Oxford et al.: Oxford University Press.

Howsare, R. (2005), *Hans Urs von Balthasar and Protestantism. The Ecumenical Implications of his Theological Style*. London and New York: T&T Clark.

Hütter, R. (1999), 'Barth between McCormack and von Balthasar. A dialectic'. *Pro Ecclesia*, 8, 105–9.

—(2000), 'Karl Barth's "Dialectical Catholicity": *Sic et Non*'. *Modern Theology*, 16, 137–57.

Johnson, K. L. (2010), *Karl Barth and the Analogia Entis*. London and New York: T & T Clark.

—(2010), 'Reconsidering Barth's Rejection of Przywara's *analogia entis*'. *Modern Theology*, 26, 632–50.

Jüngel, E. (1977), *Gott als Geheimnis der Welt. Zur Begründung der Theologie des Gekreuzigten im Streit zwischen Theismus und Atheismus*. Tübingen: Mohr.

—(2006), *Das Evangelium von der Rechtfertigung des Gottlosen als Zentrum des christlichen Glaubens. Eine theologische Studie in ökumenischer Absicht*. Tübingen: Mohr Siebeck.

Kälin, B. (1957), *Lehrbuch der Philosophie*, vol. 1. Sarnen: Benediktinerkolleg Sarnen.

BIBLIOGRAPHY

Kappes, M. (2005), 'Die Bedeutung der Theologie Karl Rahners für die Ökumene. Ein vergessenes Thema?'. *Cath(M)*, 59, 1–35.

Kasper, W. (ed.) (2006), *Logik der Liebe und Herrlichkeit Gottes. Hans Urs von Balthasar im Gespräch*, Festschrift Karl Lehmann. Mainz: Grünewald.

Kerr, F. (1999), 'Foreword: Assessing this "fiddy Synthesis"', in L. Gardner et al. *Balthasar and the End of Modernity*. Edinburgh: T&T Clark, pp. 1–13.

—(2007), *Twentieth-Century Catholic Theologians. From Neoscholasticism to Nuptial Mysticism*. Malden, MA et al.: Blackwell.

—(2010), 'By reason alone: what Vatican I never said'. *New Blackfriars*, 91, 215–28.

Klein, A. (1998), 'Möhler-Institut'. *LTK*³, 7, 375.

Kleinschwärzer-Meister, B. (2007), *In allem auf Christus hin. Zur theologischen Funktion der Rechtfertigungslehre*. Freiburg i.Br. et al.: Herder.

Kooi, C. van der (2005), 'Karl Barths zweiter Römerbrief und seine Wirkungen', in M. Beintker et al., *Karl Barth in Deutschland (1921–1935). Aufbruch - Klärung - Widerstand [...]*. Zürich: Theologischer Verlag Zürich, pp. 57–75.

Korsch, D. (1989), 'Wort Gottes oder Frömmigkeit? Über den Sinn einer theologischen Alternative zwischen Karl Barth und Friedrich Schleiermacher'. *ZDT*, 5, 195–216.

—(1996), 'Intellectus fidei. Ontologischer Gottesbeweis und theologische Methode in Karl Barths Anselmbuch' [1989], in *Dialektische Theologie nach Karl Barth*, Tübingen: Mohr, pp. 191–213.

—(1999), 'Dialektische Theologie'. *RGG*⁴, 2, 809–15.

Kreutzer, K. (2001), 'Karl Rahners Kritik antiintellektualistischer Tendenzen in der deutschen Philosophie und Theologie während der nationalsozialistischen Ära'. *TP*, 76, 410–20.

Ladaria, L. F. (1996), 'Nature et surnaturel', in B. Sesboüé (ed.), *Histoire des dogmes*, vol. 2. Paris: Desclée, 375–413.

Lambinet, L. (1938), 'Das Prinzip des Protestantismus nach J. A. Möhler'. *Cath(M)*, 7, 37–53.

Lamirande, E. (1968), 'Roman Catholic Reactions to Karl Barth's Ecclesiology'. *CJT*, 14, 28–42.

—(1974), 'The Impact of Karl Barth on the Catholic Church in the Last Half Century', in M. Rumscheidt (ed.), *Footnotes to a Theology. The Karl Barth Colloquium of 1972*. Waterloo, Ontario: The Corporation for the Publication of Academic Studies in Religion in Canada, pp. 112–48.

Lange, H. (1926), 'Protestantismus', in J. Braun (ed.), *Handlexikon der katholischen Dogmatik*. Freiburg i.Br.: Herder, pp. 237–8.

Lash, N. (2008), 'What Happened at Vatican II?', in *Theology for Pilgrims*. Notre Dame, IN: University of Notre Dame Press, pp. 240–8.

Lehmann, K. (2009), '"Einig im Verständnis der Rechtfertigungsbotschaft? – Erfahrungen und Lehren im Blick auf die gegenwärtige ökumenische Situation"' [1998], in F. Hauschildt et al. (ed.), *Die Gemeinsame Erklärung zur Rechtfertigungslehre. Dokumentation des Entstehungs- und Rezeptionsprozesses*. Göttingen: Vandenhoeck und Ruprecht, pp. 849–72.

Leiner, M. and Trowitzsch, M. (ed.) (2008), *Karl Barths Theologie als europäisches Ereignis*. Göttingen: Vandenhoeck und Ruprecht.

Leinkauf, T. and Trappe, T. (1995), 'Setzen/Setzung'. *Historisches Wörterbuch der Philosophie*, 9, 697–721.

BIBLIOGRAPHY

Lessing, E. (2004), *Geschichte der deutschsprachigen evangelischen Theologie von Albrecht Ritschl bis zur Gegenwart*, vol. 2. Göttingen: Vandenhoeck und Ruprecht.
—(2009), *Geschichte der deutschsprachigen evangelischen Theologie von Albrecht Ritschl bis zur Gegenwart*, vol. 3. Göttingen: Vandenhoeck und Ruprecht.
Liggenstorfer, R. (2003), 'Bauhofer, Oskar'. *Historisches Lexikon der Schweiz*, 2, 96.
Link, C. (2005), 'Bleibende Einsichten von Tambach', in M. Beintker et al., *Karl Barth in Deutschland (1921–1935). Aufbruch - Klärung - Widerstand [...]*. Zürich: Theologischer Verlag Zürich, pp. 333–46.
Lochbrunner, M. (2002), *Hans Urs von Balthasar als Autor, Herausgeber und Verleger. Fünf Studien zu seinen Sammlungen (1942–1967)*. Würzburg: Echter.
—(2007), 'Die schwere Geburt des Barth-Buches von Hans Urs von Balthasar. Ein Beitrag zur Werkgenese', in A. G. von Brandenstein-Zepplin et al. (ed.), *Die göttliche Vernunft und die inkarnierte Liebe*, Festschrift Joseph Ratzinger. Weilheim-Bierbronnen: Gustav-Sieverth-Akademie, pp. 631–64.
—(2009), *Hans Urs von Balthasar und seine Theologenkollegen. Sechs Beziehungsgeschichten*. Würzburg: Echter.
—(2011), 'Review of Dahlke (2010)'. *TP*, 86, 297–9.
Lösel, S. (2001), *Kreuzwege. Ein ökumenisches Gespräch mit Hans Urs von Balthasar*. Paderborn et al.: Schöningh.
Löser, W. (2006), 'Von Balthasars Karl-Barth-Buch – eine theologische Würdigung', in W. W. Müller (ed.), *Karl Barth – Hans Urs von Balthasar. Eine theologische Zwiesprache*. Zürich: Theologischer Verlag Zürich, pp. 71–96.
—(2008), 'Der herrliche Gott. Hans Urs von Balthasars "theologische Ästhetik"', in R. Kampling (ed.), *Herrlichkeit. Zur Deutung einer theologischen Kategorie*. Paderborn et al.: Schöningh, pp. 269–93.
Lohmann, J. F. (1995), *Karl Barth und der Neukantianismus. Die Rezeption des Neukantianismus im 'Römerbrief' und ihre Bedeutung für die weitere Ausarbeitung der Theologie Karl Barths*. Berlin and New York: Walter de Gruyter.
Lonergan, B. (1972), *Method in Theology*. London: Darton Longman & Todd.
Lotz, J. B. (1957), 'Akt. I. Ontologisch'. *LTK²*, 1, 247–9.
Lubac, H. de (1946), *Surnaturel. Études historiques*. Paris: Aubier.
—(1949), 'Le mystère du surnaturel'. *RSR*, 36, 80–121.
—(1989), *Mémoire sur l'occasion de mes écrits*. Namur: culture et vérité.
Madrigal, S. (2005), 'K. Barth, A las puertas de San Pedro', in *Memoria del Concilio. Diez evocaciones del Vaticano II*. Madrid: Desclée de Brouwer, pp. 277–96.
Maffeis, A. (2009), 'Karl Barth, un teologo tra le confessioni cristiane'. *Hermeneutica. Annuario di filosofia e teologia*, 27–66.
Malevez, L. (1953), 'La gratuité du surnaturel'. *NRT*, 75, 561–86, 673–89.
Manser, G. M. (1928), 'Das Wesen des Thomismus'. *DT*, 6, 385–404; *DT*, 7 (1929), 3–30, 322–47, 373–99.
Marga, A. (2010), *Karl Barth's Dialogue with Catholicism in Göttingen and Münster. Its Significance for His Doctrine of God*. Tübingen: Mohr Siebeck.
Marion, J.-L. (2002), *Dieu sans l'être*. Paris: Presses Universitaires de France.
Martina, G. (2001), *Storia della Chiesa. Da Lutero ai nostri giorni*, vol. 4. Brescia: Morcelliana.
Maßmann, A. (2008), 'Ein ambivalentes Erbe. Karl Barth zwischen Neuprotestantismus und Katholizismus'. *EvT*, 68, 144–9.

BIBLIOGRAPHY

Matošević, L. (2005), *Lieber katholisch als neuprotestantisch. Karl Barths Rezeption der katholischen Theologie 1921–1930*. Neukirchen-Vluyn: Neukirchener.
Mayer, R. J. (2008), 'Zum *desiderium naturale visionis Dei* [...]'. *Ang*, 85, 737–63.
McCabe, H. (2008), 'Aquinas Himself', in *On Aquinas*. London and New York: Continuum, pp. 1–5.
McCool, G. (1977), *Catholic Theology in the Nineteenth Century. The Quest for a Unitary Method*. New York: Seabury.
—(1989), *From Unity to Pluralism. The Internal Evolution of Thomism*. New York: Fordham University Press.
—(1994), *The Neo-Thomists*. Milwaukee, WI: Marquette University Press.
McCormack, B. (1995), *Karl Barth's Critically Realistic Dialectical Theology. Its Genesis and Development 1909–1936*. Oxford: Clarendon Press.
—(1997), 'Beyond Nonfoundational and Postmodern Readings of Barth's Critically Realistic Dialectical Theology'. *ZDT*, 12, 67–95, 170–94.
—(1999), '§ 27 "The Limits of the Knowledge of God". Theses on the Theological Epistemology of Karl Barth'. *ZDT*, 15, 75–86.
—(2002), 'What Has Basel to Do with Berlin? Continuities in the Theologies of Barth and Schleiermacher'. *Princeton Seminary Bulletin*, 23, 146–73.
—(2002), 'The Barth Renaissance in America. An Opinion'. *Princeton Seminary Bulletin*, 23, pp. 337–40.
—(2003), 'The End of Reformed Theology? The Voice of Karl Barth in the Doctrinal Chaos of the Present', in W. M. Alston and M. Welker (ed.), *Reformed Theology. Identity and Ecumenicity*. Grand Rapids, MI: Eerdmans, pp. 46–65.
—(2004), 'The Being of Holy Scripture is in Becoming. Karl Barth in Conversation with American Evangelical Criticism'. *The Princeton Theological Review*, 9, 4–15.
—(2006), 'Karl Barth's Christology as a Resource for a Reformed Version of Kenoticism'. *International Journal of Systematic Theology*, 8, 243–51.
—(2008), 'The Actuality of God. Karl Barth in Conversation with Open Theism', in ibid *Engaging the Doctrine of God. Contemporary Protestant Perspectives*. Grand Rapids, MI: Baker and Edinburgh: Rutherford House, pp. 185–242.
—(2010), 'Is there a Future for "Church Dogmatics"?'. *TZ*, 66, 306–17.
McDermott, J. M. (2008), 'The Path and Progress of Twentieth-Century Catholic Theology'. *Josephinum Journal of Theology*, 15, 11–42.
McGill, A. C. (1967), 'Recent Discussions of Anselm's Argument', in ibid and J. Hick (ed.), *The Many-Faced Argument. Recent Studies on the Ontological Argument for the Existence of God*. New York: Macmillan, pp. 33–110.
McGrath, A. E. (1981), 'Justification: Barth, Trent and Küng'. *SJT*, 34, 517–29.
—(2005), *Iustitia Dei. A History of the Christian Doctrine of Justification*. Cambridge et al.: Cambridge University Press.
McInerny, R. (1996), *Aquinas and Analogy*. Washington, DC: The Catholic University of America Press.
—(2006), *Praeambula fidei. Thomism and the God of the philosophers*. Washington, D.C.: The Catholic University of America Press.
Meier, H. G. (1972), 'Denkform'. *Historisches Wörterbuch der Philosophie*, 2, 104–7.
Meyer zu Schlochtern, J. and Siebenrock, R. A. (ed.) (2010), *Wozu Fundamentaltheologie? Zur Grundlegung der Theologie im Anspruch von Glaube und Vernunft*. Paderborn et al.: Schöningh.

BIBLIOGRAPHY

Mettepenningen, J. (2010), *Nouvelle Théologie – New Theology. Inheritor of Modernism, Precursor of Vatican II*. London and New York: T & T Clark.

Michel, A. (1941), 'Surnaturel'. *Dictionnaire de théologie catholique*, 14, 2849–59.

Milbank, J. (2005), *The Suspended Middle. Henri de Lubac and the Debate concerning the Supernatural*. London: SCM Press.

Morgan, D. D. (2010), *Barth Reception in Britain*. London and New York: T & T Clark.

Moss, D. and Oakes, E. T. (ed.) (2004), *The Cambridge Companion to Hans Urs von Balthasar*. Cambridge et al.: Cambridge University Press.

Müller, D. (2005), *Karl Barth*. Paris: Cerf.

Müller, G. L. (1993), 'Analogie. II. Theologisch'. *LTK*^{3}, 1, 579–82.

Nebel, D. (1999), 'Die Lehrstuhlinhaber für Apologetik/Fundamentaltheologie und Dogmatik [...]', in H. Wolf (ed.), *Die katholisch-theologischen Disziplinen in Deutschland 1870–1962. Ihre Geschichte, ihr Zeitbezug*. Paderborn et al.: Schöningh, pp. 164–230.

Neufeld, K. H. (1990), 'Jesuitentheologie im 19. und 20. Jahrhundert', in M. Sievernich and G. Switek (ed.), *Ignatianisch. Eigenart und Methode der Gesellschaft Jesu*. Freiburg i. Br. u.a.: Herder, pp. 425–43.

Neuser, W. (1985), *Karl Barth in Münster*. Zürich: Theologischer Verlag Zürich.

Nichols, A. (1998), *Catholic Thought Since The Enlightment. A Survey*. Pretoria: Unisa Press and Leominster, UK: Gracewing.

—(2007), *Divine Fruitfulness. A Guide through Balthasar's Theology beyond the Trilogy*. London and New York: T&T Clark.

Nimmo, P. T. (2007), *Being in Action. The Theological Shape of Barth's Ethical Vision*. London and New York: T&T Clark.

Nossol, A. (1986), 'Die Rezeption der Barthschen Christologie in der katholischen Theologie der Gegenwart'. *EvT*, 46, 351–69.

Oakes, K. R. (2010), 'Three Themes in Przywara's Early Theology'. *The Thomist*, 74, 283–310.

Oh, P. S. (2006), 'Complementary Dialectics of Kierkegaard and Barth. Barth's Use of Kierkegaardian Diastasis Reassessed'. *NZSTh*, 49, 497–512.

O'Meara, T. F. (1992), *Church and Culture. German Catholic Theology, 1860–1914*. Notre Dame, IN and London: University of Notre Dame Press.

—(2002), *Erich Przywara, S.J. His Theology and His World*. Notre Dame, IN: University of Notre Dame Press.

Oswald, J. (ed.) (2000), *Schule des Denkens. 75 Jahre Philosophische Fakultät der Jesuiten in München und Pullach*. Stuttgart: Kohlhammer.

Pannenberg, W. (1997), *Problemgeschichte der neueren evangelischen Theologie in Deutschland. Von Schleiermacher bis zu Barth und Tillich*. Göttingen: Vandenhoeck und Ruprecht.

Peeters, R. J. (2002), *Teken van de levende Christus. De openbaringsdynamische traditieopvatting van Karl Barth*. Zoetermeer: Boekencentrum.

Pesch, C. (1926), *Gott der Eine und Dreieine. Dogmatische Darlegungen*. Düsseldorf: Schwann.

Peterson, E. (2009), *Ausgewählte Schriften*, vol. 9/2, ed. Barbara Nichtweiss. Würzburg: Echter.

BIBLIOGRAPHY

Pfleiderer, G. (2008), 'Karl Barths Dialektische Theologie als Paradigma des 20. Jahrhunderts. Versuch einer Selbstrezension eines Rezeptionsweges'. *ZDT*, 24, 31–47.

Plasger, G. (2000), *Die relative Autonomie des Bekenntnisses bei Karl Barth*. Neukirchen-Vluyn: Neukirchener.

—(2010), 'Kirche als ökumenisches Ereignis. Die Einheit der Kirchen in der einen Kirche Jesu Christi', in M. Beintker et al. (ed.), *Karl Barth im europäischen Zeitgeschehen (1935–1950)* [...]. Zürich: Theologischer Verlag Zürich, pp. 471–83.

Pohle, J. (1952), *Lehrbuch der Dogmatik*, vol. 1, ed. J. Gummersbach. Paderborn: Schöningh.

Pozzo, G. (1996), 'La Manualistica', in Fisichella, R. (ed.), *Storia della teologia*, vol. 3. Rom and Bologna: Edizioni Dehoniane, pp. 309–36.

Premm, M. (1953), *Katholische Glaubenskunde. Ein Lehrbuch der Dogmatik*, vol. 4. Vienna: Herder.

Quash, B. (1998), 'Von Balthasar and the Dialogue with Karl Barth'. *New Blackfriars*, 79, 45–55.

—(2004), 'Exile, Freedom and Thanksgiving: Barth and Hans Urs von Balthasar', in M. Higton and J. C. McDowell (ed.), *Conversing with Barth*. Aldershot, UK and Burlington, VT: Ashgate, pp. 90–119.

Rademacher, A. (1937), *Die Wiedervereinigung der christlichen Kirchen*. Bonn: Hanstein.

Raffelt, A. (1995), 'Gratia (prae)supponit naturam'. *LTK*[3], 4, 986–8.

—(1999), 'Potentia oboedientialis'. *LTK*[3], 8, 459–60.

Rahner, K. (1939), 'Zur scholastischen Begrifflichkeit der ungeschaffenen Gnade'. *ZKT*, 63, 137–57.

—(1954), *Schriften zur Theologie*, vol. 1. Einsiedeln et al.: Benziger [English translation: *Theological Investigations*, vol. 1, trans. Cornelius Ernst (Baltimore, MD: Helicon Press, 1961)].

—(1959), 'Existential, übernatürliches'. *LTK*[2], 3, 1301.

—(1976), *Grundkurs des Glaubens. Einführung in den Begriff des Christentums*. Freiburg i.Br. et al.: Herder.

Rasmusson, A. (2007), 'Historiography and Theology. Theology in the Weimar Republic and the Beginning of the Third Reich'. *Kirchliche Zeitgeschichte*, 20, 155–80.

Ratzinger, J. (1971), 'Das Ganze im Fragment. Gottlieb Söhngen zum Gedächtnis'. *Christ in der Gegenwart*, 23, 398–9.

Reikerstorfer, J. (2000), 'Apologetische und fundamentaltheologische Momente und Modelle in der Geschichte. III. Fundamentaltheologische Modelle der Neuzeit', in W. Kern et al. (ed.), *Handbuch der Fundamentaltheologie*, vol. 4. Tübingen: Francke, pp. 242–64.

Reymond, B. (1985), *Théologien ou prophète? Les francophones et Karl Barth avant 1945*. Lausanne: Edition l'Age d'Homme.

Ricca, P. (1990), 'Barth di fronte al cattolicesimo e all'ecumenismo', in S. Rostagno (ed.), *Barth contemporaneo*. Turin: Claudiana, pp. 197–211.

Rolnick, P. A. (2002), 'Realist Reference to God: Analogy or Univocity?', in W. P. Alston (ed.), *Realism and Antirealism*. Ithaca, NY and London: Cornell University Press, pp. 211–37.

BIBLIOGRAPHY

Rondet, H. (1948), 'Le problème de la nature pure et la théologie au XVIe siècle'. *RSR*, 35, 481–521.

Rosato, P. J. (1986), 'The Influence of Karl Barth on Catholic Theology'. *Greg*, 67, 659–78.

Routhier, G. (2011), 'L'ombre de Karl Barth à Vatican II'. *Etudes Théologiques et Religieuses*, 86, 1–24.

Routhier, G. and Jobin, G. (ed.) (2010), *L'Autorité et les autorités. L'herméneutique théologique de Vatican II*. Paris: Cerf.

Rulands, P. (2003), 'Selbstmitteilung Gottes in Jesus Christus: Gnadentheologie', in A. Batlogg et al. *Der Denkweg Karl Rahners. Quellen - Entwicklungen - Perspektiven*. Mainz: Grünewald, pp. 161–96.

Ruster, T. (1994), *Die verlorene Nützlichkeit der Religion. Katholizismus und Moderne in der Weimarer Republik*. Paderborn et al.: Schöningh.

—(1998), 'Theologische Wahrnehmung von Kultur im ausgehenden Kaiserreich', in H. Wolf (ed.), *Antimodernismus und Modernismus in der katholischen Kirche. Beiträge zum theologiegeschichtlichen Vorfeld des II. Vatikanums*. Paderborn et al.: Schöningh, pp. 267–79.

Salmann, E. (1988), 'Die Anselm-Interpretation bei A. Stolz', in ibid (ed.) *La Teologia mistico-sapienziale di Anselm Stolz*. Rom: Pontificio Ateneo S. Anselmo, pp. 101–24.

Santeler, J. (1931), 'Die Lehre von der Analogie des Seins'. *ZKT*, 55, 1–43.

Sauter, G. (1997), 'Rechtfertigung VI. Das 19. und 20. Jahrhundert'. *TRE*, 28, 336–52.

Schaber, J. (2004), 'Der Beuroner Benediktiner Daniel Feuling (1882–1947)'. *Freiburger Diözesan-Archiv*, 124, 73–84.

Schelkens, K. and Gielis, M. (2007), 'From Driedo to Bellarmine. The Concept of Pure Nature in the 16th Century'. *Augustiniana*, 57, 425–48.

Schempp, P. (1928), 'Randglossen zum Barthianismus'. *Zwischen den Zeiten*, 6, 529–39.

Schmidt, J. (2003), *Philosophische Theologie*. Stuttgart: Kohlhammer.

Schönberger, R. (2004), *Anselm von Canterbury*. Munich: Beck.

Schöpsdau, W. (2011), 'Philosoph des Protestantismus? Kant zwischen den Konfessionen'. *Materialdienst des Konfessionskundlichen Instituts Bensheim*, 62, 10–3.

Schultenover, D. G. (ed.) (2008), *Vatican II. Did Anything Happen?* New York and London: Continuum.

Schulz, M. (2006), 'Friedrich Hegel', in W. Kasper (ed.), Logik der Liebe und Herrlichkeit Gottes. Hans Urs von Balthasar im Gespräch, Festschrift Karl Lehmann. Mainz: Grünewald, pp. 111–33.

Schwahn, B. (1996), *Der ökumenische Arbeitskreis evangelischer und katholischer Theologen 1946 bis 1975*. Göttingen: Vandenhoeck und Ruprecht.

Seckler, M. (2000), 'Der Begriff der Offenbarung', in W. Kern et al. (ed.), *Handbuch der Fundamentaltheologie*, vol. 2. Tübingen: Francke, pp. 41–61.

Seebaß, G. (1978), 'Antichrist. IV. Reformations- und Neuzeit'. *TRE*, 3, 28–43.

Sesboüé, B. (2005), 'La genese d'une œuvre ou comment sortir de la «néoscolastique»?', in H. J. Gagey and V. Holzer (ed.), *Balthasar, Rahner – Deux pensées en contraste*. Paris: Bayard, pp. 47–67.

Smulders, P., (1949), 'De oorsprong van de theorie der zuivere natuur. Vergeten meesters der Leuvense school'. *Bijdragen*, 10, 105–27.

Stanley, T. (2008), 'Returning Barth to Anselm'. *Modern Theology*, 24, 413–37.

BIBLIOGRAPHY

Steiner, G. (1998), *Errata. An examined life*. London: Phoenix.
Steinhoff, A. J. (2006), 'Christianity and the creation of Germany', in S. Gilley and B. Stanley (ed.), *The Cambridge History of Christianity*, vol. 8. Cambridge et al.: Cambridge University Press), pp. 282–300.
Stransky, T. (2002), 'Roman Catholic Church and pre-Vatican II ecumenism', in N. Lossky (ed.), *Dictionary of the Ecumenical Movement*. Genf: WCC Publishing, pp. 996–8.
Striet, M. and Tück, J.-H. (ed.) (2005), *Die Kunst Gottes verstehen. Hans Urs von Balthasars theologische Provokationen*. Freiburg i.Br. et al.: Herder.
Sudduth, M. (2009), *The Reformed Objection to Natural Theology*. Farnham, UK: Ashgate.
Theobald, C. (1996), 'De Vatican I aux années 1950: Révélation, foi et raison, inspiration, dogme et magistère infaillible', ibid and B. Sesboüé, *Histoire des dogmes*, vol. 4. Paris: Desclée, pp. 227–470.
Thompson, J. (1994), 'Barth and Balthasar. An Ecumenical Dialogue', in B. McGregor and T. Norris (ed.), *The Beauty of Christ. An Introduction to the Theology of Hans Urs von Balthasar*. Edinburgh: T&T Clark, pp. 171–92.
Torrance, T. F. (1952), Balthasar (1951), *The Scotsman* (14 April 1952).
—(1962), *Karl Barth. An Introduction to his Early Theology, 1910–1931*. London: SCM Press.
—(1990), *Karl Barth. Biblical and Evangelical Theologian*. Edinburgh: T&T Clark.
Voderholzer, R. (2006), 'Balthasars', in W. Kasper (ed.), Logik der Liebe und Herrlichkeit Gottes. Hans Urs von Balthasar im Gespräch, Festschrift Karl Lehmann. Mainz: Grünewald, pp. 204–28.
Wagner, J.-P. (2001), *Henri de Lubac*. Paris: Cerf.
Wainwright, W. J. (ed.) (2005), *The Oxford Handbook of Philosophy of Religion*. Oxford et al.: Oxford University Press.
Webster, J. (2000), *Karl Barth*. London and New York: Continuum.
—(2004), 'Barth', in D. Moss and E. T. Oakes (ed.), The Cambridge Companion to Hans Urs von Balthasar. Cambridge et al.: Cambridge University Press, pp. 241–55.
—(2005), 'Karl Barth', in J. P. Greenman and T. Larsen (ed.), *Reading Romans through the Centuries. From the Early Church to Karl Barth*. Grand Rapids, MI: Brazos Press, pp. 205–23.
Weiß, O. (1995), *Der Modernismus in Deutschland. Ein Beitrag zur Theologiegeschichte*. Regensburg: Pustet.
White, T. J. (ed.) (2011), *The Analogy of Being. Invention of the Antichrist or the Wisdom of God?* Grand Rapids, MI and Cambridge: Eerdmans.
Wiedenhofer, S. (1980), 'Ökumenische Theologie (1930–1965). Versuch einer wissenschaftsgeschichtlichen Rekonstruktion'. *Cath(M)*, 34, 219–48.
Wigley, S. D. (2003), 'The von Balthasar thesis. A re-examination of von Balthasar's study of Barth in the light of Bruce McCormack'. *SJT*, 56, 345–59.
—(2007), *Karl Barth and Hans Urs von Balthasar. A Critical Engagement*. London and New York: T&T Clark.
Wilde, M. J. (2007), *Vatican II. A Sociological Analysis of Religious Change*. Princeton, NJ and Oxford: Princeton University Press.
Wildi, H. M. (revisor), (1992), *Bibliographie Karl Barth*, vol. 2. Zürich: Theologischer Verlag Zürich.

BIBLIOGRAPHY

Wobbermin, G. (1932), 'Ein neuer Fall "Peterson"'. *Das Evangelische Deutschland*, 9, 180.

Wolf, E. et al. (1956), *Antwort*, Festschrift Karl Barth. Zollikon and Zürich: Evangelischer Verlag.

Wolfes, M. (1999), *Protestantische Theologie und moderne Welt. Studien zur Geschichte der liberalen Theologie nach 1918*. Berlin and New York: Walter de Gruyter.

Woolverton, J. F. (1997), 'Hans W. Frei in Context. A Theological and Historical Memoir'. *ATR*, 79, 369–93.

Wurm, H. J. (1897), 'Protestantismus'. *Wetzer und Welte's Kirchenlexikon*, 10, 480–533.

Yoccum, J. (2002), 'What's Interesting about Karl Barth? Barth as Polemical and Descreptive Theologian'. *International Journal of Systematic Theology*, 4, 29–44.

Zachhuber, J. (2005), 'Friedrich Schleiermacher und Albrecht Ritschl. Kontinuitäten und Diskontinuitäten in der Theologie des 19. Jahrhunderts'. *Zeitschrift für Neuere Theologiegeschichte*, 12, 16–46.

AUTHOR INDEX

Adam, Karl 18–24, 72
Allers, Rudolf 54–6, 60
Althaus, Paul 34
Anselm of Canterbury 30fn. 22, 53–60, 132fn. 48, 139–40, 143, 156
Augustine 15, 17, 43, 47fn. 31, 67, 83

Baius, Michael 97, 122, 130
Balthasar, Hans Urs von viii–ix, 6–7, 53fn. 3, 87, 92, 93fn. 150, 94–155, 157, 159
Bartmann, Bernhard 4fn. 13, 54fn. 7, 63fn. 5, 66–8, 80, 89, 118
Bauhofer, Oskar 64, 71–2, 91–2
Baur, Ferdinand Christian 49
Böminghaus, Ernst 42
Bonaventure 83
Bouillard, Henri 128fn. 32, 146
Brinktrine, Johannes 57, 97fn. 8, 137fn. 72
Brunner, Emil 5, 29fn. 17, 33, 39, 62fn. 2, 74–7, 81, 84fn. 102, 91, 137, 140
Bultmann, Rudolf 5, 146

Calvin, John 20
Chenu, Marie-Dominique 106
Cohen, Hermann 37fn. 62
Congar, Yves 51fn. 50, 138fn. 75, 159fn. 10

Daniélou, Jean 6, 159fn. 10
Descartes, René 55
Diekamp, Franz 54fn. 7, 63fn. 5

Engert, Joseph 11–15, 17, 22–3

Fehr, Jakob 66, 70–9, 83
Feiner, Johannes 79fn. 78, 126
Feuling, Daniel 66, 68–70
Frei, Hans W. 142–4

Garrigou-Lagrange, Réginald 151
Geiselmann, Josef Rupert 22–4, 49fn. 40
Gierens, Michael 26–9, 31, 38–9
Gilson, Étienne 58
Goethe, Johann Wolfgang von 152
Gogarten, Friedrich 5, 10, 16, 29fn. 17
Grosche, Robert 41–52
Gutwenger, Engelbert 127

Haecker, Theodor 92
Hamann, Johann Georg 152
Hamer, Jérôme 137
Harnack, Adolf von 4, 16, 42
Hasenkamp, Gottfried 41fn. 2, 42, 48, 50
Hegel, Georg Wilhelm Friedrich 34, 102, 110–11, 128, 132, 137fn. 70, 138–41, 153
Heiler, Friedrich 5, 13, 17, 23fn. 71, 48–9
Heinrich, Johann Baptist 118
Heim, Karl 21

Jaeger, Lorenz 52
John XXIII 3

AUTHOR INDEX

Kant, Immanuel 25–6, 30, 37–8, 55, 152
Keller, Hermann 57fn. 24
Kierkegaard, Sören vii, 6, 8fn. 3
Kirschbaum, Charlotte von 85
Kolping, Adolf 59–60
Küng, Hans 146–8

Lercher, Ludwig 118
Lubac, Henri de 7, 102, 121–3, 127, 129–30
Luther, Martin 17, 20, 30, 62fn. 2, 81, 147

McCormack, Bruce 53fn. 3, 141–5
Merz, Georg 5
Möhler, Johann Adam 43, 49–50

Nossen, Annemarie 42

Peterson, Erik 44fn. 15, 57fn. 22, 64
Pius IX 3
Pius XII 3, 123
Pohle, Joseph 118, 123fn. 5, 137fn. 72
Pribilla, Max 90
Przywara, Erich 15–19, 22–4, 31fn. 27, 60fn. 40, 63, 65, 80–1, 83–9, 92, 101, 106–8, 112–13, 116fn. 64, 117, 159

Rahner, Karl 26, 31–5, 38–9, 93fn. 150, 104, 117–20, 126–9, 129fn. 32, 159fn. 10

Ripalda, Juan Martínez de 118
Ritschl, Albrecht 34fn. 39
Rosenmöller, Bernhard 42–4, 49, 50fn. 44, 51

Scheeben, Matthias Joseph 43
Schleiermacher, Friedrich 1, 20, 28, 30, 34fn. 39, 38, 45, 63, 133, 155
Schmitt, Franciscus Salesius 54–6, 59fn. 37, 60
Söhngen, Gottlieb 79–83, 87, 148fn. 130, 159
Stählin, Wilhelm 52
Stolz, Anselm 54, 56–60, 159

ten Hompel, Max 48, 50
Thomas Aquinas 7, 24fn. 71, 43fn. 12, 55, 68, 74, 77, 79, 106, 116–17, 130, 131fn. 42, 132 with fn 48, 135fn. 60
Thurneysen, Eduard 5, 15–6, 29fn. 17, 43, 45fn. 20, 72, 86fn. 116
Torrance, Thomas F. 142
Troeltsch, Ernst 4, 16

Volk, Hermann 24fn. 73, 26–7, 35–9

Weisweiler, Heinrich 56fn. 18, 66, 89
Wittig, Joseph 9–11, 18, 22–3
Wobbermin, Georg 63–4

SUBJECT INDEX

analogia entis viii, 6, 15–18, 21, 61–94, 101, 103, 106, 109–10, 112–13, 115–16, 128, 137, 156–7
analogia fidei 61, 63fn. 6, 66, 70, 75, 80–1, 83, 84fn. 101, 87, 94, 108, 112

Dialectical Theology 4–5, 9, 11, 16–24, 26–31, 34–5, 38–40, 42, 44–7, 50–2, 64, 71–80, 92, 98, 138, 141–5

Ecumenism/ecumenical dialogue 41, 46–52, 64, 90, 101, 107–8, 126, 128
Enlightenment viii, 11, 25, 46, 90, 93, 96–7

Heilsgeschichte/Salvation History 79–83, 105fn. 6, 135, 159
Humani Generis 7, 121–3, 127, 146

Idealism 25, 28–9, 31, 36–7, 46, 133

infinite qualitative distinction/ difference vii, 8, 20, 29–31, 36, 38–9, 111, 138–9, 156

Liberal Theology/Neo-Protestantism 5, 12, 17, 23, 34, 43, 52, 63–5, 69, 76, 80, 90–1, 112, 139, 142–4, 155–7

natura pura 97, 115, 122–3
Neo-Scholasticism/Neo-Thomism vii–ix, 3, 6–7, 25–6, 39, 43, 54, 57–8, 60, 63fn. 6, 66, 68, 71–7, 79, 80fn. 78, 81fn. 85, 83, 90, 91fn. 139, 93, 96–9, 102, 104–5, 107, 113–20, 126, 128–33, 135–7, 142, 151–9
Nouvelle Théologie 7, 119, 121–7, 129

Vatican I 55–6, 67–8, 71, 107fn. 16, 114, 135fn. 60, 158
Vatican II, vii, ix, 2–3, 41, 50, 94–5, 98fn. 11, 151, 154–5, 157–9

Lightning Source UK Ltd.
Milton Keynes UK
UKOW04f1534141013

219044UK00002B/70/P